# Managing People in Changing Times

*Coping with change in the workplace—
a practical guide*

## Robert Burns

**ALLEN & UNWIN**

© Robert Burns, 1993

This book is copyright under the Berne Convention.
No reproduction without permission. All rights reserved.

First published in 1993
Allen & Unwin Pty Ltd
9 Atchison Street, St Leonards, NSW 2065 Australia

National Library of Australia
Cataloguing-in-Publication entry:

Burns, Robert, 1939–
    Managing people in changing times.

    Includes index.
    ISBN 1 86373 356 6.

    1. Organizational change – Management.  I. Title.

658.406

Set in 10/11pt Times by Graphicraft Typesetters Limited, Hong Kong
Printed by Kim Hup Lee Printing Co Pte Limited, Singapore
10  9  8  7  6  5  4  3  2  1

# Contents

# Preface

This book is written by a psychologist and therefore focuses on some of the psychological effects of technological, structural and economic change in the workplace and how management involved in such a context can ameliorate these effects and related problems for themselves and others. It is not a text on organisational management but contains information and advice from a psychological perspective that bears upon the management of self and others in an era of rapid technological and structural change. It will aid managers to understand themselves, how they respond to change and their mode of personal interaction with others. This self-understanding will in turn help them think positively and constructively about how they respond to the needs of colleagues and employees at a time of stress and insecurity, so that problems involved in reskilling, enforced transfer, lack of opportunities for promotion, redundancy, and involuntary early retirement are handled sensitively and supportively. Symptoms of stress, low self-esteem, depression and the like are discussed so that people suffering from the stresses of current workplace problems can be identified. Additionally some simple but effective techniques for helping those with such psychological problems are offered.

The book contains numerous activities that enable readers to assess their psychological status in a number of problem areas, and practice techniques that enhance adjustment. The activities have been written assuming readers will work on them by themselves. However, they can be easily adapted for groups working with a leader such as a trainer or counsellor. The activities have been chosen to have the widest possible relevance to readers of all ages and positions in organisations. However, should you find that a few of the activities and skills do not suit your particular needs, it is perfectly in order for you to skip them and move on to more relevant activities.

To gain the maximum benefit from this book, readers should carry out as many of the activities as possible. While the photocopying of books is not acceptable, completing the questionnaires would require marks to be made in this book. In these circumstances a limited copying of some of the questionnaires for *personal* use is permitted.

The writer hopes that this book will help to obviate some of the stress found within the workplace and facilitate the development of more positive and constructive behaviour among those who would otherwise feel considerable distress at a time when their control of what happens to them appears to be declining.

While the book will be of general help, a few readers will have more serious problems which they cannot cope with alone. In such a case it is essential that they seek professional help, especially if psychological and/or physical health is deteriorating. There are a number of private and voluntary organisations that deal with sudden crises and emergencies. Their phone numbers are usually prominently displayed in newspapers and telephone directories. Contact them; they are there to help you.

*R. B. Burns*
*Canberra*

# Introduction

*The art of progress is to preserve order amid change, and to preserve change amid order.*

Alfred North Whitehead

## The exponential era

Every manager, supervisor, human resources person and trainer is well aware that the structure and processes of work, industry and business are changing, not only in Australia but also throughout the world. In some cases these changes are gradual and indiscernible but in others rapid and tumultuous. Few managers and even fewer workers are able to comprehend what these changes mean for them and their families, what effects will be wrought on their work practices or their lifestyle and whether they will still be working at all within the near future.

The future has always been sort of 'out there'; we have always been too busy with the 'here and now' to give it too much thought. While it can be amusing to look at the years ahead, à la *2001: A Space Odyssey*, *Star Wars* or *Star Trek*, underlying all this fantasy is a sense of cold reality that requires a seriousness of purpose. Present conditions initiated in the past force us to consider the future. We are where we are because of our past behaviour. We can do nothing about that. There is relatively little we can do to change the events of today. But the decisions we make today will have much to do with the shaping of our future environment and way of life as a culture and as individuals.

Since the future does not exist, we must all play a part in inventing it. We are not victims of predestination. We can attempt to shape the changes and prepare ourselves to cope with them and with inevitable life transitions in a way that will bring positive consequences for ourselves, our families, our colleagues and society in general. As managers, counsellors, colleagues and friends, we can contribute to facilitating these changes for ourselves and our employees. It is important to remember that there is no single determined future but a panoply of potential futures depending on which purposeful decisions and actions we take. The past is gone forever but the future is still ours to determine.

In other to cope with change and prepare for life transitions we need to know what changes are occurring or are likely to occur. Change has always been with us. Each of us changes or matures from infancy to senescence. If we didn't, in adulthood we would be 210cm-tall bouncing babies! We have experienced changes in our home circumstances as children grow up, leave and marry; in the government of the day at election time; in the weather, often on a daily basis; in our health; we adjust to new TV programs, to new modes of travel, to new forms of electronic communication and so on. But life continues and we cope. In my lifespan, we have moved from small uncomfortable piston-engined planes to large comfortable jumbo jets, video cassette recorders enable me to watch late-night sport at a more convenient time, and I can obtain money from automatic teller machines without going into a bank.

So change is always with us—particularly, since the industrial revolution, technological change. Each change has affected social, economic and political life. One of the first major technological changes in Britain was the introduction of artificial waterways or canals. This had a profound effect on the location of industry and where workers lived. Then followed the technology of steam, and after that the technologies of steel and electricity. All these innovations caused far-reaching changes to production methods, skill requirements, industry location and the social and economic infrastructure needed to support the changes. The social and economic implications of these changes even played a role in the march of Europe to war in 1914. The biggest changes of the mid twentieth century were the introduction of the production line and of complex corporate organisations. The latest changes have been in microelectronics and biotechnology.

What is so different now is that the pace of change is far more rapid. It is hard to keep up with the innovations and understand their applications before other innovations supersede them. Sudden change like this can trigger a forced restructuring of lifestyle. Just as the death of a parent or divorce imposes a need to sit down and rethink the future, so too do new work processes, organisational restructuring, relocation, redundancy and early retirement. We cannot carry on exactly as before. A new dawn is breaking on our lives and we must choose a path that will provide satisfaction and new possibilities for the days ahead.

Granted, it is difficult to predict the future. But we can discern a number of major trends that are with us now. 'Futurists' such as John Naisbitt, Alvin Toffler and Tom Stonier, as well as Australian analysts such as Gruen, Economic Planning Advisory Council (EPAC), and Barry Jones have published their ideas on the future.

Toffler has proposed three waves in the development of mankind. The first was a move from an itinerant pastoral to a sedentary agricultural society; the second was when agricultural society gave way to industrial society. The third wave is on us now as we move from an industrial society to a technology and information society. We are across the frontier now into the new land. The drumbeats of high technology, robotics, fibre optics, superconductors, telecommunications, lasers and biotechnology, *inter alia*, reverberate around us with messages that the future ain't what it used to be. We possess a rough sketch of the beckoning environment. Each twist in the trail ahead will reveal new visions, new experiences, new ways of living, new uncertainties. Consolidation will hardly have begun before further new sights greet us. The shift from a society based on centralised industry to one based on information and technology is as dramatic as that from an agricultural to an industrial society. This shift will bring new values, new relationships, new ways of living out one's life, new sources of identity and esteem and new career structures. Toffler argues that the transition from one wave to the next is accompanied by great social upheaval and insecurity, or *future shock*, a pathological anxiety condition which increasingly afflicts people who cannot cope in an age of profound and widespread change. It is the psychological effect of impermanence, a state of continuous adaptation. Too high a rate of change produces a physical stress reaction in the body, a reduction in emotional stability, degradation of physical health and a decline in the general quality of life.

All the signs are present in Western economies and societies that such vast transitions, and the accompanying personal and societal distress, are here. Toffler visited many organisations and interviewed numerous people in his study of future shock. He concluded that future shock was no longer a distant potential danger, but a real sickness from which increasingly large numbers already suffer. To give some perspective on the rate of change, Toffler divided the past 50 000 years into lifetimes of around 60 years each to give about 800 human lifetimes. The first 650 lifetimes were spent living in caves, writing has only been available for the last 70 lifetimes, print for the last six, and the electric motor in the last two. Most of the material goods we use and the technological advances we are accustomed to have been crammed into less than one lifetime. We are living in an era of exponential change. In Australia we are witnessing increasing unemployment, and the failure of many of the institutions of industrialism. The industrial society is on the wane and the technology and information society is waxing strongly. New concepts in science and technology are reducing many of us to the status of naive visitors in a world we have ceased to understand.

# 1

# The context
## *The future ain't what it used to be*

*To me you speak not. If you can look into the seeds of time and say which grain will grow and which grain will not, speak them to me.*

Banquo to the three witches in *Macbeth*

*I think mostly about the future; that's where I am going to spend the rest of my life.*

Charles Kettering

## The developing scenario for the world of work

Tumultuous changes in the world of work are going on around us now. Some of the changes are a result of technological innovation which began in the last decade and is continually extending its scope and complexity, resulting in alterations to work practices and to the structure of industry before consolidation of and acclimatisation to previous changes have been effected. Other changes to the world of work are a function of the seesaw of boom and bust, of the recession we 'had to have' and of economic uncertainties. As a result of these technological and economic changes to the structure and processes of work, some workers' jobs are disappearing while for others new job opportunities arise, possibly accompanied by the need for re-training or relocation. Many managers and employees are finding that their career paths are crumbling, job satisfaction is diminishing, and the future appears threatening and bleak. While the unspoken 'R' word of politicians in 1991 was Recession, the four often-invoked 'R' words of the 1990s in the world of work are **Restructuring, Re-skilling, Relocation** and **Retrenchment**.

Such changes in society and work contexts lead, in human terms, to life transitions and life crises. In such a context, human resource and training professionals, as well as those in general management, must learn new skills, particularly people skills and coping skills, and teach these to their employees. Unfortunately these economic, technological and structural changes have not been accompanied by organisational and managerial support systems to protect and nurture employees. Indeed, during this period of rapid change we have also witnessed the decline of the extended family. The nuclear family too has come under pressure as more women enter the workforce, and the natural support system in the community has been undermined as occupational and geographical mobility becomes a way of life. A country's greatest resources are its human resources but humans can only operate to the benefit of themselves and the general good if they are living and working in physical and psychological conditions that are secure, satisfying, and unthreatening. Managers and employees need to be given the skills to enable them to cope with the changes that are reverberating around them so that they can live satisfying lives at work and at home. Managing stress, building self-esteem, learning decision-making skills and relationship-making skills, knowing how to adjust to new work practices and job expectations, are among the central coping skills needed to prepare employees to 'ride the tiger of change' and not be unseated, trampled underfoot, and left to wallow in misery in an unwanted and unprepared-for life transition. In effect we must help ourselves and others gain some control over our lives rather than being helpless flotsam amd jetsam, tossed directionless in the tempest of life.

A famous satire written in the 1930s entitled 'The Saber-Tooth Curriculum' recounts how a Palaeolithic school curriculum became inappropriate when the Ice Age came. A different curriculum was required to teach the community how to survive under the new conditions. However, attempts to change the curriculum encountered stern opposition. 'But that wouldn't be education,' the elders of the tribe argued when new subjects were suggested that would enable the tribe to learn how to survive in the snowy wastes. Of course the tribe died out! This satire is still relevant today. If we do not learn to adjust to change, accept the need to learn new skills, and develop appropriate practices with regard to our human resources, then Australian workers, their families, communities and the whole fabric of industry and society may deteriorate psychologically, socially, emotionally and physically over the next decade. Our future society could have some very unpleasant aspects, particularly for the unskilled, the young, minority-group members or those made redundant in their late 40s. Capitalism appears to some to have some unacceptable faces yet the alternatives are more frightening and even less successful. If we do not prepare and help colleagues and employees to cope with current and future changes then economic and social opportunities will be swallowed up in the chasms of a society split between rich and poor, employed and unemployed, rural and urban, Left and Right. An embittered and divided society would be a bitter harvest to reap from technological advances and economic change.

This book is not a political document; no ideology is being placed before you, no new political platforms or economic strategies. There are no arguments for or against import controls, union legislation, pollution, ethnic discrimination, the Green movement or sustainable development. This book is an attempt to handle at a personal level the human problems of dealing with change in the context of work. How do you manage change in this context? How do you handle your own insecurity and that of others? How do you help others to manage their stress? How do you counsel others in a work situation? How do you build constructive relationships and communication between staff and workers, and between worker and worker, in conditions of threat and insecurity? How do you help others and yourself manage career change, increased leisure time, relocation, retrenchment and other life transitions? This book will attempt to answer these and other questions. Each of these issues may appear small fry when set against the great dramas on the world stage but for the health of the nation they are not. Sound houses are built from individual bricks; sound organisations are founded on the people who work in them.

## Activity 1    Your future

What do you see as your future? It might be useful for you to start thinking about it so that you can start planning for it. The following activity invites you to start prognosticating. What do you believe will be the major changes:
  in your career;
  in the organisation you work for;
  in the way you do your work;
  in your lifestyle;
over the next ten years?

Check your own responses to Activity 1 against the following trends, which are already affecting the world of work in Australia and many other countries, and will continue to do so over the next decade.

## Technological innovation

There will be more use of technology in the workplace. This will lead to a reduced demand for labour and emphasise the relentless movement from blue-collar to white-collar work. Producing, processing and distributing will increasingly be done with the aid of microchip processors, communications satellites and home-based computers networked into larger systems. Capital equipment will be increasingly substituted for labour in order to produce maximum outputs in terms of value added with minimum investment in labour. In place of conventional jobs, more people will adopt new ways of supporting themselves such as job sharing, multiple part-time jobs and working from home in self-employment. Historically, the introduction of a new invention has created new jobs and new potential. Yet the technology currently being introduced makes it possible to have economic growth without increasing employment. Microelectronics has made most of this possible and is all-pervasive. It is likely that no business, industry or occupation will be untouched by it.

The technology and information society will not be static, but will be transformed all the time by new discoveries. The cost of robots is declining as wages spiral upwards. A fibre-optic cable can transmit in one second the same volume of electronic signals it would take the traditional copper wire 21 hours to transmit. Biotechnology will be to the twenty-first century what physics and chemistry were to the twentieth, as genes are altered to turn living organisms into industrial products. The superconductors which won Bednorz and Muller the 1987 Nobel Prize for Physics are transforming transport systems (via magnetic levitation), information transmission and medical technology.

'Intelligent' automation replaces workers and, because it uses microelectronic devices, requires significantly less labour to produce than formerly because fewer parts are involved. For example, one telex machine uses one microprocessor to replace 936 moving parts. Continuing occupations require new job skills. For example, the formerly labour-intensive garment industry now requires operators who can use computer systems for cutting out patterns using laser-guided cutters; car mechanics use computerised diagnostic equipment to perform tasks traditionally done by hand and eye.

The introduction of information processing and transmission systems have a marked effect on most people's daily lives. Innumerable spin-offs from microelectronics are changing the world far more comprehensively than the printing press or the steam engine. Among these are automated banking, interactive education systems, remote conferencing, bar-coding, automatic checkouts, stock control, computer-aided design. Improved telecommunications will enable work to be done from home with computers, faxes and 'seeing telephones' all contributing. Businesses will be dispersed, professional people will have the chance to move to rural areas, reversing the attraction of urban living, while decaying cities will have a higher proportion of the unemployed, the unskilled and the service industries. The producing, processing and distribution of information will be the basis of a communications and information society. Electronics rather than physical space connections will be the order of the day. The mining of knowledge is mind-numbing. The sheer quantity of information, indicated by the publication of research papers, is now doubling every ten years.

The high-tech revolution presents a challenge to managers, leading to new management styles that can replace the old adversarial management–labour relationship. Information technology in particular can bring about the internal restructuring of companies, flatten the management pyramid, and put masses of information at the elbow of each manager. For unions the innovations present a challenge. Still afflicted with outdated attitudes, distrustful of technological innovation, and beset by adverse economic conditions, unions and many of their members are in danger of being left out in the cold.

Even for the person in the street there is an inevitability about technological change. You can refuse to use cash dispensers and always go into the bank but the day will come when you need money and the bank is closed. Resist technology as we may in the home or at work, it will still creep in.

## Structural change in industry and award restructuring

Structural changes are linked to technological innovation. Labour-intensive industrial society is changing into an automated information society. All Western industrialised countries are moving from dependence on agricultural activities and heavy industry to white-collar, communication and service industries as newly industrialised countries and Third World countries provide cheaper competition for manufactured goods. Australian government subsidies are being removed, causing much hurt in the agricultural and industrial sectors, as other countries maintain their subsidies. Australian car manufucturers such as Ford and GM-H are closing down plant for a few days at a time to reduce production, and requiring employees to work shorter weeks. The development of specialised industries processing raw materials into expensive exports and investment in industries based on new technology and 'know-how' will speed up, changing the face of Australian industry and job prospects for all time. All aspects of society are becoming increasingly dependent on information, and the number of people employed in collecting, processing, storing and retrieving this welter of information will continually increase. Forty per cent of Australia's workforce is in that sector of work now. However, the very use of new and increasingly sophisticated microelectronics will cause an eventual decline in the service industries as technology takes over even these roles, for example those of bank tellers, petrol station attendants, stock controllers.

When the electronic circuit learns your job, what can you do with yesterday's skills?

The job skills required in the future will be very different as the types of jobs alter and as technology and capital equipment are substituted for labour. According to the National Alliance of Business's 1986 report, 'Looking to the Year 2000', workers aged between 25 and 35 will change the nature of their work five times during their working life, and 75 per cent of currently employed workers will need retraining by the year 2000.

Many industrial awards are reflecting these changes and needs; awards that separate jobs into numerous narrow classifications are now seen as restrictive and obsolete. Award restructuring is giving employers and employees opportunities to change work practices and to promote new ways of thinking about and managing the workplace. The benefits of award restructuring are seen to be:

- replacing outdated methods with more efficient ones
- giving workers more interesting work, better career paths and higher pay, and broad-banding similar jobs and pay rates together
- developing multi-skilling so that workers can do the whole job, not just one small, repetitive part
- introducing more flexible working conditions tailored to an enterprise's needs
- improving job training, and
- facilitating the introduction of new technology.

However vital for the health of Australia's industry and business, such restructuring has its costs for managers and employees. They must be capable of learning new skills, returning to school or training if necessary, and be willing to adopt and operate within new work practices. Some will have to learn to adapt to redundancy, relocation and temporary unemployment. Decentralisation and enterprise bargaining will put a premium on communication skills at all management levels.

## The labour market is changing and shrinking

Structural shifts in the production of goods and services combined with technical change involving the introduction of new equipment, restructuring, new production techniques and new services—all currently overlain by a deep local and world recession—are affecting the number of jobs available as well as modifying job content and the skills and qualifications required in the workplace. Table 1 summarises the trends in Australia.

The most important features of the table are:

**Table 1 Some trends in the Australian labour market (per cent)**

|  | 1968 | 1980 | 1986 | 1989 | 1992 (Feb) |
|---|---|---|---|---|---|
| Unemployment rate | 1.6 | 5.9 | 8.0 | 5.8 | 10.5 |
| Average length of unemployment (weeks) | 7.4 | 32.0 | 46.8 | 45.2 | 49.8 |
| Participation (males) | 83.2 | 77.8 | 75.2 | 74.9 | 69.2 |
| Participation (females) | 31.6 | 42.6 | 48.6 | 51.1 | 49.7 |
| Manufacturing employment/total employment | 25.0 | 19.7 | 16.4 | 16.0 | 15.2 |
| Service employment/total employment | 56.2 | 62.0 | 66.4 | 68.1 | 65.3 |
| Part-time/total employment | 10.5 | 16.4 | 18.9 | 20.8 | 19.8 |

*Sources*:  Australian Bureau of Statistics: The Labour Force. Cat 6203
  Treasury: Economic Round-up
  Reserve Bank: Occasional paper 8A
  Telephonic information ABS.

the increase in part-time employment since 1980
the continuation and recent growth of high rates of
    unemployment
the increase in female labour-force participation rates
the growth in service-sector employment in the last decade

These developments in turn generate other trends such as a decrease in male labour-force participation, a decline in male full-time employment and a decline in the share of employment in manufacturing.

New industries do not require as much labour as the ones being displaced. Most of the jobs that disappear are at low levels of skills and training where the process can easily be automated. Jobs are not being lost to other people. Unemployment rates are reaching high levels, with more than 900 000 unemployed (10.6 per cent of the workforce) in May 1992, an increase of more than 13 700 on the previous month. The grim reality is that Australia may soon be carrying more than one million unemployed people. The Australian Bureau of Labour predicts an unemployment rate of more than 10 per cent until the end of 1993.

During the year July 1990 to July 1991 more than 300 000 workers were retrenched, with construction and manufacturing industries the hardest hit (*The Weekend Australian*, 26 October 1991). Another 100 000 are expected to go in the next decade as a result of structural changes. At least one-third of the job cuts are due to restructuring but were brought forward because of the recession. These losses are permanent losses as both public and private sectors struggle to become more efficient and productive. Private-sector investment in new plant and equipment in 1992 is the lowest for 30 years, suggesting the manufacturing sector is still locked into recession. In early 1992, 34 per cent of companies plan further cuts in their workforces. Given that unemployment lags behind movements in the GDP, it will keep rising for a time after GDP recovers. Alongside all this there has been an increase in the duration of unemployment, a reduction in the length of working life, an increase in part-time work and self-employment, an increase in female workforce participation rates, increasing exposure to unemployment in some groups (e.g. up to 40 per cent for unskilled school leavers in some parts of Victoria) and growing hidden unemployment. Many of these unemployed people may never know full employment again as the dynamics of the labour market change. Full employment, or rather an irreducible minimum rate of 3 per cent unemployment, has always been the goal of Western democracies. This inevitable 3 per cent minimum was due to seasonal factors, workers moving between jobs and voluntary unemployment. Now we have a combination of structural unemployment—in which a few, if no jobs existed in their own field, could find jobs if they changed fields—and demand-deficiency unemployment, where there are no jobs even for workers willing to change fields.

There is ample evidence from Australia's last recession almost a decade ago that labour-market dynamics do indeed change. Employment patterns in the post-recession period were different from those before it, as were employer and trade-union attitudes. This recession is very different from that of ten years ago. Other economic and political factors have been brought into play—deregulation, privatisation, and the general breaking up of government-controlled monopolies. Overseas evidence suggests that such combinations of events contribute to long-term job losses. The current growth in part-time employment does not augur a future increase in full-time employment. It is simply a tactic on the part of employers to maintain a workforce sufficient to meet their needs at any particular time yet minimise their exposure to hefty redundancy and other employment costs. Business investment is at its lowest for twelve years.

By the end of 1991, job vacancies were at their lowest level since data collection began. There will be pockets of growth in service industries and the new technologies (which now employ about 76 per cent of employed people) and these people will require far greater technical skills than in the past. The Department of Education, Employment and Training report 'Australia's Workforce in the Year 2001' (August 1991) claims that over the next ten years the number of jobs requiring a degree will increase by 50 per cent and those requiring other training qualifications will increase by 25 per cent.

It is estimated that up to 70 per cent of new jobs are generated in small businesses. The traditional employment model of unionised male full-time employment in manufacturing enterprises no longer applies. The majority of the labour force will no longer be located in

**Table 2 Employment level changes**

| Area | Peak Aug. 89 | Feb. 92 |
|---|---|---|
| Mining | 107 400 | −21 600 |
| Manufacturing | 1 240 900 | −124 400 |
| Construction | 611 800 | −79 000 |
| Wholesale/retail | 1 639 200 | −66 500 |
| Public admin and defence | 325 900 | +20 200 |
| Recreation and other services | 1 348 400 | +98 900 |

**Table 3 Balance sheet of job losses and job gains**

| Losses | Little change | Gains |
|---|---|---|
| Industrial crafts | Professional/advisory | Computer based employment |
| Retailing | Personal services | Health/Welfare |
| Mechanical operators | Vocational education and training | Manufacture of electronic devices |
| Clerical and secretarial | School teaching | Information systems |
| Manual labourers | | Security |
| Farm work | | Leisure |
| Science | | Psychology |
| Typesetting | | Engineering |
| Banking | | Recurrent education |
| Transport | | Recreation |
| Public sector | | Fast food |
| Textile manufacture | | Taxation |

manufacturing, mining, agriculture or construction industries, each of which has lost more than 10 per cent of its workforce. Manufacturing and agriculture now employ only around 16 per cent and 5 per cent respectively of the working population compared to 27 per cent and 16 per cent in the 1960s. Table 2 shows the changes of employment levels over the last two and a half years in major areas of the economy.

In 1970, 60 per cent of the Australian labour force was unskilled. That ratio has now halved and will continue to decline. Flourishing small businesses and the informal economy will be the future lifeline for many people seeking employment. Informal economies fill needs in the community and can grow, thereby providing work for others. Table 3 lists some of the main areas of job losses and job gains.

According to the Australian Bureau of Statistics, 40 per cent of Australian workers have changed their job in the three years mid 1989 to mid 1992. Thirty per cent of workers are in jobs that did not exist twenty years ago. There will even be a decline in employment in the service industries as economic recession reduces the ability of the general public to purchase services. Job losses are inevitable as businesses shrink or 'rightsize' their labour forces to maintain profitability in the current recession. At the time of writing, Telecom has retrenched 5000 employees, Qantas around 3500, the state of Victoria about 18 000 public servants and Nissan is closing its car manufacturing plant in Victoria. Middle managers in the manufacturing and financial areas are seriously affected by restructuring and technological developments. Their traditional lines of command have been reduced and redefined so that one manager bears a greater degree of responsibility over more areas. Thus multi-skilling is also taking place at the executive level. The old work pattern of our parents' era commonly known as 48 cubed (i.e. 48 hours for 48 weeks for 48 years of your life), is likely to become 35 cubed in future—and even the 35 years are unlikely to be consecutive.

Australia's ability to compete in world markets is eroding. The productivity growth of competitors outstrips our own. The capability of our economy to provide a high standard of living for all Australians is increasingly in doubt. As jobs requiring little skill are automated or go offshore, demand for a pool of highly skilled and talented employees grows and the backwater of unemployable people will rise. The dilemma that Australia faces is that without technology the country will not be competitive in world markets and unemployment would soar even higher. The new technology does help to maintain competitiveness and prevent countless others from joining the ranks of the jobless. But it also means that soon there will not be enough jobs for all the people who want fulltime jobs. Women will find the new forms of work more to their liking than men will, as white-collar and white-coat activities replace blue-collar jobs. House husbands may become as common as housewives, with new technology enabling even the most incompetent to maintain a household. Atypical employment styles such as casual, part-time, and self-employment are growth areas, particularly within the service sector. More unconventional work and periodic unemployment will make it more difficult to separate work from the rest of life, and will make a nonsense of categories like redundant or unemployed.

A tradition already established in the armed services will spread to other areas, as some workers and managers come to expect retirement at 45 and find other work in self-employment or smaller companies with a capital grant or part-pension to start them off. Workers are now almost divided into two tiers: 'core' and 'periphery'. Core workers are fulltime with secure jobs and good conditions of service. Periphery workers are typically those on temporary contracts, part-time, self-employed or employed by subcontractors. Core workers are functionally flexible in return for security. Periphery workers are hired to do specific jobs and fired when no longer needed.

These developments suggest a greater flexibility in the labour force to suit demand and conditions by adjusting the numbers employed and the hours worked. This is indicative of a developing, deregulated, more privatised labour market in which award coverage and union-isation have less of an impact.

Hence training policies, human-resource policies and the content of training programs need to be modified to prepare workers for what lies in their future. Training should no longer be seen as education to earn a living but as education for living. We need to teach people how to cope with unemployment and how to survive without a formal employer, and also furnish them with the knowledge and skills to create their own employment.

## The development of work outside formal employment

Full-time employment has crashed by 5 per cent in the last two years (*SMH*, 25 February 1992) and many people are now seeking to earn a living outside formal employment. Three types of work can be distinguished outside the formal economy; these comprise what is popularly known as the informal economy. The informal economy is made up of the household economy, the voluntary economy and the 'black' economy. These are growing as people find other ways to support themselves, make money and occupy their time. The informal economy has been called the 'self-service economy' as people grow their own vegetables, make their own clothes etc. Many aspects of the informal economy often originate in the household and then extend into the voluntary or black economies. For example a housewife with skill in quilting may make cushion covers for the home. These are seen by guests, who ask her to make some for them and for the school fete; before long a little one-person industry is flourishing, with cash exchanged for products on a private basis. A whole new economy is emerging which is based on relationships rather than bureaucracy, on self-help, on self-employment. It builds networks rather than organisations, and requires skills and expertise rather than qualifications. It thrives on personal energy and initiative. The need is to develop proactive individuals who will refuse to accept that being jobless is the same as being hopeless. The alternative to employment is not necessarily unemployment.

## Decline of the Protestant work ethic

Western society tends to emphasise the ethic of personal success through hard work and suggests that if people are jobless it is their fault because they must be lazy, unreliable and incompetent. This is coupled with a belief that every individual can achieve success through his or her own efforts, and that hard-working individuals, while not gaining much enjoyment from this hard work, will reap their rewards in the afterlife. Hard work is good for the individual, even spiritually cleansing, and prevents sloth and temptation. Thrift is particularly admirable, and future orientation is beneficial, for deferring gratification is an indication of good character.

This Protestant work ethic is no longer tenable if there are not enough jobs to go around and if work cannot function as an indicator of the quality of an unemployed person. It is important not to be locked into a model stemming from the industrial revolution. We may need to develop a new community ethic embodying a concept of one's contribution to society rather than to the economy. The rigid view that salvation lies only in employment must be countered. As early as 1955 Spindler developed a set of what he called emergent values, as opposed to the traditional Protestant ethic. These new values put an emphasis on group relationships, concern for others, relativistic morality and present-time orientation. Rather than being the sum of what one can accomplish, one's career becomes a human project placing not one's work but oneself on display. We need to help ourselves and employees explore a variety of aspects of our lives to discover potential sources of satisfaction other than the work role. We must stop assuming that work is at the core of human functioning. But we must first know what our values are.

A value is a belief we hold that causes us to act the way we do. It is something that we believe to be important in our lives. Examples of values are knowledge, power, money, recognition, friendship. Those who do not know what their values are will drift and make last-minute decisions because they have never thought about what is important to them. People who know their values are purposeful, positive and decisive. To this end, here is an activity to help you assess and explore your own values.

## Activity 2   Your values

The following is a list of 25 values frequently sought by individuals. Choose the five that are most important to you.

- Being an honest person
- Being a reliable person
- Opportunity to enjoy fine food/entertainment/culture
- High self-confidence/self-esteem
- Enjoyment of nature and beauty
- A life with meaning, purpose and fulfilment
- Continuing to learn and gain knowledge
- A chance to help the sick/disadvantaged
- A physical appearance to be proud of
- Some honest close friends
- A long and healthy life
- A meaningful relationship with God

- A good marriage relationship
- Satisfaction/success in career/job of choice
- An equal opportunity for all people
- Freedom to live your life as you want
- A financially comfortable life
- Accomplishing something worthwhile
- A secure family life
- An enjoyable leisurely life
- Possibility of travel
- Being an innovator
- A beautiful home in a setting of own choice
- Opportunity to use creative ability
- Owning possessions of great value.

Look at your five choices and place the number '1' next to the most important one. Continue to rank the other four. Then ask yourself the following questions.

1 Do my actions in my life right now reflect these values and the priorities that I have given to them?
2 If my actions in my life do not reflect my values, how can I change them so they are more in keeping with my values?
3 If there are some aspects in my life that I cannot change now, what is my timetable for bringing my life more into harmony with my values?
4 What kind of career or career change would be most in keeping with my values?

Here is another values clarification exercise.

## Activity 3   Clarifying your values

1 List 20 things you enjoy doing
2 After completing your list do the following:
   - Place a dollar sign next to each item that requires an initial outlay of at least $5
   - Place an O against those items that you prefer to do with other people and an A next to those things that you prefer to do alone
   - Place a 5 next to any item you would not have thought of doing five years ago
   - Place an M next to any item you really enjoy doing
   - Record the date when you last did any of the items you marked with an M
   - Place an S next to items that you do because they give you status

- Place a P next to any item you do because it gives you power

By analysing your responses you can see the basis on which you should choose to live your life, and where you ought to direct your career to gain most satisfaction.

## From state help to self-help

In this century there has been a steady development of social welfare, with its proliferation of schemes for unemployment, old age, health, children's allowances etc. Disillusion has set in not only because such schemes fail to deliver help where it is most needed but also because their cost is enormous and continually rising. The Australian government, along with other Western governments, is looking increasingly to the individual to provide the social welfare the state once provided. Superannuation schemes are encouraged, cut off points for support payments are declining relative to the cost of living, membership of private health schemes will need to increase. In these conditions, there is an increase in the number of community groups providing assistance with housing development, legal aid, child care etc. Self-reliance, resourcefulness and entrepreneurial spirit will be required in an age where state support declines as the needs of unemployed and disillusioned people grow.

## Declining influence of the trades unions

All the above changes tend to shift the balance of power in the labour process towards employers. High unemployment, structural and technological change, and the growing informal economy are placing pressure on trades unions whose membership is declining, and whose leverage on employers is weakening. Only by accepting insignificant or no wage increases will some employees keep their jobs and unions may have to accept changes in awards if they wish to see their members retain jobs. For example, the big SPC cannery in Shepparton, Victoria, stayed in business in 1991 because its employees recognised the plight of the company, realised their jobs were on the line and accepted terms that at one time no union would have contemplated. Luddite attitudes have no place where it is a matter of automate or liquidate. There is now greater willingness on the part of the workforce to accept flexible working arrangements.

## The extension of the third age

The period after the end of working life will start earlier and last for twenty years or more. Working life is shortening as the average lifespan increases. The gap between the end of working life and the end of life itself is going to be a chasm which some will find difficult to fill if they do not plan for early retirement and organise their leisure. A 30-year period of active life is possible. The third age is not a life sentence of boredom or unfulfilment. But it needs to be planned for and used constructively. We can develop hobbies, learn new skills, involve ourselves in the community and in our families. The University of the Third Age will flourish as retirees return to study to develop and enjoy education and interests.

## High-tech–high-touch paradox

The impersonality of a high-tech society will generate the demand for more satisfying personal relationships and groups, therapies, human potential movements, and born-again religions that focus on self-knowledge, self-fulfilment and self-awareness. In a technical world jobs become more specialised, standardised and synchronised as they become more related to the technical means of production. Work can then lose its meaning, and workers in these sorts of environments can become frustrated, bored and alienated in what Studs Terkel has called 'a Monday to Friday sort of dying'. The personal, high-touch corollary develops as a counter to this trend, to satisfy human needs in social, emotional and spiritual areas of life.

The scenario presented above suggests continuing, rapid, and drastic changes to the world of work in Australia, to the lives of those involved in it, and to their families and communities. There is a touch of the inevitable about it. In summary, economic growth will be small, and conventional jobs in the market economy will continue to decline as structural and technological changes ensue. Many people will have to find new possibilities in the informal or part-time sector and develop new work skills through leisure activities. Many business organisations will become smaller, flatter and more spread-out. The world is going to be very different for many people. The message of this book is, When change is inevitable, be proactive, help to shape it and enjoy it. Help others, particularly employees and family members, to do the same by increasing their awareness of what is happening and facilitate their adaptation by providing them with the opportunities to learn the work and personal skills that will be needed in the brave new world ahead. The trick is to prepare for the budding of spring in the midst of the bleak midwinter.

The sorts of skills and characteristics that will help individuals to cope with the challenges (apart from some basic intellectual ability and a sound general education) are listed in Table 4. This list is of general or portable skills, not job-specific skills. That is, they can be applied in a wide variety of settings.

**Table 4  Personal coping skills that can be taught**

How to manage stress
How to make decisions
How to develop positive self-esteem
How to think positively
How to manage time
How to use leisure time
How to communicate effectively
How to be assertive
How to make, keep and end relationships
How to cope with unemployment
How to find a job
How to study effectively
How to use community resources
How to keep informed about the future
How to build and use a network

Any future in-house training programs should incorporate, in addition to industry-based requirements, such components as those listed in Table 4. In short, we can no longer train people for a single skill but rather give them the foundations on which they can come back to training and education again and again in the course of a lifetime. The purpose of these skills is to produce employees who are able to cope with change and life transitions. All of them can be seen as relevant to the scenario raised earlier. Indeed Prime Minister Hawke referred to such skills in his 1986 address to the nation on the economy. A current buzz phrase is that Australia must become a 'clever country'. However, cleverness of itself will not help individuals or the nation. Financial fraud by senior executives can be very clever, as can manipulation of work practices by union members. What is needed is certainly some intellectual skill, knowledge and creativity, but these by themselves may lead to intellectual virtuosity bereft of emotional and social balance and maturity. What must be sought rather than a 'clever country' is an enterprising and hard-working country where future and established workers and management are provided with satisfying work and work conditions *plus* personal growth skills.

There is of course a context in which this training and preparation can be done. This is the mandatory training requirements imposed by the federal government under its training guarantee scheme. All Australian employers have to spend in the year July 1991 to June 1992 1.5 per cent of their wages bill on employee education and training. This ratio will inevitably be increased over time. The Taxation Office has the responsibility to ensure employers meet these requirements. Under the Act, an approved training program must fulfil three criteria: it must be concerned with employment-related skills; it must be structured around defined objectives and details must be provided of how such objectives will be assessed; and it must have been constructed by a qualified training officer. Currently only a minority of employers are committed to in-house training. Before July 1990, of Australian public and private companies with payrolls of $200 000 to $2 million, 62 per cent allocated nothing to training.

## Summary

People today are subject to enormous stresses as a result of the rapid changes that are proceeding at an ever-increasing pace in technology, in the home, at work, and in the environment. According to Alvin Toffler, many people will suffer from 'future shock' because they have not anticipated the changes, and are not prepared to face them. This chapter has provided an overview of the technological, economic and social changes that are transforming the world of work, particularly in Australia. Technological innovation, world and local recession and the consequent restructuring are creating a different employment environment for the future, with employment opportunities expanding for some, and diminishing for others. New concepts of career and employment, new work practices, new values and philosophies about work are emerging. All these have far-reaching implications for managers in their management of employees and themselves in this time of change.

The changes are not ephemeral, but will be with us for many years to come. Businesses need to be well aware of these trends and provide, for their managers and other staff, training in general, personal and portable skills that will enable individuals and companies to survive, adapt and prosper.

# 2

# Change
# *A personal issue*

*Change is not made without inconvenience, even from worse to better.*

Dr Johnson

*God grant me the courage to change the things I can, the serenity to accept the things I cannot change, and the wisdom to know the difference.*

*All changes, even the longed for, have their melancholy, for what we leave behind us is part of ourselves; we must die one life before we can enter another*

Anatole France

*There is nothing permanent except change*

Heraclities (535–475 BC)

## Change: danger or opportunity

Several times I have moved to a new job in a new country, which meant that as I was learning about a new task in a new work environment, my family and I were also adjusting to a new culture, new schools, new house, and the absence of old friends and ways of living. On each occasion the whole process has been traumatic, and fraught with stress as each family member tried to come to terms with a changed personal world. This book is about how to cope with the stress of change and the life transitions that accompany change, and how best it can all be managed with reference to the world of work.

A life transition is any event or time passage that results in a change in the way you live, in how you see yourself and the world around you, and in your relationships with others. Some transitions you can anticipate and plan for: marriage, the birth of a child, obtaining a university degree. Other transitions are unexpected: the death of someone close to you, the sudden loss of a job, the unanticipated promotion, the unrequested transfer to a branch in another state.

Every change and transition involves loss and gain. The old environment must be given up, the new accepted. People come and go; one job is lost, another begun; territory and possessions are accrued or sold; new skills are learned, old ones abandoned; expectations are fulfilled or hopes dashed. In all these situations the individual is faced with the need to give up one mode of life and accept another. Change, or as it is termed in the human context, life transition, is a life crisis, but of course—as the Chinese recognised with their word for crisis, *wei chi*, a compound of the words for danger and opportunity—there are both dangers and opportunities in life transitions. The aim is to recognise the dangers and seize the opportunities. In a dynamic universe nothing remains the same. Humans can cope with change if it takes place at a steady pace and if they can incorporate it gradually into their lives. But evolving change has been replaced by revolutionary change and humans do not cope well with rapid change. They prefer stability. Stability is the known; change is the unknown with its confusions and disturbances to settled and known ways of doing things. Even those who have never had quite as traumatic an experience as that of moving to a new country are well aware of recent changes to their lifestyles. A day out in the car has to be calculated in terms of petrol costs, overseas holidays are too expensive, dining out is rare, bankruptcies escalate in number, large companies shed staff or close for extended holidays to stay in business, houses cease to be a good investment as they fail to appreciate much in value. Our lives are altering. Things will never be the same and we must adjust to the changes. Yet we would prefer things to be the same as they were. Most of us are unready and perhaps even unwilling to meet the future and will suffer from 'future shock'. Personal wellbeing is best assured where order, security, stability and predictability are common features of the environment.

## Life events

There are well-researched links between having to cope with too much change and stress-related illness. Living at a time of rapid change can induce feelings of powerlessness, apathy and alienation. It can increase the incidence of mental illness, anxiety and neurosis, and is likely to produce social symptoms such as increases in violent crime, less-stable family relationships, and even political unrest. If the features of the future are more options, fewer certainties, more pressures and more ambiguities, then this is likely to call for individuals who are resilient, confident, adaptable. In Chapter 3 we will be considering more fully the effects of stress on health.

Any change in an individual's life, whether pleasant or unpleasant, requires some readjustment. In *Future Shock*, Alvin Toffler suggests that even though change is a necessary element in the lives of individuals and society, if it occurs at too great a rate or on too massive a scale we may cease reaping the rewards of change and begin contemplating the devastation it causes and the effort—physical, psychological and emotional—needed to keep up with and adjust to it. This sequence can last from two minutes to a lifetime. There is no definite timespan. Each stage can recur. It is normal and healthy to experience feelings of anger, despair, guilt and even elation in response to both chosen and forced life transitions. Those who take longer to adjust are those whose transition was forced, or imposed. They have made no free choice; understandable and strong anger, depression, and guilt may last a long time.

*The transition curve*

It is not possible to predict how someone will react to change as every experience is affected by a host of variables. There is, however, a distinct and recognisable pattern in the stages of response to change or life transitions. The type and depth of event will obviously affect the strength of the reaction and the time taken to complete the process—promotion is more welcome than redundancy, marriage more positive than divorce.

Figure 1 shows a common sequence of reactions to change where change is imposed and perceived as negative. It is often called the transition curve.

*Recognising the symptoms*

Accepting and talking about negative and upsetting feelings is an effective way to let go of them. One woman I know went through most of the reactions of the transition curve in one awful day, two months after she accepted voluntary redundancy. She almost telephoned her former workplace to beg them for a few hours upaid work. Others report being irritable, having headaches and colds, eating and drinking more than usual, altered sleep patterns, avoiding going out and spending the day in front of the TV. If you are concerned

**Figure 1   The transition curve**

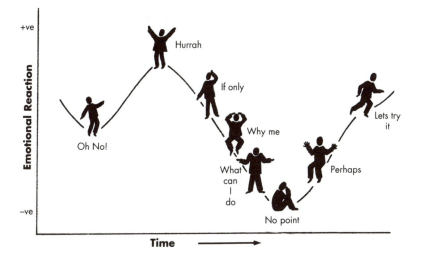

Shock:    Unable to believe it has happened. 'You are joking.' Sometimes frantic, useless activity.

Euphoria:    'Didn't like the job anyway'; 'She'll be right.'*

Guilt:    Blame self. 'If only I'd . . .'

Anger:    Blame someone—the boss, the government, the company, me.

Despair:    'What am I going to do?'

Apathy/depression:    Lack of motivation . . . to get up, to plan, to do anything. At worst, it seems too much effort to stay alive.

Gradual acceptance:    Letting go—taking up old and new activities.

about your behaviour or that of a colleague, do find someone to talk to about it. A sympathetic listener is the best medicine. Many of these transition reactions can occur before the change itself. This situation arises when there is a winding-down process before to the final act. Papers have to be sorted, desk cleared, responsibilities re-assigned, career or retirement counselling meetings attended, discussions held about new duties or training a successor, relocation planned. All these activities and many more are potent daily indicators of the change to come.

Change, regardless of whether it is desirable or undesirable, will produce stress. Negative, or distressful, events are usually the most harmful as they stimulate fear, self-doubt and catastrophic imaginings.

Holmes and Rahe (1967) have devised a Life Change Stress Index which emphasises that any change in a person's life, whether pleasant or unpleasant, requires some readjustment. The index lists 42 life-change events ranked in order from the most serious (death of spouse), through such events as being fired, retirement, change in financial status or working hours, to the least serious (minor infringements of the law). To arrive at this scale the investigators interviewed thousands of people and examined hundreds of medical records to identify the kinds of life events and transitions that people find stressful, the subjective degree of stress felt and the consequent health effects. The Life Change Stress Index is included as Activity 4.

Studies using this index have found a consistent relationship between the number and type of changes in a person's life and their emotional and physical health. Each item on the index is given a numerical value depending on the strength of its effect. Using the Holmes-Rahe scale, a consistent relationship has been found between emotional and physical health and preceding stressful events. A number of studies have found that more than half the people whose life-change score for one year totalled between 200 and 300 had health problems the following year. Of those with scores over 300, 79 per cent became ill the following year.

These illnesses are not caused so much by the crisis itself as by the way in which the individual perceives it. If the event is threatening to the person's self-identity, self-esteem or personal survival, the resultant fear or insecurity may trigger the illness—particularly where some personal loss has occurred, such as bereavement, redundancy or early retirement. Some researchers believe that this sense of loss (actual, potential or imagined) can give rise to an emotional response of hopelessness and helplessness which results in the individual literally 'giving up' as his sense of being a worthwhile, complete and useful individual is fractured.

Of course it is impossible to say that there is a direct cause and effect at work here. When people are stressed they often seek solace in habits such as smoking, overeating and drinking, all of which have adverse implications for health. Stressful life-change events do appear to play a role in personal health but they may do so in interaction with other life habits, pre-existing susceptibilities to certain disorders and the psychological characteristics of the individual. It is important to remember that it is the accumulation of events over a concentrated period, not one event, that is predictive of illness.

# Activity 4

**Table 5  Life change stress index**

| Event | Scale of impact | Your stress score |
|---|---|---|
| Death of spouse | 100 | _____ |
| Divorce | 73 | _____ |
| Marital separation | 65 | _____ |
| Jail term | 63 | _____ |
| Death of close family member | 63 | _____ |
| Personal injury or illness | 53 | _____ |
| Marriage | 50 | _____ |
| Fired at work | 47 | _____ |
| Marital reconciliation | 45 | _____ |
| Retirement | 45 | _____ |
| Change in health of family member | 44 | _____ |
| Pregnancy | 40 | _____ |
| Sex difficulties | 39 | _____ |
| Gain of new family member | 39 | _____ |
| Business readjustment | 39 | _____ |
| Change in financial state | 38 | _____ |
| Death of close friend | 37 | _____ |
| Change to different line of work | 36 | _____ |
| Change in number of arguments with spouse | 35 | _____ |
| Mortgage over $80 000 | 31 | _____ |
| Foreclosure of mortgage or loan | 30 | _____ |
| Change in responsibilities at work | 29 | _____ |
| Son or daughter leaving home | 29 | _____ |
| Trouble with in-laws | 29 | _____ |
| Outstanding personal achievement | 28 | _____ |
| Spouse begins or stops work | 26 | _____ |
| Begin or end of school | 26 | _____ |
| Change in living conditions | 25 | _____ |
| Revision of personal habits | 24 | _____ |
| Trouble with boss | 23 | _____ |
| Change in work hours or conditions | 20 | _____ |
| Change in residence | 20 | _____ |
| Change in schools | 20 | _____ |
| Change in recreation | 19 | _____ |
| Change in church activities | 19 | _____ |
| Change in social activities | 18 | _____ |
| Mortgage or loan less than $80 000 | 17 | _____ |
| Change in sleeping habits | 16 | _____ |
| Change in number of family get-togethers | 15 | _____ |
| Change in eating habits | 15 | _____ |
| Vacation | 13 | _____ |
| Minor violations of the law | 11 | _____ |

*Source*: Adapted from Holmes, T. & Rahe, R., 'The social readjustment rating scale'
Journal of Psychosomatic Research 1967, no. 11, pp. 213–218.

You can interpret your score as follows:

What was your score? Look at the items you marked and think about the following:

- Which items you have marked had a negative/unpleasant effect?
- Which items had a positive/pleasant effect?
- How did you respond at the time?
- In future would you respond differently?
- Did the activity suggest that you need to learn how to cope more adaptively with events?
- Did the scoring of the scale match your responses in terms of how you felt they affected you/stressed you?

If you scored in the moderate or high range you should try to ward off the effects of these events by learning relaxation techniques, positive thinking and self-esteem enhancement (Chapter 5).

Your score on the above scale only indicates your probable level of resistance to stress and how likely you are to become ill from the changes you have been through during the past year. Remember, these are *probabilities only*. Given a group of people who have filled out the rating scale and received the same score, all of them will have the same probability or odds of becoming ill as a result of the changes they have experienced. But only some will succumb to illness. Part of the reason for this is that those who cope successfully are more likely to be healthy. Whether you remain well or become ill will depend more on how you perceive, cope and deal with the issues than upon the actual score you got. A high score should, however, serve as a warning that you may need to attend to the stress that is building up in your life and devote yourself to more effective ways of coping.

Changes in your life are not necessarily to be avoided. The nature of human life, growth and development requires change at various stages. But too much change in too short a time exacts its toll on the body's adaptive capabilities, thus increasing the risk of major health problems. Another factor that influences how a person reacts to change is their subjective interpretation of the change.

## Perception of change: Seeing is believing, or is it believing is seeing?

Perception is an active and subjective process in which distortion of reality is likely to occur. Every experience is given meaning by the individual doing the experiencing. 'We don't see things as they are; we see them as we are' (Gibran, *The Prophet*). We can complain that rose bushes have thorns or rejoice that thorn bushes have roses. If a young male administrative assistant offers his seat in a full staffroom to a middle-aged female computer-input clerk, she may interpret it as a kindly act, as an insult about her age, or even as an improper advance. Each of these interpretations is dramatically influenced by the view that the woman has of herself. In another example, two hat salesmen went to a foreign country to sell hats. On arriving, they found that everyone wore hats. One salesman went home immediately, perceiving no sales in a saturated market; the other stayed, enthusing over the size of the market and the possibilities for different types of headgear.

So what we see, hear or feel is not always a true reflection of reality. Each of us organises our perception of events or items into something that is meaningful to us as individuals, that makes sense to us personally. Every experience, change, life transition is turned into a subjective and personally meaningful perception as it is filtered through a plethora of feelings, expectations, past experiences, and emotional mood states. New experiences are interpreted in terms of meanings we already hold, whether those meanings are true or not. Obviously, changes and life transitions are also filtered into these subjective meanings. Subjective interpretation is the way we make sense of the environment—it provides a frame of reference without which we would have great difficulty understanding and interpreting events. So in a sense we distort reality and try to make things fit our own preconceived notions. That which does not fit in is denied, distorted, ignored. Our perception also can fill things in if they do not fit with what we expect, deliberately giving pattern and meaning to seeming anomalies.

*Perception of self*

Our emotional response to events, and particularly the way we see ourselves—as valuable, worthless, intelligent, lazy—affects our perception and interpretation of the situation. We react or respond to other people and to ourselves in the light of our previous experiences. For example, a person who perceives herself as a failure (even if this perception is erroneous on objective grounds) may attribute any success she has to luck, or see encouragement from others as a kind of deceit, since in her opinion it is undeserved. We often believe naively that the way to improve self-esteem in employees with low self-esteem is to provide them with positive reinforcement or positive feedback, for example by praising their work. We do this to demonstrate how competent we feel they are. But there is no guarantee that the employee will perceive such actions in the way they were meant. The employee could well perceive the situation negatively, saying to himself, 'I must be incompetent, or why would the boss keep trying to tell me I'm not'. It makes a great deal of difference to how you perceive your work situation, a change in your work practices, a sideways move or a redundancy if you usually see yourself as a respected, successful and competent manager, supervisor or employee—or alternatively, as an incompetent failure.

Work role is a vital part of self. The perception and interpretation of changed work roles, in a sense looking at yourself in a new way, working out new accommodations with those around you, worrying whether you are meeting or even can meet the demands of the changed role, all combine to produce stress. A woman placed in authority over men, a younger person supervising older colleagues, a transferee to another department all have to revise in some way their self-concepts as both they and the others involved perceive the new situation from their own perspectives. A supervisor promoted from the ranks will start to perceive the work context, relationships with workers, relations with staff, and union activities in very different ways as the new role restructures perceptions.

*The role of words in perception*

The use of words to describe items or events determines to a large extent how these items or events are perceived and interpreted. Simple examples are illustrated in the Punch cartoon (Figure 2) and in the way verbal labels affect the interpretation of an ambiguous sketch (Figure 3).

Figure 3 summarises an experiment conducted in the 1930s. Subjects were shown a set of ambiguous figures, as in column A. Half the subjects were informed that these figures represented the items named in column B; the other half were told they portrayed those listed in column C. When the subjects were asked to reproduce what they had originally seen in column A, they modified the drawings towards the verbal labels they had been given.

Our ability to take in accurately what we see or hear or read is certainly nowhere near perfect. Try the next activity.

## Activity 5

Have a look at the following sentence. Count the number of 'f's in the sentence. The number will be revealed when you turn the page.

FINISHED FILES ARE THE RESULT OF YEARS OF SCIEN-TIFIC STUDY COMBINED WITH THE EXPERIENCE OF MANY YEARS

*Stereotypes*

In our perception of others we tend to rely on stereotypes. Stereotypes are generalisations based on limited experience and inference.

**Figure 2  Punch lines**

JOINT WINNERS:  *'Well, it started as a rag stunt years ago.'*

P. Haywood of Leeds.

AND: *'Try not to look too conspicuous, Constable.'*

S. Dexter of Horley, Surrey.

1933 caption—Watchman. *'Yes, it's my old box all right, Fred, but I've thought of a new idea for more comfort.'*

Words may alter what we read into a picture—as with these 'then and now' examples of humour from *Punch*. They provide a frame of reference which the picture alone cannot supply.

On meeting a Scotsman or an Italian for the first time some people will assume without evidence that the former is a Scrooge, extra careful with money, and the latter a Lothario, libido-loaded. They may respond to the Scotsman or Italian in the light of these stereotypes, ignoring any evidence to the contrary. Stereotypes are often based on syllogistic reasoning. For example,

- all bald managers are mean and uncaring
- Mr X is bald and a manager
- therefore Mr X is mean and uncaring

People hold onto these sets, prejudices, stereotypes and idiosyncratic ways of construing their environment because they provide a frame of reference in which to produce a habitual response. These perceptions and responses make a kind of sense. Evidence that does not fit in is threatening and is therefore ignored or distorted.

**Figure 3  Verbal labels**

*Perception of drawings and illusions*

Many drawings and illusions demonstrate that we can interpret things in different ways.

## Activity 6

Have a look at Figure 4. What do you see?

**Figure 4   Illusion A**

Some of you will see two faces; others will perceive the outline of a vase. In fact, once you have settled on one interpretation it is hard to let go of it for long enough to see the alternative.

Look at the illusion (Figure 5). Which of the three lines is longest? Measure them. The Kanizsa Triangle (Figure 6) appears to be an erect white triangle with a black disc beneath each corner, superimposed upon a shaded-bordered inverted triangle.

Things do not look as they do because of what they actually are, but more because of the way we interpret them. Each of the lines is the same length and of course there is no white triangle. Do you remember counting the 'f's over the page? How many did you count? There are actually six 'f's in the sentence!

**Figure 5    Illusion B**

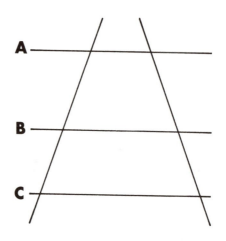

**Figure 6    Illusion C**

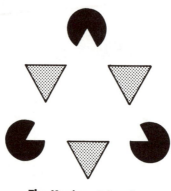

**The Kanizsa Triangle**

*Expectations*

Perception and interpretation are influenced by expectation too. In one experiment a class of students was shown a new born baby. Half of the group was informed it was a male; the other half was told it was a female. They were then asked to observe it and describe its characteristic behaviour. Those students who believed it to be male saw the baby as vigorous, active, strong; those who believed it to be female reported it to be placid and quiet. Clearly, the students' expectations of how male and female babies should behave were affecting their subjective perceptions.

The examples of these experiments and the illusions show that people's needs, moods, motives and expectations strongly influence their subjective perception of events and other people. Our subjective perception can make the difference between feeling good and reacting positively about something or someone, or feeling bad and reacting negatively. People are not disturbed by things but by the views they have of them. Changes in organisations hold no uniform meanings for members. Depending on individuals and circumstances, a change in work practices could be equated with a wide range of concepts ranging from innovation, growth, transformation, opportunity, involvement, renovation, through standardisation, decentralisation, automation, to confusion, coercion, repression and destruction. Our individual perception of terms like 'redundancy', 'bosses', 'unions', 'restructuring' and 'unemployment' influences our reaction to them. Whether we interpret redundancy as the end of the line or as a God-given opportunity to develop some new skills is a complex reaction based on our needs, moods, past experience, expectations. Our perception of ourselves also influences our reaction to changing circumstance; it can be a threat, another confirmation that we are a failure, or it can be a challenge, a learning experience. Others, such as managers bearing the news of change, colleagues not affected by the change, family members who are affected by the change, may be perceived in a variety of ways depending on our emotional state. Thus the same event can be viewed by different players in very different personal ways.

## Activity 7

1 Your organisation borrows money from the bank to finance the introduction of new technology that will enable it to expand its business. The staff object and go on strike.
How might each of the following perceive the situation:

   the staff
   the management
   the bank manager?

2  A customer returns a faulty product and demands a refund. How might the following view the situation:

  the customer
  the sales person
  the department manager?

## Activity 8

Write down three situations in which you have experienced some mental, emotional or physical tension and your interpretations and perceptions of those situations.
Example:

| Situation | Feeling | Perception |
| --- | --- | --- |
| A colleague told me that he didn't think the report I wrote was very good. | Anger, hurt | He's got it wrong. He feels threatened. |

Now write your own, and as you will see, each situation can be interpreted in a variety of ways.

*Your perception of a transition*

How we perceive ourselves—our self-concept—affects how we perceive the world. The lover sees everything through rose-coloured glasses, the child's happy optimism makes the world appear to be his oyster, while the unemployed person may see everything in depressing and morbid terms. Figure 7 shows how an event such as having to relocate can be perceived in two very different ways.

The subjective element in the perception and interpretation of our life situations is a major cause of stress, since perceiving ourself and what happens to us with a negative tinge reduces our ability to cope and adapt and increases tension. Your perception of a transition affects how successful you are in dealing with it. Some factors to consider are,

a)  Do you see the transition as a gain or a loss?
We have already seen that every change may involve both, but as with the force-field analysis below, what at first seemed to be a major loss can in the long run turn into a major gain. Try and focus on the positive aspects of each transition you face.

b)  Do you have control over the transition?
You react differently if you have some control over the transition rather than it just happening to you. You may choose to resign, to marry someone, to buy a car. On the other hand, you may have little

**Figure 7 Married male aged 40 made to relocate**

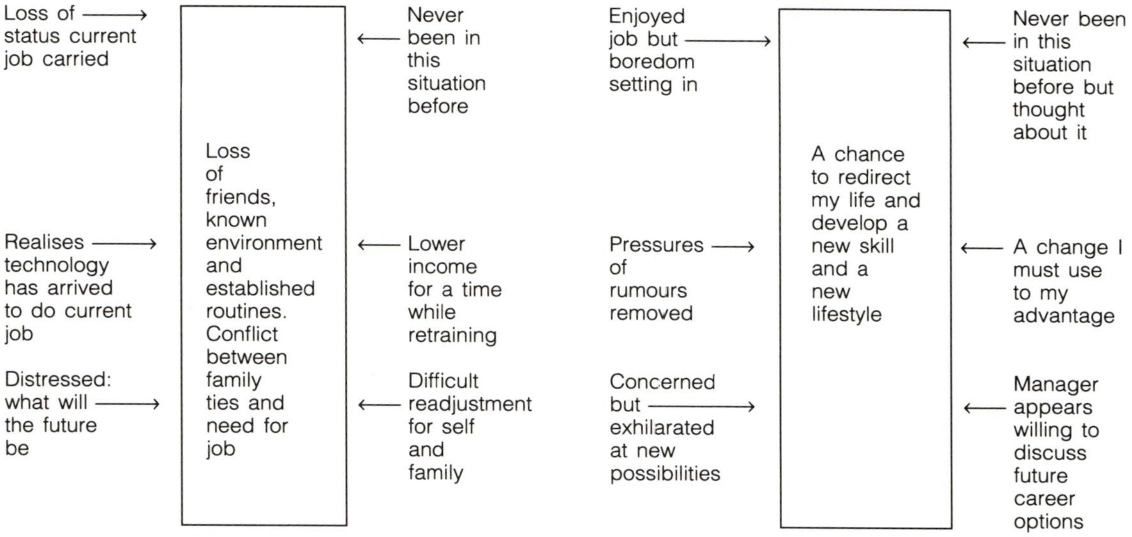

Loss of status current job carried ⟶ Never been in this situation before

Realises technology has arrived to do current job ⟶ Lower income for a time while retraining

Distressed: what will the future be ⟶ Difficult readjustment for self and family

Loss of friends, known environment and established routines. Conflict between family ties and need for job

Enjoyed job but boredom setting in ⟶ Never been in this situation before but thought about it

Pressures of rumours removed ⟶ A change I must use to my advantage

Concerned but exhilarated at new possibilities ⟶ Manager appears willing to discuss future career options

A chance to redirect my life and develop a new skill and a new lifestyle

control over whom your child marries, over the firm you work for
becoming bankrupt, or over the loss of financial aid due to a change
in government policy. But often you may have far more control than
you think.

c)   Is the timing of the transition on time or off time?
You expect certain changes in your life at certain times. Retirement
in the early 60s can be anticipated and planned for. On the other
hand, forced retirement unplanned-for in the 40s is quite difficult to
deal with.

d)   Does the transition come suddenly or gradually?
You can plan for a gradual transition such as a coming marriage, but
a sudden transfer to another city, a sudden loss of financial resources
or even a sudden promotion presents immediate adjustment problems.

e)   Is the transition permanent, temporary or uncertain?
A permanent transition, though stressful, can sooner or later be adjusted to by most people. A temporary transition—say a six-month
move to another country—can again be coped with, as you can anticipate the re-establishment of the old routines at the end of the
transfer. An uncertain transition, such as the removal of overtime,
makes it much more difficult to plan ahead since a return to the
original conditions may never eventuate.

Thus change has both quantitative and qualitative aspects. In the
quantitative sense change is measurable. We can count, for example,
the increasing number of people out of work, or note the frequent
increases in the price of petrol. Change is also a qualitative experience. In this sense, change is less a result of actual changes around
us and more a product of our perception of how things seem to be.
Qualitative change therefore includes our feelings, attitudes and
expectations about events and people. Thus each of us 'knows' or
experiences change in a unique way. Do you look at a glass of water
and see it as half full or half empty? You can take a negative, even
catastrophic view and look on the dark side of most changes. But
you can also take the positive view and concentrate on potential
opportunities.

Perceiving change and managing change are thus closely inter-
locked; the perception influences the reaction and the strategy used.
It is interesting to note that it is change itself, not simply negatively
perceived events, that has a significant impact on our physical and
mental health. A new job or promotion can be a happy event, but it
requires adaptations that have far-reaching consequences for personal adjustment.

So it all depends on how you perceive a particular event, for every
event is open to innumerable interpretations. It is vital that as far as
possible each person's explanation of what is happening around them
and to them is viewed as positively as possible, so the person's re-

sponses to the situation are those that will lead to beneficial outcomes and not to self-defeat.

## The elements of change

Change usually involves four elements. First there is **loss**: the loss of known and accepted routines in your life, the loss of security that goes with those routines and behaviours and the loss of previously made life plans. Things will never be as they were. This loss is often termed 'letting go'. But if change is to be a learning experience we have to learn to let go. Letting go is most difficult in cases such as bereavement, divorce, children leaving home, redundancy, a house fire and burglary. We need to accept that the past is really past. The stolen car has gone for good; the firm has closed down for ever. It does not mean we should try to deny that we ever owned the car or held the job but we should turn them into happy memories and accept that these events are over. When couples have a trial separation before divorce or when management discussions are held about the possibility of employee redundancy, it may give the impression to some that the past is not necessarily past. Things could still turn out all right. Immediate divorce or notice of redundancy without the moratorium of hope is far more enabling for letting go, for the acceptance that a change in lifestyle is now mandatory. Similarly in wartime, it is infinitely more disturbing to receive the message 'missing believed killed' than just 'killed'. The roller-coaster of hope and despair prevents early adjustment to a finality.

The second element of change is **replacement**: this involves the conditions that newly impose themselves: a new environment, new plans, new conditions of work, new roles to play. These replacements need adjusting to just as much as the losses do.

Third, there is the **risk** attached to all changes: is the replacement better than the loss? How will it all work out? There will always be negatives as well as positives. An entrepreneur will not succeed with every scheme, gold miners do not strike gold in every shaft, sales representatives do not get orders with every sales pitch. Such failures could cause some people to withdraw from the activity. Having failed, they regard themselves, rather than the activity, as a failure. However these failures must be perceived as enabling a possibility to be crossed off the list. They can also be perceived positively—as a learning experience providing guidelines about what to do and what not to do in some future similar event.

Fourth, there is **continuity**. This involves the continuation of elements from the past through the present and into the future. Such elements are usually core elements in our lives. One is our own self; we can never leave it behind; it travels with us. The more positive and secure we feel about ourselves, the easier we find it to cope with change. The role of the self-concept in enabling us to cope with change will be considered in depth in Chapter 3. We are a stable element in our environment.

Another core element of continuity is memory. We can enjoy recollections of departed loved ones, of jobs once held, of former homes and friendships. However, in order to maintain some continuity with the past, our behaviour may betray that our self has habitual ways of operating, ways that are incongruous with the needs of the present and the future. The divorcee may engage in a hectic pursuit of amorous affairs to replace the loss, and the redundant person may submit a plethora of unsuitable job applications just to gain employment again.

A balance between letting go and continuity is needed to permit a person to cope with change. There should be a thread of continuity through any change—a secure and steady rock that is the core of our life. This core of continuity could be one or some of the following: family, friends, religious commitment, work, leisure pursuits and so on. So long as change does not remove all such elements at once, those which remain provide the continuity and lifebelts that prevent us drowning in the maelstrom of personal upset. The security of home support, of continuing friendships, of an interest-group membership can all help Mary through the unsettling period of learning new skills in a job-restructuring program at work. On the other hand, such an occupational trauma is made more difficult for Jack to cope with if he is going through a divorce and has little involvement with other leisure, interest-group or community activities. If one's only focus in life disappears, stress, ill-health and emotional disturbance are the heirs.

For those such as recent immigrants who are involved in changing their entire lifestyle, the only continuity may be their immediate family, and the debit side of loss may weigh them down. Continuity here can only be fostered through expectations: a looking forward and planning for what life will be like. The continuity is in the mind first of all, a dream which one hopes will come to pass.

Generally, change is easier to manage when:
- the change is voluntary and predicted
- other changes are kept to a minimum
- there are supportive relationships
- self-esteem and confidence are high
- there are many interests outside the job
- employers offer opportunities for gradual change
- there are opportunities to exchange one job for another
- employees are offered formal opportunities to join in the planning and exploration of future options.

## Role and role change

A person's role is the set of expectations others have of his or her behaviours and attributes with respect to a particular job, position or status. Mary's knowledge of how to do the job and the kinds of interactions expected of her are all part of her role. We all occupy many roles in the course of a day—parent, citizen, committee member, employee and so on. Role is the dynamic aspect of position and status. Roles are aggregates of the expectations of numerous others. The expectations transmitted to us about the particular roles we fill are perceived by us with a lesser or greater degree of accuracy and, when we are figuring out how to behave in the role, are assessed against our own predispositions and experience. But there is far more latitude in the social role of parent, say, than in a job role, where there is frequently a detailed official description which acts as an index of others' expectations and against which one is measured.

Since a particular work role applies to anyone occupying a given position, it follows that changes in work practices and in one's position or status require a change in role behaviour. There is now a different role to play, different expectations of self and of others to be met. So it is not simply a matter of coping with promotion, demotion, transfer, retraining, redundancy and so on. Part of the adjustment, perhaps a major part, involves learning a new role, learning the expectations that flow from that new role and getting comfortable with the new role behaviour. In a study by Lieberman (1956), employees promoted to foreman became more positively disposed toward management, while those promoted to shop steward became more hostile to management. In changing roles, the employee must also change attitudes, values and behaviour and rework them into a congruent matrix. Social role and status changes such as marriage are accompanied by known and specific rites and ceremonies. Such rites often clarify and describe expected behaviour in the new position and make the life transition easier. In the work context, however, exactly what must be changed and learned is often unclear, ambiguous, and anxiety-provoking.

Figure 8 shows how roles are learned. At the outset are group expectations about a particular position. These expectations may not always be congruent, as they may derive from various groups. For example, one's fellow employees may have a different set of expectations about a particular position than management does. These expectations are communicated in formal ways (job descriptions, safety regulations) and informal ways (colleague pressure, shop-floor norms). The third stage is the way this mixture of expectations is perceived and interpreted by the incumbent, whose personal input affects the role as he plays it. The fourth and final stage is the actual role behaviour.

**Figure 8   Role learning**

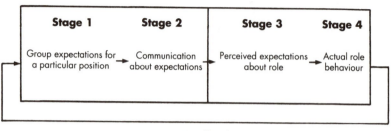

| Stage 1 | Stage 2 | Stage 3 | Stage 4 |
|---------|---------|---------|---------|
| Group expectations for a particular position | Communication about expectations | Perceived expectations about role | Actual role behaviour |

**Feedback**

*Role ambiguity*

When the expectations are unclear, and the occupant is uncertain about what he or she is supposed to do—'I don't know exactly what my boss expects of me in this new post'—then role ambiguity exists. This can occur when internal reorganisation, unsupported by detailed thought and planning, is the order of the day. Jobs are switched around or combined or new jobs created without detailed job descriptions being provided or discussed with the employees concerned. Role ambiguity contributes to low employee job satisfaction, low commitment to the organisation and lower performance, since unclear goals reduce motivation.

*Role overload*

When expectations are too numerous, role overload occurs—'I cannot cope with two people's jobs now my assistant has been made redundant'. The common trend to reduce staff may well result in such an overload and also involve ambiguity, as in the examples above. Job disatisfaction, fatigue and stress can result from overload. Role overload more frequently appears in supervisors and members of lower management, who act as troubleshooters and go-betweens between workers and upper management on a variety of issues simultaneously.

*Role conflict*

When there is disagreement over the expectations of others about what a job involves, role conflict is present—'Everyone has a different idea about what I will be doing in the new set-up'. This situation often results from sudden change in an organisation with employees being placed in new and ambiguous roles. Sometimes the different expectations arise from people at different levels of the organisation. People in the middle of an organisational hierarchy, such as supervisors, tend to be in this dilemma, receiving one set of expectations from above and another from below. The man in the middle is often dependent on his superior for career prospects, resources and support and must focus in his work role on efficiency, performance and cost, yet his subordinates expect similar support in their endeavours and in representing their interests to management, particularly with regard to wages, security, and comfort. Managers have to learn to balance the organisation's need for tough and effective management with their role in supporting, encouraging, reinforcing and motivating staff to perform.

Role conflict also exists where there is incompatibility between two or more roles played by the same person. The accountant may also be a wife and mother. In Australia women now comprise nearly half the workforce. The conflict between role demands can often create disharmony, with shift work, work brought home or absence abroad all capable of interrupting the adequate playing-out of either role. Promotion, relocation, internal transfer, redundancy can all cause stress as new roles interrupt or impede other roles, particularly in the home. Some jobs actually contain conflicting roles. A human-resources manager in a small company may find herself acting as a counsellor and career adviser one minute and as a disciplinary agent the next.

It is unlikely that any work or work-related role will be conflict-free, particularly when considerable and rapid changes are occurring in the workplace, altering old roles, creating new roles, fusing roles, substituting and removing roles. Management must ensure that role conflicts and ambiguities do not overwhelm employees. Role conflict has a potent effect on job satisfaction, job commitment and job involvement.

*Stigmatised roles*

Some roles are stigmatised because the incumbent and others recognise their undesirability. Being made redundant is such a role: it is demeaning, lowers self-esteem, reduces motivation and invites criticism from others who may view it unsympathetically as one's own fault, an index of incompetence, laziness or both. Such devaluation reduces the individual's psychological status. Some jobs are also stigmatised, for example garbage collector, street cleaner, kitchenhand or parks and gardens worker.

*Reduction of role problems*

There are three essential strategies to reduce potential role problems. First, jobs need to be clearly defined and as changes in work practices occur, new job descriptions need to be worked out in consultation with employees. Second, employees will need training to adjust to new or changed roles so that they know the expectations, the lines of authority, the skills required and so on. Third, effective selection techniques should be employed to ensure that those selected or appointed are able now, or will be able after training, to cope with the specific requirements of the job. So by means of detailed job analysis, job design, job specification, training and selection, role problems can be reduced in an era of change.

## Change strategies

There are three major strategies for initiating change, according to Chin and Benne. Which strategy is chosen depends on the people and situations involved. The three strategies are:

- rational (cognitive)
- power–legislative (behavioural)
- re-educative (affective)

*Rational strategies*

These are based on the assumption that people are rational and will therefore respond to a clear presentation of the facts and to the common sense of the approach being advocated. If change can be shown to be desirable and beneficial, reasonable people will accept it. The emphasis is on cognitive processes. If people understand why change is needed, they are likely to change with less trouble. The education system, research and development centres, government offices and senior management are areas where a rational approach to change might work best. That is, one can assume that in these organisational groups are people who will respond to a clear presentation of facts and to the common sense of the argument.

*Power–legislative strategy*

If you believe some form of power applied from the appropriate authority, be it political, legal, moral or economic, is the only way change can be effected, then you will use this strategy. Unions and pressure groups which believe they cannot exert influence without showing muscle tend towards this technique. Non-violent actions such as strikes, work slowdowns and peaceful demonstrations are typical examples. At times this strategy can involve violent means such as rioting, looting and terrorism. Changes are also mandated through state and federal laws and judicial decisions. This in effect makes the change compulsory, but ensuring compliance with the new rules can be difficult. Desired change does not come about simply because a law has been passed. People are more likely to resist changes they dislike when they are imposed on them by law. Issues related to sexual equality and racial intolerance often fall into this trap.

*Re-educative strategy*

This is based on the assumption that personal change involves some readjustment and clarification of attitudes and values, which can occur in a climate of openness and personal support. Change is effected as attitudes and values become congruent with the change. It is felt that knowledge alone is not enough to effect change and even if a person has sound knowledge of the issues, antagonistic attitudes and values will be too powerful to permit rational consideration. If you have traditional attitudes to the work roles of men and women in industry and are hostile to women entering occupational roles which were previously a male preserve, no amount of information on the equal efficiency and performance of the sexes will convince you of the need for or acceptability of the change. Your attitudes need changing first and attitude change can take a long time, as many of our attitudes and values are central to our habitual behaviour. An atmosphere of trust, openness, support and sometimes even therapy is required for attitude change.

## Activity 9   How I react to change

How you cope with change and life transitions depends to some extent on how you react to change. Mark an X at the point on the continuum which best represents your response to the following questions.

1   When I'm trying to change or influence others I tend to be
    dogmatic ........................................................................ flexible
2   I believe conflict in the form of argument and debate serves to
    impede harmony and progress ..................... stimulate thinking
3   When others try to influence my thinking I tend to be
    closed-minded; dismissive of others' views ..............................
    ............................... considerate of others' views; open-minded
4   I believe the best way for social and economic change to occur
    is through
    discussion and participation .................. imposition from above
5   I tend to
    set ambitious goals and never deviate ......... flow with the tide

From your responses to Activity 9, can you see what strategies you adopt?

## Individual adaptation

These three approaches to change are strategies from the point of view of someone trying to change someone else. But how does change take place within the individual? Kelman has proposed three mechanisms by which individuals respond to attempts to change them.

*Compliance*

This is a frequent response to imposed change from physical, resource or position power. The person is unable to counter or resist the pressure placed on them. The change may become permanent or internalised if there is no cost or even reward to the individual—'I may not like it but if it means promotion, then so be it.' The change becomes acceptable. This is not the best way to create acceptable change, for if the pressure is removed or the costs become too high then ingenious and counterproductive steps may be taken to negate or avoid the change.

*Identification*

Change occurs because the individual wishes to resemble the source of the power initiating the change. This may be because of admiration or inspiration. Many religious conversions occur this way but it is also apparent in therapeutic contexts, where the client changes behaviour or attitudes because of increasing attachment to the counsellor. Identification with pop stars and football heroes also comes into this category and has great power to change the behaviour of young people in particular.

*Internalisation*

This is a potent form of change which in some cases stems from a continued and deep identification. In internalisation the individual accepts the change and makes it an integral part of herself and of her self-image. This takes time, as the individual develops a commitment. In internalisation the person changes to adapt to the organisational or life transition. This occurs more readily where a professional change agent, using counselling skills, enables the individual to reinvent herself and incorporate the life transition as an acceptable and motivating element for the future. Change that is internalised is relatively permanent and causes less stress to the person. Compliance always has the aura of imposition from outside; identification is not stable, as new identifications are always possible. Only internalisation involves a new self-concept.

## The change agent

The change agent is a person who actively works to bring about change in individuals, groups or organisations. His skills are a key factor in facilitating change. It is important that the change agent be seen as independent and not linked to any specific part of the organisation. For this reason many organisations bring in change agents from outside. An independent external perspective makes it more likely that a clear, unbiased view will be obtained of how individuals and a group interact and what functions they perform. Like a marriage guidance counsellor, the change agent is able to observe, analyse, understand and advise on the problems of change from the perspectives of all parties and help them develop solutions. The change agent works like a therapist rather than an expert, facilitating change and supporting people as they face new life transitions rather than prescribing a cure and leaving the patient to take the nasty medicine. Knowledge is crucial to success as a change agent. A change agent who understands the structure, interdependence, functions and purpose of an organisation is more likely to succeed.

Being able to identify and utilise formal and informal channels of communication and key individuals within an organisation is essential for influencing change. Interpersonal skills also make a significant contribution to a change agent's effectiveness. In particular, the change agent must have empathy to understand the way the other person sees things, listening skills so that the other person feels he is being paid attention, and communication skills. Another vital skill is the ability to create a climate for growth—basically a warm, caring, accepting and supportive environment. In such a positive environment change is perceived as less of a threat, self-esteem is enhanced, and there is freedom to explore available opportunities and develop new skills and attitudes. Change agents are most successful when they involve others actively in the process.

Finally the change agent must himself have high self-esteem. We can only accept others, be warm towards them and open in our dealings with them if we accept ourselves, feel good about ourselves and have no need to be defensive. In Chapter 3, we will consider this important relationship between feelings about the self and ability to help others.

## Organisational change

Organisational change takes place on three levels: the organisation, the group and the individual. Individual change is the basis of all the other levels of change, for if the individual does not change then neither can the group or the organisation. Any development or training program for change must devote a large portion of time and effort to individual change.

Change in the workplace is often resisted. The initial reaction is that change is going to be disadvantageous to the majority and is only going ahead because it will be advantageous to the few (top management) who are initiating it. This may be true sometimes. The secretive way in which change is often foisted on employees also leads to resistance, fear and resentment. Some managers believe any changes must be kept close to the chest because employees would find ways of blocking them if they knew about them in advance. Of course secrecy and the rumours that it generates lead to precisely the outcome management fears, with workers spurning proposed changes, no matter how valuable and positive they are.

Few managers appear to realise that just wanting staff to do something is rarely enough motivation for them to actually do it. Memos and directives will not convince them. Staff are more concerned with local workplace issues than with the overall goals of the organisation, which are often remote, poorly communicated and lacking in local interest. Change is often resisted by ignoring it or blocking it. Symptoms of resistance are absenteeism, strikes, reduced performance levels, unpunctuality, low morale, negative attitudes and rumour, errors, waste and stealing.

*Why we resist change*

**Lack of control**   At work many people feel they have very limited control over decisions affecting them compared to the decision-making and planning they can indulge in at home. A sense of powerlessness is created when changes to work practices are imposed from above.

**Insecurity**   Change causes insecurity about what is to happen and whether we will cope. Insecurities stem from anticipation of failure, fear of looking incompetent, a feeling that existing skills are threatened, and misinformation. It is scary to let go of something you are familiar with.

**Force of habit**   How many New Year resolutions have you broken? It is very difficult to change old habits. Patterns of behaviour built up over years of practice and repetition are difficult to break. We are used to the procedures at work, 'the way we do things here'. The old methods are easy and familiar; the new—the break-up of a team, new working hours, redesigned order forms etc—are disruptive.

**Exhaustion**   The pace of change for some has been so rapid, with more changes coming before the first ones have been assimilated, that we can become dispirited and lethargic. This is especially so where previous changes brought no real benefit or were abandoned before they were effective. Increased workload, new paperwork requirements, too little reward all wear people out.

**Loss** The principal loss is usually the job, but other losses include benefits such as the company car, status in a merger, friends if we relocate, and self-esteem if the change seems to imply that our job was of little importance. When you are the one initiating the change the benefits may seem obvious; if you are on the receiving end you may feel your performance is being criticised.

*Overcoming blocks to change*

Resistance to change and emotional upset in the face of change are understandable. But they do not always mean the change is wrong. Rather, they may indicate that the approach to introducing the change was misconceived. What appears to be necessary to reduce anxiety, insecurity and blocking by individuals and groups is a policy and ethos of openness, trust and involvement. Such an ethos is exactly the one psychotherapists have found the most facilitative in changing their clients' behaviour and it can be engendered in colleagues and employees with the help of a change agent. Individuals and groups involved in diagnosing, planning and implementing change are far more likely to feel positive towards the change and actively seek its implementation. It is hoped that problems will have been ironed out, and fears recognised and alleviated, leading to internalisation of the change rather than simply compliance.

## Activity 10   Your potential

Many people resist change because they aren't aware of their own potential. The average person only uses a small part of what they are capable of. List three work activities/areas in which you feel you are not using your full potential. Can you change this? How?

*Openness and resistance to change*

Whether we are open or resistant to change depends on such things as:

• who is bringing about the change
• what change is being suggested
• how the change will be implemented
• how the change will affect us
• our level of self-esteem.

Generally we are less likely to resist change if we feel some ownership in the change. However, if we sense that the change is being imposed on us by others, we are likely to resist. For example, supervisors are more likely to invest time and effort in evaluating employees' work technique if they have been involved in its development or if their ideas have been sought during its development. Supervisors told to implement a new procedure over which they have not been consulted are likely to put up strong resistance. We are more likely to support a change if we think the change will benefit us—for example, enable us to be more productive and earn more money. Changes in keeping with our values, attitudes and interests will also stand a better chance of acceptance. Finally, our reaction to change is more likely to be positive if the proponents of change are able to listen, empathise, and reduce the fears and concerns of those affected by the change. We are also more positive if we feel that our views are being listened to and if details of the change are open to revision during this discussion period. In summary, change is perceived as less threatening if we have a role in initiating it, do not feel powerless in controlling it, and can see how it will benefit us. When we assume the role of trying to change others, we need to recognise that they need to be involved, and understand their needs, values and self-esteem. Self-esteem seems to be a vital factor in attitudes to change and coping with life transitions. Those who feel good about themselves are willing to try new skills, recognise and develop opportunities. Those with low self-esteem tend to be resistant and closed-minded because they feel threatened. Self-esteem and self-concept enhancement will be considered in more depth in Chapter 5.

*Implementing change*

If you are in a position to implement change that affects others you must ensure that you adopt a procedure that will minimise the deleterious effects on the others and ensure that the change sought is acceptable and implemented properly. We have already outlined three change strategies—the rational, the re-educative and the power–legislative—and emphasised the fact that our response to change depends on:

- who is bringing about the change
- what change is being suggested, and
- how it will be implemented.

Generally, we are less likely to resist change if we feel some ownership in it. If change is imposed we are more likely to resist it or feel threatened by it. If the change is in keeping with our values, priorities and interests, again, we will tend to support it. Finally, our reaction to change will be more sympathetic if the proponents of change

- present their plans openly for discussion
- permit contribution and modifications as a result of group discussion, and
- clarify concerns.

Overall, we need to feel part of the change through consultation rather than feeling powerless, which leads to resistance and feelings of threat.

This theoretical knowledge about implementing change is interesting but only meaningful when it is used. You should now be ready to involve yourself in a change implementation. Assuming that you have already established rapport within the organisation or environment in which you want to initiate change, you are ready to develop a plan of action. The plan of action should include the following steps.

### 1 Identify goals and objectives

Here you are clarifying what the problem is; what change needs to take place. If there are a number of changes, decide which are most important, which are achievable, which are priorities. Identify alternative ways of bringing about this change. Now project yourself into the future—say six months ahead—and in specific terms describe what should have happened by then and again in one year's time. These will become the objectives.

### 2 Identify resources

What resources—financial, human, information and physical—will you need? People resources are often the most important. Who can and is willing to do what? What special knowledge and expertise do they have? Some of these people may already be within the system, others will be outside it. Information is often very valuable. Have you data to support your position?

### 3 Identify potential support and opposition

Identify who is likely to support the effort. One of the best ways to do this is to think about who will gain most from the change. Who is likely to lose? Are there ways you can gain their support—some offset? Who will continue to oppose the change? The opposition usually comprises people who feel change will mean loss of power, role, status or money. As we have discussed, these sorts of changes are tremendously threatening because they strike at the very core of one's identity. Once potential opposition has been identified, try to determine the objections so they can be countered with facts and arguments.

### 4 Plan action strategies

Now is the time to plan action strategies to accomplish the objectives. Do not limit possibilities, be creative and identify all potential strategies. Evaluate all the strategies and determine which one will lead most readily to achievement of the objectives given the resources available, the time constraints set, the availability of change agents and any other relevant factors. Then clarify responsibilities: who will do what and by when.

**5 Implement the planned change**
Using the action plan as a guide and an organising point for the change efforts, begin implementation. Sometimes plans that appear effective on paper are not so in practice. Be flexible, ready to modify the plan in consultation with others.

**6 Evaluate results**
No plan for change is complete until it has been evaluated. Some of the questions to ask are:

• Were the objectives appropriate?
  Were the objectives clearly stated?
  If not, go back to step 1.
• Were some important resources ignored?
  Were some important resource persons not involved?
  Were some people affected by the change not consulted?
  Were all potential opposition and support groups identified?
  Did everyone involved understand their role in the change and what the outcome would be?
  If not, go back to steps 2 and 3.
• Was the most appropriate action strategy selected?
  If not, go back to step 4.

## Activity 11   Design your own plan

Using the six-point plan above, develop a plan of action for some change you may wish to introduce at work or at home, or for some change which is likely to impose itself on your work or home context. Remember, the six steps are:

1  Identify goals and objectives
2  Identify resources
3  Identify potential support and opposition
4  Plan action strategies
5  Implement the plan
6  Evaluate the results.

There is a positive side to change, in that it can be regarded as a learning experience. Many people benefit from developing untapped potential and coping mechanisms which stand them in good stead for future stressful situations. People who adapt easily to other cultures and countries tend to be those who experienced most change in their childhood and coped with it. They have learned from these early experiences how to cope with change and developed the personal qualities that enable them to adjust to new ways of living without psychological pain. People can learn and benefit from change. Change may not necessarily be bad. It can lead to improvements in work conditions, in lifestyle, and in life chances. It all depends on how you perceive and respond to change and how you perceive particular changes. Whether any or all of the trends discussed in the scenario in Chapter 1 continue precisely in the ways suggested is not important. The point is that we can anticipate volcanic upheaval, not only in our economic and social structures but also in our personal values, our attitudes, the ways we live our lives, and the ways we perceive reality. You can assess your attitudes to change by trying the following questionnaire.

## Activity 12   Your attitudes to change

Individuals' attitudes to change affect how effectively they manage change. This activity invites you to consider your attitude to change. Rate each statement on the following scale:

Always = 3; Sometimes = 2; Never = 1.

1  Before I try something new I have to be sure I can do it and won't fail
2  When I hear about something new I can't wait to try it
3  I prefer things as they are
4  I like seeing new places and meeting new people
5  I prefer to use tried ways of doing things
6  I like rearranging my living environment
7  I am always trying out new ways of doing things
8  People waste too much time trying out new ideas which aren't fully developed
9  I usually wait for someone else to try out new things first
10  New procedures only cause problems and stress
11  I make an effort to keep up with new developments in my field
12  I worry about learning new skills
13  I encourage staff/others to make suggestions about any change
14  I like doing things the same way
15  Implementation of change is a management issue only
16  Change leads to improvements
17  It's worthwhile to give something a go even if it doesn't work out well in the end.

Reverse the scoring on items 1, 3, 5, 8, 9, 10, 12, 14 and 15. Total your scores. High scores indicate a positive attitude to change and a willingness to be open-minded and try new things.

## Basic survival strategies in change situations

- Get as much information as you can about what is happening or about to happen in your organisation, and try to be involved in the change
- Practise stress management and relaxation techniques (Chapter 5)
- Express and acknowledge your feelings; live for the present and let go of the past
- Set new goals; make decisions; look for alternatives (Chapter 6)
- Develop and use a support network. List all the useful people you know (Chapter 6)
- Think positively about yourself and about the future (Chapter 5)

## Summary

Sudden changes and life transitions can be psychological risk factors and show a high degree of correlation to later health and emotional problems. However, whether some event or life transition is traumatic or not depends on our subjective perception of it. What we see, hear and feel is not always a true reflection of reality. Each of us organises our perception of events into a model that is meaningful to us as individuals, that makes sense to us. New experiences are interpreted in terms of our expectations and previous experiences. Every life transition involves loss, replacement, risk and continuity.

Changes in work roles involve a complex interaction of the expectations and perceptions of oneself and others which can lead to role overload, role ambiguity and/or role conflict. These situations give rise to stress as the individual tries to cope with competing, inconsistent and unclear demands. Thus change is usually easier to manage if one is involved in negotiating the role change, if the change is predictable and voluntary, if self-esteem is high and if there are supportive relationships. Organisational change will be resisted if those whom it affects are not involved or consulted. Individuals and groups involved in planning and implementing change are more likely to feel positive about it. The use of an external independent change agent to create an ethos of trust, openness and support improves the chances of individuals and groups coping well with change.

# 3
# Coping with change
## *The human response*
## *Personal strategies*

We have already seen that change is inevitable and that in the world of work in particular, tremendous changes are currently imposing themselves on organisations and their employees at all levels. Such changes lead to major and minor life transitions, whose consequences impinge powerfully on the emotional, social and personal well-being of each individual and, as a corollary, on the business organisation. Most managers understand and accept the fact that human resources are the most costly form of capital for any organisation. Employee problems cost money in absenteeism, in poor job performance and in difficult labour–management relationships as well as reducing the well-being and quality of working life of all employees from the top of an organisation to the bottom.

This chapter will discuss some responses to change and to life transitions and the psychological factors that underpin them, to help managers identify (a) which staff may be most affected by change and (b) the main behavioural characteristics of a person reacting poorly to potential or actual changes. As the focus of this book is how to identify and help those having difficulty coping with current transitions in the world of work, theories of personality and personality development will only be considered insofar as they enable differences in response to change to be identified and understood.

Every person is, in certain respects, (a) like all other people, (b) like some other people, and (c) like no other person. This means that while all people are very much alike every individual is in some ways unique and therefore will respond in a unique way and require a personalised approach. Everyone is alike in the overall way they respond to a given situation. This is a general principle. But of course each person is a specific amalgam of heredity and past experiences (their life history) and each event is a subjective interpretation of what the context really is, as we read in the previous chapter. So the individual's response is a subtle interaction between heredity and a subjective interpretation based on experience and expectations.

Person with life history (experiences and expectations)
↓
Situation as subjectively interpreted and perceived
↓
Behaviour or response to situation

Thus, while it is possible to generalise to some extent about how most people will respond to particular events, it is impossible to predict how a particular individual will respond. In this chapter we can offer clues only to how most people respond to change and life transitions.

## Stress and its symptoms

A vital element in any person's being is their sense of identity, their way of living, their understanding of their place in society and how well they fit into it. As we move into a different sort of world we have to accept changes in our identity, roles and status, which can bring about confusion of identity, a disturbing and bewildering state. If the degree of change and its speed are even remotely close to what some futurists predict, the shifts to come will place considerable stress on many people as a result of uncertainty, fear of the future and fear of failure. Change basically requires people to be deviants. To cope with change, one has to deviate from existing behaviour patterns; but deviation creates stress.

The term stress was introduced into medicine in the 1930s by Hans Selye. Early research focused on physiological reactions to stress; only since the 1970s has stress been considered in its occupational context. Stress refers to any demand, whether negative (unpleasant) or positive (pleasant), that requires some kind of physical or emotional adjustment. A negative demand could be failing a job interview or losing an argument with a colleague; a positive demand might be winning Lotto or gaining promotion. Every experience we have contains an element of stress. It is a 'lack of fit' between the environment and the person. What is stressful to one person may not be so to another because the stressfulness of an event is subjectively perceived. The strident sound of rock music excites some but disturbs others. Crowding makes some people agitated while others feel uncomfortable without it.

Moderate levels of stress and stimulation are necessary for healthy functioning and optimum performance. With very low levels of stress we are very undermotivated and less efficient. With very high levels of stress performance is dislocated, and efficiency and healthy functioning are greatly impaired. Since we cannot avoid stress, we must learn to manage it and maintain it at moderate levels. We must allow ourselves enough challenges to make life interesting and fulfilling.

## Factors affecting individual reaction to stress

It is important to note that there is no fixed pattern of behaviour that follows a stressful event. Each individual's response will be determined by many factors including personality—especially the inner resource of self-esteem—previous experience of similar or related situations, the context, age, current health status and so on. Remember too the discussion on perception in Chapter 2, where it was emphasised that our views of reality are subjective; any event is open to a variety of interpretations. The degree of stress an individual experiences will largely depend on his interpretation of what is going on.

The above factors, plus the person's ability to manage stress using techniques such as relaxation exercises (Chapter 5), positive thinking skills (Chapter 5), self-esteem enhancement skills (Chapter 5), and decision-making skills (Chapter 6) determine whether the person's health or behaviour will suffer as a result of a potentially stressful event. Speaking before a large audience is a traumatic event for some managers, but those who are experienced in public speaking, who are well prepared, who feel positive about the task, and who have used relaxation techniques before the presentation usually enjoy and master the context.

Bear in mind that the personality attributes which make a person stress-prone are often positive and desirable ones such as commitment and conscientiousness. If expended in the face of environmental and man-made obstacles, however, these qualities can lead to frustration and stress.

An overload of stress at any one time or an accumulation of it over time may predispose people to physical and emotional illness. Research into the links between stress and illness suggests that stress is involved directly or indirectly with high blood pressure, ulcers, coronary heart disease, asthma, diabetes, and a range of psychological and psychiatric disorders.

Stress also has emotional effects. Anxiety, anger and depression are the most common. In their train come other side effects such as headaches, abdominal cramps, limb tremors, fatigue, insomnia, withdrawal, drug abuse, self-doubt, inability to make decisions, and eating problems.

Here is a short checklist which will help you assess whether you are under stress.

## Activity 13   Your stress level

Have you experienced any of the following symptoms during stressful occasions or on a persistent, longer-term basis? Respond to
each statement by circling the appropriate response category for
you. Do not think too long over each one, as your first thought is
usually the most accurate.

None = 1
Slight (fewer than four times in the last month) = 2
Moderate (more than four times in the last month) = 3
Severe (more than four times in the last two weeks) = 4

| | | | | |
|---|---|---|---|---|
| Face feels flushed/hot | 1 | 2 | 3 | 4 |
| Frequent need to urinate | 1 | 2 | 3 | 4 |
| Acid stomach | 1 | 2 | 3 | 4 |
| Skin rash | 1 | 2 | 3 | 4 |
| Dry mouth/throat | 1 | 2 | 3 | 4 |
| Butterfly stomach | 1 | 2 | 3 | 4 |
| Nail-biting | 1 | 2 | 3 | 4 |
| Heart pounding | 1 | 2 | 3 | 4 |
| Rapid breathing | 1 | 2 | 3 | 4 |
| Eye twitching | 1 | 2 | 3 | 4 |
| Sweaty/shaky hands | 1 | 2 | 3 | 4 |
| Grinding teeth | 1 | 2 | 3 | 4 |
| Headaches | 1 | 2 | 3 | 4 |
| Backache | 1 | 2 | 3 | 4 |
| Diarrhoea or constipation | 1 | 2 | 3 | 4 |
| Eating too much | 1 | 2 | 3 | 4 |
| Increased alcohol consumption | 1 | 2 | 3 | 4 |
| Increased cigarette smoking | 1 | 2 | 3 | 4 |
| Temper easily lost | 1 | 2 | 3 | 4 |
| Lack of concentration | 1 | 2 | 3 | 4 |
| Depression | 1 | 2 | 3 | 4 |
| Reduced sex drive | 1 | 2 | 3 | 4 |
| Anxious | 1 | 2 | 3 | 4 |
| Poor memory | 1 | 2 | 3 | 4 |
| Circling/confused thoughts | 1 | 2 | 3 | 4 |
| Pressed for time | 1 | 2 | 3 | 4 |
| Awake most of the night | 1 | 2 | 3 | 4 |
| Restless/overactive | 1 | 2 | 3 | 4 |
| Tense | 1 | 2 | 3 | 4 |
| Over-emotional | 1 | 2 | 3 | 4 |
| Unexplained fears | 1 | 2 | 3 | 4 |
| General tiredness | 1 | 2 | 3 | 4 |

Total the points ringed. Your score will be between 32 and 128. The
higher it is, the more stress you are reporting.

## Activity 14    Awareness of stressful situations

The aim of this activity is to enable you to gain awareness of the specific situations in which you get anxious, irritable, frustrated and/ or tense. Observe the specific situation, what was said, what you saw, how you felt, how you reacted etc.

Write down three situations in which you have experienced physical tension or an emotional reaction.

| Situation | Physical or emotional stress at the time |
| --- | --- |
| A colleague pushed in front of me in the queue in the staff dining room. | My facial muscles got tight; I felt irritated and shouted a rude word at him. |

*Occupational factors*

The contemporary workplace is a source of stress. Occupational stress occurs when discrepancies exist between occupational demands and opportunities on the one hand and the worker's capacities, expectations and needs on the other. Needs include such things as economic security, physical safety, acceptance and recognition as a person, a sense of effectiveness through the use of skills in meaningful tasks, and an appropriate measure of autonomy. Economic and structural changes are imposing severe tensions on workers at all levels, with demands for new skills, decreasing personal satisfaction and life chances, growing time pressures, financial constraints, interpersonal tensions and environmental hazards.

In addition, the Protestant work ethic, which maintains that work is a duty and that salvation lies in hard work and success, still holds sway. Although its importance is declining, strong conditioning at home and school present work as the central preoccupation and achievement of adulthood. It is not surprising that in the face of such conditioning, the prospect of career dislocation and reduced job opportunities causes anxiety and stress. Cooper (1983) found that lack of promotion, over-promotion, lack of job security and thwarted ambition were all significantly associated with stress reactions.

All in all, it is no wonder that job stress is becoming a major part of many lives and resulting in high levels of absenteeism, illness and low productivity. Even trying to reduce stress through changes in work habits, work environments and worker relations can actually add to the stress, as innovation is threatening. While these changes are needed, they should be accompanied by some form of training in stress management, or the personal skills to keep stress under control.

It is not surprising that given the strength of the Protestant Work

Ethic in our society, lack of promotions, decreasing job security and thwarted ambition are significantly associated with stress reactions.

Many jobs involve specific sources of stress, such as a poor physical working environment (e.g. noise, pollution), task problems (e.g. work overload/underload, shift work), and unsatisfactory psychosocial organisation (e.g. no participation in decision-making, poor job definition, job dissatisfaction).

In a context of change, these common job stress factors, listed below, will become manifest in a variety of combinations and act as a major basis for stress reactions.

• career development thwarted
• lack of job security
• too much or too little work/responsibility
• inability to adapt to new work practices
• boring/meaningless work
• little support from management
• lack of required skills
• inability to use existing skills
• inadequate training/reskilling
• lack of involvement in decision-making
• lack of socioemotional support/counselling
• rumours about future change, and
• uncertainty about the future

The type of work, as well as the physical and social attributes of the work environment, has been found to be associated with workers' stress levels. While a stressful job and difficult working conditions may be adjusted to over time, any additional stress load from potential changes in work practices or possible retrenchment can lead to marked changes in stress levels and subsequent health status and emotional behaviour. Shift work is associated with stress because it disturbs the circadian (daily) rhythm as well as social behaviour. Work involving long sessions, or work performed in physically adverse conditions—cramped, noisy, poorly illuminated, hot and so on—can also lead to increased stress levels. Change to a different line of work or a different level of responsibility has been associated with increased stress and a significantly increased risk of heart attack in the year following such change. Health deterioration has been shown to arise from the extremes of job demands, for example those engaged in boring and repetitive work suffer more frequently from depression, sleep difficulties and digestive disorders. Increased responsibility at work has been shown in some cases to lead to high blood pressure and ulcers.

Thus work conditions and practices in many obvious and subtle ways can lead to increased stress and subsequent health and behaviour problems. In changing work practices and in countering the effects of restructuring and recession, managers must never forget that they are dealing with humans whose bodies respond physically and psychologically to these changes. Therefore employees need to be prepared for the changes by giving them the work skills and personal skills needed to help them manage stressful change.

*Executive stress*

Executives and managers are susceptible to job stress too. Not only do they have to contend with the possibility of retrenchment, with learning new skills, with managing change in the workplace with a potentially upset workforce, they also have to deal with top management. The workplace for many middle managers is a battlefield in which they are getting squeezed from both ends. The demands from above can create threatened and stressed managers who in turn become abrasive and abusive and find it difficult to develop positive, motivating relationships with employees. This creates a tense atmosphere, with negative feedback, insubordination and hatred from employees. A stressed executive can be of no help to his employees when they are facing problems, as he displaces his problems onto the workers. To assist workers with their needs, a manager must be in control of his. Stress management is as vital for executives as it is for employees.

In male managers job stress mainly manifests itself in coronary heart disease and ulcers, while in female managers stress tends to result in mental illness. In both, however, the main factor associated with stress is a Type A personality (see below).

*Home–work pressures*

A common danger in the current economic situation is the effect of work pressures such as fear of job loss, blocked ambition and work overload on the families of middle managers and employees. During an economic crisis the problems increase as individuals strive to cope with some of their basic economic and security needs. Under normal circumstances most people find home a refuge from the competitive and demanding environment of work, a place where they can get support and comfort. However, in a job or career crisis the tensions an individual brings home to the family disturb the domestic environment. This increased tension is then carried back to the workplace, compounding the problems there. Work is so central to a person's being that no other aspect of life can escape its influence.

# Activity 15 Work stress

For each statement, circle the appropriate number. Work quickly and do not think too long over each item, as your first thoughts are usually most correct

| | | Seldom | Sometimes | Always |
|---|---|---|---|---|
| 1 | I feel angry at work | 1 | 2 | 3 |
| 2 | I feel I have to succeed all the time | 1 | 2 | 3 |
| 3 | I find myself withdrawing from colleagues | 1 | 2 | 3 |
| 4 | I feel that others place excessive demands on me | 1 | 2 | 3 |
| 5 | I find myself increasingly callous/insensitive to clients/ colleagues/employees | 1 | 2 | 3 |
| 6 | Work has become boring/tedious | 1 | 2 | 3 |
| 7 | I feel I am at a standstill in my career | 1 | 2 | 3 |
| 8 | I feel negative about work | 1 | 2 | 3 |
| 9 | I accomplish less than ever before | 1 | 2 | 3 |
| 10 | I have trouble organising my work and time | 1 | 2 | 3 |
| 11 | I'm more short-tempered than I've ever been | 1 | 2 | 3 |
| 12 | I feel inadequate to deal with changes at work | 1 | 2 | 3 |
| 13 | I find myself taking out my work frustrations at home | 1 | 2 | 3 |
| 14 | I avoid personal contact more than I ever have | 1 | 2 | 3 |
| 15 | I feel I am not in the right job for me | 1 | 2 | 3 |
| 16 | I find myself thinking negatively about work most of the time | 1 | 2 | 3 |
| 17 | I don't enjoy my work | 1 | 2 | 3 |
| 18 | I feel that my superiors do not appreciate what I do | 1 | 2 | 3 |
| 19 | I spend a lot of time avoiding work | 1 | 2 | 3 |
| 20 | I feel exhausted at work | 1 | 2 | 3 |
| 21 | Deadlines are a daily part of my job | 1 | 2 | 3 |

| | | | | |
|---|---|---|---|---|
| 22 | I have a problem completing work on time because of many interruptions | 1 | 2 | 3 |
| 23 | I find it necessary to work during some lunches | 1 | 2 | 3 |
| 24 | I complete work at home at night | 1 | 2 | 3 |
| 25 | I find it difficult to work with some colleagues | 1 | 2 | 3 |
| 26 | I need to update my skills | 1 | 2 | 3 |
| 27 | I find it difficult to find meaning in my job | 1 | 2 | 3 |
| 28 | There is little variety or challenge in my job | 1 | 2 | 3 |
| 29 | I accept too many new responsibilities | 1 | 2 | 3 |
| 30 | I find my working environment unpleasant | 1 | 2 | 3 |
| 31 | I feel overwhelmed with the demands of my job | 1 | 2 | 3 |
| 32 | My work environment is noisy | 1 | 2 | 3 |
| 33 | I feel I should be more satisfied with what I have achieved at work | 1 | 2 | 3 |
| 34 | When I am under pressure at work I lose my temper | 1 | 2 | 3 |
| 35 | I do not feel confident of my management skills | 1 | 2 | 3 |
| 36 | I feel uncomfortable giving instructions to those I supervise | 1 | 2 | 3 |
| 37 | I have lost enthusiasm for my job | 1 | 2 | 3 |
| 38 | I feel I speak badly at department meetings | 1 | 2 | 3 |
| 39 | I find it difficult to make decisions | 1 | 2 | 3 |
| 40 | On my way to and from work I tend to rehash the problems of the day | 1 | 2 | 3 |
| 41 | When I come home from work I still have the household chores to do | 1 | 2 | 3 |
| 42 | I don't have time to take breaks at work | 1 | 2 | 3 |

| | | | |
|---|---|---|---|
| 43 | I think about problems at work even when I am on vacation | 1 | 2 | 3 |
| 44 | I feel I have not enough staff to get the work done | 1 | 2 | 3 |
| 45 | I am a perfectionist | 1 | 2 | 3 |
| 46 | I find it difficult to tolerate mistakes | 1 | 2 | 3 |

Scoring:  90–138 Severe stress
          57–89 Moderate stress
          46–56 Managed stress

The higher your score, the more stress you are likely to experience in your job.

Many people can cope with adverse or demanding work environments and some even thrive in the most trying conditions. Therefore the findings that stress is associated with such contexts does not inevitably apply to all individuals.

## Stress symptoms in a changing work environment

The fear of being unemployed or of being unable to cope with the demands of a changing job can trigger a variety of reactions such as asthma, viral infections and heart attack. The increased stress stemming from anxiety about job security or from sudden retrenchment can result in acute or chronic illness. It may also lead to poor eating habits, increased consumption of prescribed, social or illegal drugs, and an increase in domestic violence.

All this results from the predominant feeling of anxiety and fear as employed people become more and more insecure about their future. Emotional responses in turn have physical effects. When the body chemistry changes, the immune system can become depleted and people become vulnerable to illness. Stress can trigger short- and long-term illness. Short-term responses to a stressful event such as sudden retrenchment are increased blood pressure, increased heart and breathing rates, and increase in muscle tension. Long-term responses include increases in cholesterol production, blood sugar levels and blood viscosity. All these are physically dangerous. Stress makes us more vulnerable to viruses and infections, and there is a direct relationship between stress and heart disease. Stressed people become more irrational and erratic in behaviour. Those still working but worried become less productive and take more sick leave. Stress promotes domestic violence, as people unable to cope with the pressure take it out on their spouses and children. Stress may also lead to or exacerbate addictive behaviours such as drug abuse, alchoholism, smoking and overeating. These give short-term satisfaction and some drugs enable people to withdraw and forget reality. The most-used forms of escape from stress are:

1 Drinking alcohol
2 Frequent or heavy eating, especially of sweet foods
3 Smoking
4 Excessive drinking of high-caffeine drinks, e.g. coffee
5 Drug use, especially of marijuana, cocaine and mind-altering pills
6 Use of prescription drugs, e.g. tranquillisers and pain reducers
7 Use of sleeping pills
8 Withdrawing psychologically, e.g. escapism via continual TV or movie-watching
9 Self-destructive behaviour
10 Lashing out at others physically and verbally to displace anxiety and anger
11 Antisocial behaviour, e.g. crime, vandalism

All these reactions to stress allow the individual to substitute a pleasant feeling for the unpleasant stressed feeling, a form of anaesthesia and synthetic experience.

*Emotional reactions to stress*

We all experience emotions. New experiences, new problems, new lifestyles all purvey a mixture of frightening and happy feelings. Mixed feelings can bring confusion, as with the elation and dread of a new job. It is the response to feelings that is important. You cannot control how you feel but you can control your response to the feelings. You may rightly feel angry with a worker who refuses to accept your decision, angry enough to hit him, but you can choose not to and deal with the issue in another way. As Figure 7 shows, your perception of a situation colours the way you feel about it; this emotional response then affects your bodily response.

# Anger

This emotion is often expressed by name-calling ('You are the incompetent one'), by accusation ('You are the cause of this mess'), by destructive behaviour (e.g. smashing equipment, sabotaging work practices), by swearing, and ultimately by physically lashing out. Some people feel uneasy about talking directly with the person who has caused their angry feelings. You can ventilate your feelings in a diary, by exercising vigorously or by talking things out with a friend.

Western society tends to regard such emotional reactions as anger, sadness, fear and crying as bad, and not to be shown in public. However, in trying to hide these emotions we create stress and still other manifestations of obnoxious behaviour. We must not try to hide such feelings with alcohol, drugs or denial. It is possible to cope with negative feelings by expressing them in appropriate ways and being honest about our feelings, e.g. being angry when someone has done something wrong to us, crying when a devastating event occurs. It is also possible to re-evaluate the situation in which the negative event has occurred to see if there are not some positive things to respond to as well. We can also use relaxation techniques (see Chapter 5) as an aid in managing negative emotions.

**Depression**
Depression is a common result of important life-transition events such as death or divorce. It may also come from achieving a goal or a success, as it signals the end of a project or period of hard work.

If one or more of the following symptoms recur, last or worsen, you are experiencing significant depression:

- Strong feelings of sadness, inadequacy and disappointment about the past and future
- Strong pessimism about the future
- Feeling tired all the time
- Dreading mornings
- Crying without knowing why
- Not taking care of yourself
- Excessive eating or continual nibbling
- Feeling worthless and behaving as though to prove it by doing things that are self-destructive, illegal, offensive, or disturbing
- Persistent feeling of anger against others and against self
- Inability to enjoy usual pleasures—lack of interest: everything is too much bother, even going to work or getting up in the morning
- Poor sleep patterns
- Absenteeism from work

Severe depression requires medical treatment and counselling. Depressed people can help themselves too by trying to move towards others, not away from them, and by sharing their feelings and worries with those they trust. Forcing the body back to normal routines by a return to usual eating patterns, exercise, recreation and sleep is a strong counter to depression. Chemicals called endorphins, secreted during exercise, are believed to make people feel more alive and positive. Depression interferes with work and home commitments and general zest for life.

**Suicide**
Sadly, suicide is becoming more frequent among people whose depression becomes too great to handle, particularly those made redun-

dant or bankrupt, whose world has collapsed around them, whose raison d'être and self-esteem have gone. Suicide occurs among all groups in society, among urban professionals too old to find another job at 40, among workers in the rural sector as drought and recession bite, and among redundant industrial workers. There is an alarming tendency for suicidally depressed people to kill close family members before killing themselves to 'save' them from the troubles of the world. Suicidal thoughts reflect a desire to seek relief from psychological pain or conflict. If you or someone you know starts to show suicidal tendencies, recourse must be made to Lifeline or a similar organisation, a religious group, or a local medical centre or hospital. The following appear to be risk factors:

• Death of a close relative
• Family arguments/fights/separations (often happens after job loss as one member loses self-esteem and meets accusations of failure/loss of income from others)
• Moving house; loss of friends/relatives close by (often occurs on relocation or promotion or on selling to move to an area with better job prospects)
• Family splits (which may include arguments and moving house)
• Illness (may be induced by stress)
• Drug/alcohol dependence (often used as a way to avoid reality)

Clues to suicide risk:

• Long-standing depression and despair
• Severe neglect of appearance
• Claims to have a suicide plan
• Has tried it before
• Threatens to do it
• Rapid decline in work performance
• Reckless, self-destructive behaviour (fast driving; drug abuse)
• Unhealthy interest in death, weapons, methods of suicide etc.

## The self-concept

A major psychological element which appears to lie behind human behaviour is the self-concept. It is a compound of life experience and situational feedback, and appears to be considerably affected in many people as they adjust to new events and contexts. The self-concept is the set of beliefs, attitudes and feelings you have about yourself; in other words how you see or feel about yourself, with all the evaluations that implies.

Everybody has a self-concept. In reality each person has many self-concepts, each relating to a particular role played in life, e.g. how we see ourself as a parent, car driver, colleague, manager, do-it-yourself person and so on.

In coping with the stress of change and life transitions it is vital that people possess or develop positive feelings about themselves. An important way of managing stress is to be predominantly hopeful, to believe in one's ability to cope and to see life as a source of potential opportunities. It is important to know who you are, about your abilities, your needs, your values, your relationships, your limitations and your potential. Only by understanding yourself, being positive about yourself and building on your strengths can you get the most out of life now and in the future, and do what you feel you are able to do. *Until you know who you are you will never know what you can become.*

The self-concept is formed of two elements: one's *self-image* or picture of oneself, and one's *self-esteem*, or how we feel about that picture.

*The self-image*

The self-image is a picture made up of beliefs about oneself. As a result of life experiences and feedback from others, we construct a picture of ourself and behave according to it, so that it becomes self-validating. It is a description of self based on objective evidence and subjective belief. The objective evidence could be position in the company, qualifications, skill level etc. The subjective belief could be the personally interpreted comments of others at work or at home about one's competencies. Hence the self-image is composed of the limitless ways in which individuals can describe themselves.

## Activity 16   Your self-description

At this point it might be helpful for you to write down a list of descriptions about what you are and how you see yourself. How do you describe yourself? Shy? An efficient manager? Supportive? A cold fish? Short-tempered? Financially astute? My list when I tried it included: male, psychologist, married, broken-down rugby player, ambitious, overweight, sociable, enjoys travelling.

This sort of listing can continue *ad infinitum* and contain all sorts of descriptions, goals, roles, status, attributes. Some of the elements are important to our well-being, others are more peripheral. Holding the post of personnel manager may be a very important element in your array of self-conceptions; being bald may not be very important. Of course the relative importance will vary between individuals. What is important to my self-picture may not be very important to yours. But it is obvious that each of us has dozens of labels we have given ourselves over the years. These labels govern our behaviour as we act the way our self-image says we should. Our behaviour is based on our perception of ourselves, no matter how accurate or inaccurate the picture.

## Self-esteem

In each role we not only have a picture of ourselves but we also evaluate that picture. This evaluation can be positive or negative. For example, we may feel we are good at driving a car but not so good as a fix-it person round the house. Many of the evaluations we attach to our self-pictures are derived from feedback from others and from societal values. We may see ourselves as too fat, not tall enough, not intelligent, not good at our job. Alternatively, we could perceive ourselves as having a good build, as being intelligent, as being competent in our job. The former image will lower self-esteem and make us feel inferior; the latter will boost self-esteem and enable us to feel good about ourselves.

Self-esteem is the evaluation or judgment placed on each element of the self-image. Because conceptions of what one is like are so personal, each one is imbued with some degree of positive or negative connotation. It is this combination of images of self and the evaluation of these images that constitute the self-concept. The self-concept is not a singular entity but a plethora of evaluated pictures relating to our many roles and behaviours. You can hold different self-concepts about yourself as a parent, training officer, car driver, gardener, tennis player etc. As a car driver you may evaluate yourself as first-rate; as a gardener you may consider yourself the world's worst. However, whether your self-concept is raised or lowered by a particular self-evaluation depends on whether that element is important to you. To possess a generally positive self-concept simply means that you evaluate yourself reasonably positively in those things that matter to you. Imperfection, incompetency or failure in things that don't really matter in your life do not deflate the self-concept.

It may appear dogmatic to assert that all the images or pictures you have of yourself are invested with evaluative overtones. But think about it. To be male or female, a success or a failure, hardworking or lazy, employed or unemployed, the boss or a member of staff, rich or poor, tall or short or any other descriptive attribute, involves some evaluation derived from subjectively interpreted feedback and from comparison with subjectively interpreted cultural, group and individual standards and values. The more important the element is in your self-concept, the more the evaluation, be it positive or negative, will affect your feelings about yourself. These feelings about self, involving the image and the esteem in which you hold it, affect behaviour considerably. Since the evaluative significance of many self-concepts is taken from the surrounding culture, many evaluations have become normative. To be dull, fat, an unsuccessful interviewee, redundant, all tend to have negative connotations while being clever, promotable, healthy, cheerful, skilful, bear positive ones.

### How does the self-concept develop?

What you come to think of yourself is based largely on what you believe important others in your life, such as parents, peers, spouse and colleagues, think of you. Other people act as mirrors, reflecting back at you how they see you. The way they respond and act towards you is a major part of this reflection. Their words, as well as their nonverbal signals, are interpreted by you as indications of how they feel about you. Of course you may be correct or incorrect, because your interpretation is subjective. But whether correct or not, you will build up a picture of yourself and behave in accordance with that picture.

For example, at some point in your childhood, a teacher may have given you the idea that you were not very bright. Suppose you believed the teacher even though his imputation was incorrect. You stopped making an effort. Why bother if you are not going to do well anyway? You left school at the earliest opportunity and thereby severely limited your employment and career opportunities. You still believe you could not go back to study successfully. Yet you feel doubtful about holding onto your present job, as more and more of the work is computerised. This reveals the limiting nature of a negative self-concept and, more importantly, the role others such as teachers, trainers, supervisors and managers play in modifying the self-concepts of their clients and staff.

What we believe others think of us is an important source of feelings and beliefs about ourself, irrespective of the validity of the perception. As we are loved or rejected, praised or punished, as we fail or succeed, we come gradually to regard ourselves as important or unimportant, adequate or inadequate, honest or dishonest, handsome or ugly, or any of the terms we hear used about ourselves. We are likely to be affected by the labels which are applied to us by other people. This rather direct feedback has been shown in many studies to affect people's self-concept and subsequent behaviour. One researcher, in a well-known example, describes how a dull, unattractive, overweight female student was treated by some male students for a joke as though she were tremendously popular and attractive. Within a year she developed an easy manner, confidence and genuine popularity, which in turn elicited even more positively reinforcing reactions from others.

If you are inclined to perceive yourself in negative terms and demean yourself, then the rigours of life and its challenges will defeat you before you have even set out. The stresses and strains that come from feeling negative, incompetent and inferior are then supplemented by the stresses and strains of not coping in reality—for self-doubt becomes self-validating prophecy (sometimes called the expectancy effect). You are your own worst enemy.

If at the outset you believe you cannot cope with the new equipment, with the redesigned job, with the promotion, with the threat of redundancy, this belief creates feelings and behaviours which tend to make it come true. Have you ever started a task and said to yourself 'I'll never manage this'? The result was certainly that you didn't.

## Activity 17   The expectancy effect

1   Have you had a positive expectancy experience? What expectations did the other person have of you? How did you feel?
What was the outcome?
2   Have you had a negative expectancy experience? How did you
feel? What expectations did the person have of you? What was
the outcome?

## Activity 18   Self-beliefs

List five beliefs you feel are correct about yourself (include positive
and negative beliefs). Who are some of the people who have led
you to think about yourself in these ways?

So in coping with new conditions, whether they be positive or negative, the possession of a positive self-concept will facilitate the way
those changes are perceived and tackled.

*Low-self-esteem behaviour*

How you see yourself influences your behaviour. Those with low
self-esteem tend to be unhappy, anxious, self-critical people who have
difficulty building positive relationships with others. Many people
with low self-esteem bitch, find fault, boast, and try to devalue others
around them. These are futile ways to raise self-esteem, for if there
are others below you, you are not the worst. Attack is the best form
of defence if you feel inferior. Others may try to raise self-esteem
by showing off, while others simply withdraw from as many social

situations as possible. They feel unable to meet environmental demands and respond to mistakes as though they were failures. Depression, self-blame and stress-related physiological and psychological problems emerge in the downward spiral as self-esteem continues to be eroded. Persons of low self-esteem tend to underestimate their abilities and potential, thus overestimating the difficulty of various tasks. They are often unwilling to try new experiences or anything they think might confirm their expectancy of failure. They set low goals for themselves and have difficulty establishing sound interpersonal relationships. Change is very threatening to them, with their external locus of control.

*High-self-esteem behaviour*

Those with positive self-concepts tend to have the confidence to cope with most situations and generally have an internal locus of control. Such people are more resilient in coping with life's ups and downs, and are therefore less likely to succumb to stress. Confident, self-reliant, happy and friendly, they feel secure in themselves and find change a challenge, something to be mastered and adapted to. They are able to accept both their strengths and their weaknesses. They are secure in themselves and can express feelings appropriately. They lead happy and satisfying lives.

It is easy to see why a person with a positive self-concept is more likely to cope with change in the workplace and any consequent transitions in other aspects of their lives. It is apparent, too, that the self-concept is not fixed but changes with life experiences. Each person sees different aspects of self with varying degrees of clarity at different times.

Since the increasingly rapid rate of change is threatening and requires adaptation to life transitions and new lifestyles, people with positive self-concepts are best able to cope. Below is a scale that will enable you to assess your self-concept, whether you see yourself in positive or negative terms.

## Activity 19   Your self-concept

Rate yourself on a scale of 1 to 7 for each pair of descriptions by placing a cross in the appropriate box. As you see, each pair are opposites. The more you believe you are like a particular description the closer your cross should be placed to that description. If you feel that you are average, i.e. would describe yourself as neither item in the pair, then your cross should be placed in the middle, at number 4.

**Myself**

| | 7 6 5 4 3 2 1 | |
|---|---|---|
| good | :—:—:—:—:—:—: | bad |
| coping | :—:—:—:—:—:—: | not coping |
| * unsuccessful | :—:—:—:—:—:—: | successful |
| * unstimulating | :—:—:—:—:—:—: | stimulating |
| purposeful | :—:—:—:—:—:—: | aimless |
| * boring | :—:—:—:—:—:—: | interesting |
| important | :—:—:—:—:—:—: | unimportant |
| * remote | :—:—:—:—:—:—: | accessible |
| stable | :—:—:—:—:—:—: | changeable |
| * worthless | :—:—:—:—:—:—: | valuable |
| cautious | :—:—:—:—:—:—: | rash |
| friendly | :—:—:—:—:—:—: | unfriendly |
| intellectual | :—:—:—:—:—:—: | unintellectual |
| positive | :—:—:—:—:—:—: | negative |
| enthusiastic | :—:—:—:—:—:—: | indifferent |
| happy | :—:—:—:—:—:—: | sad |
| ordered | :—:—:—:—:—:—: | chaotic |
| * a loser | :—:—:—:—:—:—: | a winner |
| * pessimistic | :—:—:—:—:—:—: | optimistic |
| * tense | :—:—:—:—:—:—: | relaxed |
| * critical | :—:—:—:—:—:—: | uncritical |
| tolerant | :—:—:—:—:—:—: | intolerant |
| * excitable | :—:—:—:—:—:—: | calm |
| hardworking | :—:—:—:—:—:—: | lazy |
| * failing | :—:—:—:—:—:—: | successful |
| even-tempered | :—:—:—:—:—:—: | aggressive |
| * unambitious | :—:—:—:—:—:—: | ambitious |
| confident | :—:—:—:—:—:—: | lacking confidence |
| sociable | :—:—:—:—:—:—: | unsociable |
| * unreliable | :—:—:—:—:—:—: | reliable |

Now reverse the scoring of items with an asterix against them. Thus 1 becomes 7, 2 becomes 6, 3 becomes 5 and so on. Add up all the numbers. The maximum possible score is 210 and the minimum is 30. The higher your score, the more positive you feel about yourself.

*Self-talk*

A person's self concept is firmly based in feedback from others and from self-perpetuating thoughts. If these are generally positive, then a positive self-concept should be developed and maintained. We act like the person we talk ourselves into being.

*Positive strokes*

Eric Berne has called the positive responses people give each other *strokes*. Strokes from others make us feel valued, worthwhile and accepted. This makes our self-concept blossom. Not to be stroked means to be ignored, that you don't count, you're a failure, you're not accepted. Most people have an unhealthy tendency to focus on others' mistakes and failings, thereby demeaning them and creating feelings of inferiority, failure and defeat. By focusing on what a person does correctly, on effort, on motivation, rather than seizing on some weak point, one is more likley to build their self-esteem. Some success, however limited, will encourage further effort and more success. Remember how good you feel when you receive praise; others feel the same way when you recognise their successes. This helps us all to develop self-esteem, confidence and motivation. It also improves personal relationships, as no-one needs to behave badly to be noticed. Success can mean a variety of things. A nervous person may feel successful if she makes a verbal contribution in a work meeting. Someone who has never used a word processor before is successful every time he learns a new word-processing skill.

*The Pygmalion effect: The role of expectations*

With the use of strokes, each of us is a sculptor with the power to shape other people's lives. If we can modify our own self-esteem so powerfully by the way we speak to ourselves, we can also modify the self-concepts of others for better or for worse by the sort of feedback we give them, particularly if the feedback is in the form of *expectations*. The concept of the Pygmalion effect, or the self-fulfilling prophecy, has been expressed in many ways over the years. A modern example of the Pygmalion myth is found in George Bernard Shaw's play *Pygmalion*, which later became the musical hit *My Fair Lady*. In it, Dr Higgins changes Eliza Doolittle from an uncultured flower girl into a polished lady through his belief in his own ability and his expectation of influencing Eliza's behaviour. Most people influence others by communicating, by verbal and nonverbal means, either positive or negative expectations of the other person. People, more often than not, do what is expected of them. Most people do not realise the power of expectation. Expectation can become a self-fulfilling prophecy.

We can build up our colleagues and employees, giving them a greater capability to manage the changes impinging on them, through phrases or strokes such as: 'That's good'; 'You're on the right track'; 'That's an interesting idea'; 'You can do it'; 'I'm very pleased with what you have done'.

## Activity 20  Expectations

Do you give negative or positive expectations to those whom you influence at work? What are some of the expectations you are locked into? Will these expectations help or hinder their ability to cope and perform?

## Activity 21   Positive strokes

List some phrases or strokes you could use in your organisation to encourage others. Avoid phrases like the following as they suffocate and destroy people: 'It won't work'; 'You never seem to learn'; 'You don't seem to understand'; 'You are not much good at this, are you?'; 'I've told you before how to operate this machine'; 'You are useless'; 'You'll never make the grade'.

## Activity 22   Negative strokes

List some phrases you have used in your organisation which you will try not to use again. What effect do you think each one had?

You must quickly affirm what employees and colleagues have done competently. Managers should give constructive feedback in a form that does not damage an employee's self-concept. If you want to maintain competent performance, then self-esteem must remain high too. When you or any employee are called upon to step out of your normal role, out of your comfort zone, to take on a more challenging post or a different role, that is when high self-esteem is needed. The only way to achieve it is to control self-talk to create an enhanced self congruent with the new advanced comfort zone. The more you or your employees' self-concept can be elevated, the more you and they will reach for the stars without sweat or strain. We will be discussing the role of affirmations again in Chapter 5.

It has been found that in school, most poor readers do not improve with remedial help as long as they see themselves as poor readers. Only when their self-concept includes a component that says 'I am able to read' does an improvement start to occur. Similarly, if employees see themselves as unable to master a new technique or machine, they will not succeed, whatever training they are given. Only when they can talk positively about their potential to manage the new task and incorporate it into their self-concept will they succeed. How many people have failed exams because they talked themselves into failing with negative thoughts and images? If you believe you will fail at the outset, there is little hope for you. Set off with the intention of coping—'I'm going to master this'—and more than likely, you will. Positively motivated persons are likely to be self-starters, they look for solutions not excuses, they have drive and energy, confidence and resilience, and they want to succeed.

# Positive self-feelings create positive feelings about others

There is a very sound reason for managers and supervisors to be more positive about themselves. If they cannot cope with the pressures of change, they will be unable to offer help and support to subordinates and other colleagues. It has been found consistently in therapy situations (particularly in Rogerian client-centred therapy) that people with more positive self-concepts are more able to act positively toward others and help others see themselves more positively. The ability to interact with others in a warm, accepting way, facilitating sound personal and professional relationships, depends on a positive self-concept. This is because people with a positive self-concept feel no need to defend themselves against others, as they do not feel threatened. The interaction then acts as a therapeutic mechanism, promoting positive self-concepts in the others, who feel accepted and acceptable. So the quality of any work or professional relationship depends to a large extent on what the manager, supervisor or professional is like as a person. What a person thinks of himself is not a closed system encapsulated within the boundary of his own being; on the contrary, it reaches out to manipulate and influence relationships with others. It is very difficult to help someone else cope, to support another in a time of need, to provide wise counselling if one does not feel good about oneself. Social scientists concerned with the psychological health of individuals and of the community focus on developing strategies and invoking processes to build up the constructive and proactive aspects of personality which enable people to function adequately in all areas of their lives. It is a case not only of trying to manage problems as they arise but also of generating, as part of educational, industrial and professional training, those human capabilities that strengthen individuals psychologically and enable them to deal effectively with the transitions and stresses they will inevitably face. The parallel in medicine is that it is better to immunise against infection than to treat the infection later. The development of a positive self-concept is regarded as crucial in building up the psychological strength to manage change.

## Roles and the self-concept

The roles people play—particularly gender and occupational roles—also affect self-concept. We have already (in Chapter 1) considered occupational roles and the way in which changes in job status and conditions can influence attitudes to self. Fear of future insecurity and unemployment affect self-concept and behaviour. It is generally accepted that in Western society, an individual's work is an integral part of their identity, of their self-concept.

If work is so crucial to self-concept, then it is also crucial to our relationships with others, because the way we relate to others depends largely on how we see and feel about ourselves. The consequences of technological and structural change should not be viewed primarily in terms of the numbers who may need help to find work but more in terms of their effects on the way people feel about themselves. 'What do you do?' remains the most illuminating question to ask someone on meeting them for the first time. It is illuminating because a person's work, or the fact that they do not need to or cannot work, is indicative of so much else about them and their lifestyle. The higher a person's position in the occupational hierarchy, the higher is their probable level of self-esteem. The answer 'I am *just* a homemaker' explains why so many women have low self-esteem. An occupation provides a place in the social division of labour and the kudos that goes with it. Given the current economic climate and structural changes, the self-esteem of many thousands of people is likely to become eroded—full-time homemakers, retired people, the unemployed, the under-employed, those forced to take whatever job is available, those who feel locked into an unsatisfying job. To be unemployed places one outside the accepted, taken-for-granted system and calls into question one's capacity to be a normal, responsible citizen contributing to the general good. The following statements, made to me recently by unemployed people, suggest that the unemployed feel set apart from those with jobs, that they feel undesirable, worthless and ashamed:

'I've become a statistic'
'If you can't find any work to do, you have a feeling you are not human'
'I don't like being seen looking at the Situations Vacant at the CES'
'My little boy asks why I don't go out to work like other boys' dads'

To be unemployed is to feel different, to feel inferior, to feel excluded from the normal pattern of life. In losing work the individual loses not only his job but his social identity, and his existing self-concept is replaced by a more negative one. Many employees develop low self-esteem because they consider themselves expendable in management's eyes; severe loss of self-esteem arises when actual redundancy occurs. In their own eyes and in the eyes of others too, they believe, they have failed, it is their fault. This creates tension within marriage and with children as the breadwinner fails to live up to expectations. Additionally, there is a feeling of purposelessness, resignation and depression, with withdrawal from social situations. The self-concept contains a forlorn 'what I was' as it restructures to assimilate the negative 'what I have descended to now'.

The problem with insecurity about potential job loss or job change is that people translate a change in their objective environment into a subjective judgment of self-worth. The self-concept has to be revised, sometimes drastically and often in a less than positive way, to accommodate the new labels of unemployed, or redundant, or out of the running for new, more skilled jobs. The effect is proportional to the relative importance of employment status in the individual's self-concept and the perceived expectations of others in their close familial and other networks. Another influential factor is the presence of alternative components of the self-concept, e.g. hobby skills, that lessen the importance of the employment status component.

It is unlikely that a change in job status would affect only the employment-status component of the self-concept. Other components of the self-concept will also be directly affected as a result of the accompanying change in social role. This may accentuate the effect of the job-status change on self-attitudes by changing the person's evaluations of other components of self-concept. The attribution of the cause of the status change affects the change in self-concept. If the status change is positive and the attribution is internal, i.e. 'I brought this about', then the self-concept will be enhanced. If the change is positive and the attribution external, i.e. 'Others did this', then the enhancement of the self-concept will be minimal. Negative status change will lower self-esteem more if it has an internal attribution than if it has an external one. Research shows that becoming unemployed leads to greater dissatisfaction with self.

The importance of the employment-status component in a person's self-concept appears to determine whether unemployment leads to lower self-esteem. Where there is a lack of other sources of self-esteem, where there are no alternative roles, where there have been fewer prior achievements, the self-concept suffers much devaluation. The availability of an external source to which job loss can be attributed helps to reduce the loss of self-esteem and limit dissatisfaction.

Sex role may not appear all that relevant here, but of course many changes in the workplace affect traditional perspectives of what is men's work and what is women's work in both occupational and home contexts. Our beliefs about appropriate sex-role behaviour are created by powerful socialising agencies in childhood. Differential parental treatment and expectations of boys and girls, the presents and toys they are given, expectations about performance in different subjects at school, role models in the mass media, social attitudes in the surrounding culture all combine to encourage children to adopt culturally and subculturally appropriate views on the roles and behaviour of men and women, particularly in the home and at work.

Despite informal and formal attempts by interest groups and governments to eliminate it, sex-role stereotyping is still potent, and what is learned in childhood is often deeply ingrained and difficult to eradicate. A woman may have to restructure her self-concept when she takes on what is usually regarded as a man's job. This can create instability in her self-concept and impede her performance as she tries to adjust to the role in the face of a critical and unappreciative audience. A woman may tend to overplay what she believes is the male role and become too domineering. Or she may take others' negative attitudes to heart and underperform because she perceives herself as incompetent in the new role. On the other hand, when a man is made redundant he may have to take over the household duties while the wife works—a role reversal. If the husband sees the female role as inferior, he will come to perceive himself as inferior, with a consequent loss of self-esteem. People generally tend to change their self-concepts in the direction of their perception and valuing of the new role.

The self-concept is always changing as a result of new experiences, so we are not prisoners of the past. If it is possible to suffer a decrement in self-esteem, then it is also possible to enjoy an increment in self-esteem. This is a message of hope, for it means that even if a person has a negative self-concept, it is possible, by employing specific enhancement techniques, to increase its positive valence. In chapter 5 there is a collection of activities that can assist in the development of a positive self-concept.

## Attribution and locus of control

Imagine things haven't gone too well at work recently. There are rumours of redundancies, several orders you were handling have been cancelled, overtime is no longer available, and your work area has been designated a no smoking zone, much against your own wishes. You overhear two colleagues talking about you; another stops you in the corridor and asks whether you are feeling quite yourself. Today there is a memo on your desk from the boss, who wishes to see you. When you go to her office she starts the conversation by frankly stating that your motivation for the job seems to have gone. You might reply that though your order book is low at present due to customers feeling the pinch in the recession, you are working on new longer-term payment methods for them and this is stimulating renewed interest. You are also giving up smoking, which is causing a temporary disruption to your performance, but you intend to stick to the resolution so you can cope well in a non-smoking work environment. Or you might agree that you can't cope any more, you are over the hill, and you might as well become one of the redundancies, which is what you believe she has lined you up for anyway.

This story is entirely fictitious but does illustrate what can happen when one's life is moved out of its usual comfortable orbit. Weiner suggests that most explanations for success and failure have three characteristics.

- whether the cause is seen as external or internal (i.e. within the person)
- whether it is seen as stable or unstable
- whether it is perceived as controllable or not.

In the example above, the causes were external (e.g. the economy; the imposition of a smoking ban), unstable (temporary problems), and not controllable. The central principle behind assigning causation is the attempt to maintain a positive self-concept. Therefore when anything good happens, people tend to attribute it to their own efforts or ability. On the other hand, if anything bad occurs they attribute it to factors beyond their control, such as bad luck or discrimination. Joan is struggling to find a reason for her lack of promotion that does not require her to change her perception of herself as a competent and reliable employee. She attributes her failure to her manager, to company policy, to jealous colleagues—external factors over which she has no control. Attribution theory seeks to understand such explanations and excuses, particularly when applied to success and failure, coping or not coping.

One concept central to attribution theory is that of the *locus of control*. This term refers to the degree of control people think they have over what happens to them. The word 'locus' means place or location; the locus of control, then, is where people believe control of their lives originates. Those who see themselves as having control over their environment are less likely to be affected by stress and worry over what will happen to them in a context of rapid change. Such people are said to have an *internal locus of control*. Other people feel like broken tree branches, carried hither and thither by the flux of events. They think what happens to them and the direction of their lives is controlled not by them but by others or by outside events. They have an *external locus of control*.

Attribution theory deals primarily with four explanations for coping or not coping: ability, effort, luck, and task difficulty. Ability and effort are internal to the person while luck and task difficulty are external. Ability is a stable component, while effort is an unstable one and can be altered. Similarly, task difficulty is a stable component while luck is variable and unpredictable.

From Table 6, it is possible to see how an employee might seek to explain promotion or retrenchment differently as the attribution forms a coping mechanism to preserve self-esteem. A promotion is perceived as a result of being competent, able, reliable (internal, stable attributions), not a result of luck or the job being easy (external, unstable attributions). In contrast, an employee who is sacked would argue that she was unlucky, was picked on, was a victim of govern-

**Table 6  Attributions for success and failure**

| Locus of control | Stability | |
| --- | --- | --- |
| | Stable | Unstable |
| Internal | Ability | Effort |
| Success | I'm smart | I tried hard |
| Failure | I'm stupid | I didn't really try |
| External | Task difficulty | Luck |
| Success: | It was easy | Luck was on my side |
| Failure: | It was too hard | I had bad luck |

ment mismanagement and the like (external, unstable attributions). Such attributions allow for the possibility of success next time round and don't denigrate the self-esteem—after all, it was his fault. However such external attributions may, when not objectively true, lead into more serious defence mechanisms which involve denial and distortion of reality.

A number of animal and human studies strongly suggest that lack of control over unpleasant or stressful stimuli is associated with greater vulnerability to physical illness. In the case of human beings, many harmful and distressing situations appear to be aggravated when individuals believe they are helpless and that nothing they can do will significantly alter the outcome. This condition has been termed *learned helplessness*. In one experiment, a group of people was exposed to a loud noise that could not be controlled or turned off. A second group was exposed to the same noise but could turn it off. After exposure to the noise had ended, both groups were given a task to do. Those in the uncontrollable-noise group performed significantly worse than those in the controllable-noise group. This and other experiments suggest that when people believe they are helpless and are not in control of what is happening to them, (i) they become less able to solve new problems or adapt to new situations, (ii) their motivation to involve themselves or try anything new is reduced, (iii) depression develops, and (iv) self-esteem declines. Having developed a self-concept of which a major component is weakness and inability to achieve a desired outcome, they cease to bother involving themselves in what is going on around them. Thus, attribution of causes and belief in one's ability to control or at least exert some influence on the way one's life develops interact with the self-concept. They can be influenced positively by enhancing the pictures in the self-concept, just as the self-concept can be damaged by a life experience that engenders a sense of helplessness. Being employed, whether changes are going on or not, entails forfeiture of some control over self and the environment. One cannot do one's own thing; policies and procedures must be followed; working hours, work colleagues, work place are usually not open to discussion. In an era of rapid change, far more helplessness is imposed. To reduce feelings of helplessness and consequent self-depreciation, the methods referred to in Chapters 2 and 6 for employee involvement in planning changes, open discussion, and involvement in implementing agreed-upon change will be of considerable use.

Some kinds of depression are learned helplessness, a result of feeling unable to control one's destiny. Some psychologists have helped people whose depression stems from this feeling by encouraging and enabling them to succeed first at simple tasks then gradually at more demanding ones. Such people have to build up their own belief in themselves, progressively learn that they are capable of some personal control of their lives, and begin to feel good about themselves, i.e. develop a positive self-concept. Belief in one's ability to control events is an essential ingredient of coping and a psychological resource people draw on during stressful events.

People faced with events they perceive as uncontrollable experience a host of physiological reactions, such as increased heart rate, excessive production of adrenalin, and decreased immunological status. Lack of perceived control fosters helplessness, frustration and depression. It is less stressful never to have had control than to have had it and then to lose it. But losing it is exactly what happens to some employees in times of change. Encouraging worker participation in change is one way to reduce a sense of loss of control and the reactions that go with it.

Locus of control has been found to be an important factor in work performance. If an employee believes the performance appraisal she gets is a function of a manager's whim, luck or dislike, then of course how hard she works does not matter. So she makes no effort and gets a low appraisal—a self-validating prophecy. We have already met this situation in our discussion of the effects of a low self-concept. In contrast, those who believe that success and failure are due primarily to their own behaviour tend to succeed.

Since belief in the role of luck, in the fact one is destined to be a loser, in one's inability to control situations, leads to self-fulfilling prophecies, managers and supervisors must try to communicate to people with such beliefs the expectation that they can cope, can succeed, can perform, and that one negative event does not imply inadequacy. This will, over time, help employees in situations of change to see that their chances of coping depend somewhat on their efforts and willingness to try—an internal but alterable attribution that lets them anticipate success in the future if they are proactive. Some formal means of rewarding employees for effort as well as skill will motivate best and facilitate coping with change.

An employee who believes his working life is controlled by 'the organisation', a nameless 'them', or fate, will tend to indict such elements as the cause of their loss of a job, of their loss of overtime, of their soulless drudgery. Such accusation will be made either in anger and frustration (I'd shoot the government) or in resignation and apathy (There's nothing I can do about it; I'm finished). An internally controlled person faced with similar problems will be more proactive and attempt to find solutions to the immediate and long-term difficulties; he will not cast blame around but energetically pursue options. Internally oriented people are more able to perceive potentials and other opportunities and re-evaluate their situation in a positive way. There is a close correlation between possession of a positive self-concept and being internally oriented, and between having a negative self-concept and being externally oriented. Attribution theory is important in understanding how employees might interpret and perceive changes and life transitions. An externally oriented person can so easily reach a state of apathy and resignation about getting another job or learning new job skills that he ceases to try and joins the permanently unemployed, filled with low self-esteem and disillusion. Enhancement of the self-concept is essential in moving a person with an external locus of control towards a more internal orientation. Chapter 5 contains numerous activities to enhance self-esteem.

## Activity 23  Locus of control

To assess your locus of control, complete the following questionnaire by circling the number in the relevant box.

| Strongly disagree | Strongly agree | Agree | Disagree | |
|---|---|---|---|---|
| 1 Life is in the hands of Lady Luck | 1 | 2 | 3 | 4 |
| 2 War between countries is inevitable | 1 | 2 | 3 | 4 |
| 3 When I make plans, I am almost certain that I can make them work | 4 | 3 | 2 | 1 |
| 4 People who never get sick are just lucky | 1 | 2 | 3 | 4 |
| 5 Success is a matter of hard work | 4 | 3 | 2 | 1 |
| 6 We might as well make decisions by tossing a coin | 1 | 2 | 3 | 4 |
| 7 If I take care of myself I can avoid illness | 4 | 3 | 2 | 1 |
| 8 I have little influence over things that happen to me | 1 | 2 | 3 | 4 |

| | | | | |
|---|---|---|---|---|
| 9 | I can affect the way others behave towards me | 4 | 3 | 2 | 1 |
| 10 | Most of us are victims of forces we neither understand nor control | 1 | 2 | 3 | 4 |
| 11 | Getting on in life is a matter of knowing the right people | 1 | 2 | 3 | 4 |
| 12 | What happens to me is my own doing | 4 | 3 | 2 | 1 |
| 13 | Leadership positions tend to go to those who are capable | 4 | 3 | 2 | 1 |
| 14 | I feel that I don't have control over the direction my life is taking | 1 | 2 | 3 | 4 |

Score this questionnaire by adding up the numbers that you circled. The lower your score, the more external is your locus of control, i.e. the more you believe that external factors control your life. The higher your score the more internal is your locus of control, i.e. the more you believe that you have some control over what happens to you. The maximum score is 56 and the minimum score is 14.

## Activity 24   Career control

One major area of our lives in which we want to have some control is our career. In the current recession and period of technological restructuring many people believe they have little control over their careers. Complete this questionnaire and determine where you stand. Answer each statement using the following key:

| | | | |
|---|---|---|---|
| 1 | Strongly disagree | 5 | Slightly agree |
| 2 | Moderately disagree | 6 | Moderately agree |
| 3 | Slightly disagree | 7 | Strongly agree |
| 4 | Neither agree nor disagree | | |

a. I believe that individuals have little control over their career paths                                                                    ------
b. I will not push for promotion until I feel the time is right                                                                              ------
c. I feel that most people exaggerate the influence they feel they have over their own career paths                                          ------
d. I sometimes feel that my career is out of control     ------
e. In this organisation it tends to be who you know rather than what you do that leads to promotion                                          ------
f. I needed a great deal of luck to get my present position ------
g. I believe in the saying that you have to be in the right place at the right time                                                          ------

h.  I feel the support of powerful people is more important
    than job performance in gaining promotion                ------
i.  It doesn't matter how hard you work; if luck is against
    you, you will not succeed                                ------
j.  It is important to be well in with the powers that be
    to do well                                               ------
k.  I can improve my chances of promotion only by
    concentrating on those aspects of the job that
    superiors notice                                         ------
l.  You have to be born under the right star to get on
    in life                                                  ------

Put your score for each question into the formulae below and carry
out the calculations shown.

$(8 - a) + b + c + d =$ _____ (I)
$e + h + j + k =$ _____ (P)
$f + g + i + l =$ _____ (C)

The 'I' scale measures the strength of your belief that your career
is under your own control.
The 'P' scale measures the strength of your belief that your career
is under the control of powerful other people.
The 'C' scale measures the strength of your belief that your career
is controlled by luck.
   You might like to compare your scores with those from a sample
of British managers.

|                | Average | Range |
|----------------|---------|-------|
| Internal       | 19      | 15–23 |
| Powerful others| 16      | 11–21 |
| Chance         | 14      | 10–18 |

Remember that someone with an external locus of control person (a
low scorer) will not only perceive more stress but feel less able to do
anything about it. They will feel helpless in the face of events. Such
a person must learn some personal coping skills such as relaxation
(Chapter 5), positive thinking (Chapter 5), self-concept enhancement
(Chapter 5), decision-making (Chapter 6) in order to increase their
feeling of control over the environment and become proactive in it.

## Personality types A and B

We have known for many years that specific behaviour patterns can
adversely affect health. A prime example is the risk factors for
cardiovascular disease, which includes smoking, obesity, a high-fat
diet. Other more general behavioural traits also appear to affect the

way a person responds to the environment. One of the simplest explanations of the differences in individual reaction to stress and change is the Type A and Type B personality theory of Friedman and Rosenman. They believe that there is a correlation between the way in which a person perceives his environment and the qualities of that person's behaviour and personality. A person with a Type A personality:

- Has an intense sense of urgency; feels the need to do more in the shortest time possible
- Is aggressive and hostile, with a high level of motivation and competitiveness; is unable to play for fun; needs to make a contest out of everything
- Becomes involved in too many tasks at once
- Talks fast and listens impatiently.

Type B behaviour is more relaxed and unhurried. A Type B person is generally patient, noncompetitive and not dominated by a sense of urgency. Type B qualities are held to be the opposite of Type A. Type A people are likely to perceive more stressors in the same environment than Type B. They also experience more situations with potential stressors than Type B people do. Type B people, on the other hand, have a more easy-going manner, are patient, are not particularly competitive, and do not feel the need to set deadlines.

These two descriptions mark the extremes of a continuum. Few people are at the extremes—fully Type A or B all the time. Most of us are a mixture. Of course those with a tendency to Type A behaviour are more badly affected by the pressures of change, becoming stressed and developing a greater risk of cardiovascular illness. Everyone needs to become aware of their position on the Type A–Type B continuum. Those who find themselves towards the A end can then take some remedial action to modify their behaviour and reduce stress. In one study, regular physical examinations were carried out over a number of years on 3500 males between the ages of 39 and 59. It was found that 70 per cent of Type A persons developed coronary heart disease, as against only 30 per cent of Type Bs. Other medical research has since shown that one of the most significant psychosocial predictors of coronary heart disease is a competitive, striving, time-pressured lifestyle. This is characteristic of the Type A personality. Even when other risk factors are controlled (e.g. smoking, overweight), the incidence of coronary heart disease and the death rate from that disease are twice as high in Type A people as in Type B. Type A people appear to respond to and perceive environmental demands in less adaptive ways. It does not follow that Type As are automatically susceptible to heart disease. The danger occurs when Type As are subjected to self-perceived high demand and stress. Type As appear to be motivated by an exaggerated need for control over their environment. A questionnaire to distinguish Type A from Type B personalities is included below.

Since Type As are so deeply involved in and committed to their work, any change in work practices and conditions, in job status, in role, or in employment prospects can be devastating to them. Often, they have neglected other aspects of their lives and have nothing to compensate for loss or change at work. Already fairly stressed individuals, they experience any work change as an emotional loss which creates a void in their lives. Identification of Type As can alert management to those who are likely to be shattered by change at work and who need, through counselling, future career planning and alternative lifestyle planning, to be introduced gently to change over a period of time. It is almost impossible to change one's essential personality type. What can be encouraged is the use of techniques to manage behaviour, such as relaxation exercises (Chapter 5), and the development of other interests in life. Unfortunately, many managers are Type As. They have reached their position in many cases by selfless devotion to the job, by high levels of motivation, by ambition and competitiveness.

The following questionnaire will provide a rough idea of your behavioural type.

## Activity 25　Type A–Type B questionnaire

Read each statement carefully, then circle the number corresponding to the category of behaviour that best fits you. The numbers represent: 1 = never; 2 = seldom; 3 = sometimes; 4 = usually; 5 = always.
When you have finished, add up all the circled numbers and read the key at the end of the questionnaire.

| | | | | | |
|---|---|---|---|---|---|
| I become angry when I have to queue for more than 15 minutes | 1 | 2 | 3 | 4 | 5 |
| I handle more than one problem at a time | 1 | 2 | 3 | 4 | 5 |
| It's hard finding time to relax | 1 | 2 | 3 | 4 | 5 |
| I become irritated if someone can't explain themself clearly | 1 | 2 | 3 | 4 | 5 |
| I try hard to win at sports/games | 1 | 2 | 3 | 4 | 5 |
| I bring work home with me | 1 | 2 | 3 | 4 | 5 |
| I look at my watch when I'm sitting around doing nothing | 1 | 2 | 3 | 4 | 5 |
| I work better under pressure, meeting deadlines | 1 | 2 | 3 | 4 | 5 |
| I do not take 'time out' | 1 | 2 | 3 | 4 | 5 |
| I get angry when I lose at sports/games | 1 | 2 | 3 | 4 | 5 |
| I interrupt people when I think they are wrong | 1 | 2 | 3 | 4 | 5 |

| | | | | | |
|---|---|---|---|---|---|
| I do things quickly regardless of whether I have time or not | 1 | 2 | 3 | 4 | 5 |
| I eat rapidly in order to get back to my work | 1 | 2 | 3 | 4 | 5 |
| I feel I need to take charge of a group to get things moving | 1 | 2 | 3 | 4 | 5 |
| I feel exhilarated in a pressure situation | 1 | 2 | 3 | 4 | 5 |
| I'm inflexible when it comes to changes at work or at home | 1 | 2 | 3 | 4 | 5 |
| I become jittery when I've nothing to do | 1 | 2 | 3 | 4 | 5 |
| I eat faster than the people I am eating with | 1 | 2 | 3 | 4 | 5 |
| At work I need to perform more than one task at a time to feel productive | 1 | 2 | 3 | 4 | 5 |
| I take less vacation time than I am entitled to | 1 | 2 | 3 | 4 | 5 |
| I find myself very picky and look at small details | 1 | 2 | 3 | 4 | 5 |
| I become annoyed at people who do not work as hard as I do | 1 | 2 | 3 | 4 | 5 |
| I find there are not enough things to do in the day | 1 | 2 | 3 | 4 | 5 |
| I spend a lot of time thinking about my work | 1 | 2 | 3 | 4 | 5 |
| I get bored easily | 1 | 2 | 3 | 4 | 5 |
| I work at weekends | 1 | 2 | 3 | 4 | 5 |
| I argue with people who do not think my way | 1 | 2 | 3 | 4 | 5 |
| I take everything I do seriously | 1 | 2 | 3 | 4 | 5 |
| I interrupt others' conversation in order to speed things up | 1 | 2 | 3 | 4 | 5 |
| I have trouble rolling with the punches when trouble arises | 1 | 2 | 3 | 4 | 5 |

a.  If your score is 75 or less you are a Type B person. That is, you take life as it comes and usually don't allow problems to dominate your life.

b.  If your score is between 76 and 99 you are in the average group. For the most part you aren't very competitive or aggressive but you do take some things seriously and in certain situations like to be active and productive. You need to see which Type A traits you have and decide whether or not they are affecting your lifestyle and health. Read the section in Chapter 5 for some hints on reducing Type A behaviour and managing stress.

c.  If your score was 100 or more, you have a tendency towards Type A personality. Competitive, impatient and aggressive, you need to work on your attitudes, behaviour and priorities before you become seriously ill. Introduce a stress-reducing campaign into your life using the techniques in Chapter 5.

Since every person is different, there are no right or wrong answers. But it is a documented fact that Type A people suffer from more stress symptoms than Type B people do: Type B or AB behaviour is beneficial, as it allows us to do all the things Type As do but without being hostile, aggressive, impatient or insecure. We can achieve while maintaining composure and an enjoyment in what we do.

## Personal growth

This section has dealt mostly with your personal qualities. What is required of most people as they proceed through life with its ups and downs is increased maturity and increased competency in coping. This is often termed *personal growth*. To complete this section, fill in the following personal growth inventory. It is an inventory you can come back to later to see whether you have been able to 'grow' in those areas you designate.

## Activity 26   Personal growth

This inventory is designed to help you examine your own self-estimation on a number of important attitudes and behaviours and to project your future personal aspirations and goals. It is not a test but an instrument for gaining self-insight. Read each item and ring the number on the scale that best decribes your self-estimation. After completing all the scales, choose three or four on which you would most like to see change in yourself. On each of these, draw an arrow above the line to indicate the direction of change and mark 'F' for future on the scale at the point you feel you can realistically work towards.

**Personal growth inventory**

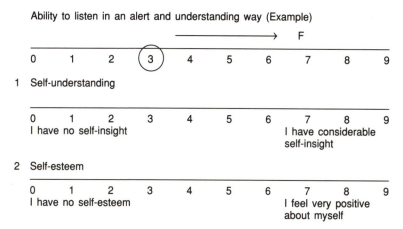

Ability to listen in an alert and understanding way (Example)

```
                              ────────────→   F
_____
  0     1     2    (3)     4     5     6     7     8     9
1  Self-understanding
```

```
_____
  0     1     2     3     4     5     6     7     8     9
I have no self-insight                    I have considerable
                                          self-insight
2  Self-esteem
```

```
_____
  0     1     2     3     4     5     6     7     8     9
I have no self-esteem                     I feel very positive
                                          about myself
```

3  Courage to fail

| 0 | 1 | 2 | 3 | 4 | 5 | 6 | 7 | 8 | 9 |
|---|---|---|---|---|---|---|---|---|---|

I am very afraid to fail                    I am not afraid to fail

4  Showing care and concern

| 0 | 1 | 2 | 3 | 4 | 5 | 6 | 7 | 8 | 9 |
|---|---|---|---|---|---|---|---|---|---|

I am a cold fish                    I am exceptionally
                                    warm and caring

5  Accepting care and concern

| 0 | 1 | 2 | 3 | 4 | 5 | 6 | 7 | 8 | 9 |
|---|---|---|---|---|---|---|---|---|---|

Makes me uneasy                    I value all I can get

6  Openness

| 0 | 1 | 2 | 3 | 4 | 5 | 6 | 7 | 8 | 9 |
|---|---|---|---|---|---|---|---|---|---|

I reveal little of                    I reveal much of
myself                                myself

7  Peace of mind

| 0 | 1 | 2 | 3 | 4 | 5 | 6 | 7 | 8 | 9 |
|---|---|---|---|---|---|---|---|---|---|

I am restless and                    I am at peace with
dissatisfied                          myself

8  Tendency to trust

| 0 | 1 | 2 | 3 | 4 | 5 | 6 | 7 | 8 | 9 |
|---|---|---|---|---|---|---|---|---|---|

Quite suspicious                    Very trusting

9  Physical energy

| 0 | 1 | 2 | 3 | 4 | 5 | 6 | 7 | 8 | 9 |
|---|---|---|---|---|---|---|---|---|---|

I tire easily and                    I am vital and
quickly                              resilient

10  Versatility

| 0 | 1 | 2 | 3 | 4 | 5 | 6 | 7 | 8 | 9 |
|---|---|---|---|---|---|---|---|---|---|

Can only do a few things                    Can do many
well                                        things well

11  Innovativeness

| 0 | 1 | 2 | 3 | 4 | 5 | 6 | 7 | 8 | 9 |
|---|---|---|---|---|---|---|---|---|---|

I like to keep the status                    Exceptionally
quo                                          creative and inventive

12  Expressing anger

| 0 | 1 | 2 | 3 | 4 | 5 | 6 | 7 | 8 | 9 |
|---|---|---|---|---|---|---|---|---|---|

I express it openly                    I repress it constantly

13 Receiving hostility

| 0 | 1 | 2 | 3 | 4 | 5 | 6 | 7 | 8 | 9 |
|---|---|---|---|---|---|---|---|---|---|
| It immobilises me | | | | | | | It stimulates me | | |

14 Clarity in expressing my thoughts

| 0 | 1 | 2 | 3 | 4 | 5 | 6 | 7 | 8 | 9 |
|---|---|---|---|---|---|---|---|---|---|
| Quite vague | | | | | | | Exceptionally clear | | |

15 Ability to listen in an alert and understanding way

| 0 | 1 | 2 | 3 | 4 | 5 | 6 | 7 | 8 | 9 |
|---|---|---|---|---|---|---|---|---|---|
| Very slow | | | | | | | Very high | | |

16 Reactions to comments about, or evaluations of my behaviour

| 0 | 1 | 2 | 3 | 4 | 5 | 6 | 7 | 8 | 9 |
|---|---|---|---|---|---|---|---|---|---|
| I ignore them | | | | | | | I take them very seriously | | |

17 Tolerance of differences in others

| 0 | 1 | 2 | 3 | 4 | 5 | 6 | 7 | 8 | 9 |
|---|---|---|---|---|---|---|---|---|---|
| Very low | | | | | | | Very high | | |

18 Feeling anxiety

| 0 | 1 | 2 | 3 | 4 | 5 | 6 | 7 | 8 | 9 |
|---|---|---|---|---|---|---|---|---|---|
| High levels of anxiety | | | | | | | Rarely feel anxiety | | |

19 Negative thinking

| 0 | 1 | 2 | 3 | 4 | 5 | 6 | 7 | 8 | 9 |
|---|---|---|---|---|---|---|---|---|---|
| Often troubled by negative thoughts | | | | | | | Rarely have negative thoughts | | |

20 Being me

| 0 | 1 | 2 | 3 | 4 | 5 | 6 | 7 | 8 | 9 |
|---|---|---|---|---|---|---|---|---|---|
| Never enjoy being me | | | | | | | Really enjoy being me at all times | | |

21 Interest in learning

| 0 | 1 | 2 | 3 | 4 | 5 | 6 | 7 | 8 | 9 |
|---|---|---|---|---|---|---|---|---|---|
| Relatively dormant | | | | | | | Very active | | |

22 Independence

| 0 | 1 | 2 | 3 | 4 | 5 | 6 | 7 | 8 | 9 |
|---|---|---|---|---|---|---|---|---|---|
| Very little | | | | | | | A great deal | | |

23   Vision of the future

| 0 | 1 | 2 | 3 | 4 | 5 | 6 | 7 | 8 | 9 |
|---|---|---|---|---|---|---|---|---|---|

Think mainly of the present                    Often try to
                                               envision and plan
                                               for the future

24   Level of aspiration

| 0 | 1 | 2 | 3 | 4 | 5 | 6 | 7 | 8 | 9 |
|---|---|---|---|---|---|---|---|---|---|

Quite low                                      Extremely high

## Personality traits

A trait is a style of behaviour in a person which is consistent in different situations. A trait is really a description, for example happy, sad, sociable etc. Traits are the innumerable ways in which we describe our own and other people's personalities. It is fairly obvious that many of the descriptors are synonymous, or closely so. For example, unhappy, miserable, dolorous, sad, all have much the same meaning; we could therefore scrap three of them as redundant and use only one. This in a sense is what some psychologists have done by using statistical factor analytic techniques to reduce the many ways we can describe people to the bare minimum number of traits. Cattell suggests we need only sixteen source traits, as these subsume all other traits. Eysenck goes even further and claims only three traits are needed. Both of these psychologists provide questionnaires by which to assess a person's standing on each of the traits. Every trait is bipolar; that is, it is a continuum running from a high end (a description) to a low end (its antonym). For example, the trait indicative of your degree of shyness runs from 'extremely shy and timid' to 'socially bold'. Cattell's sixteen factors are measured on his 16 Personality Factor scale, or 16 PF for short. This scale is often used in staff selection. The sixteen traits or factors are listed in Table 7. Using the questionnaire, an individual can be given a score from 0 to 10 on each trait. People who *may* have most problems coping with change are those who score low on A, C, E, H and Q1 and high on I, O and Q4. Such questionnaire results are not perfectly accurate but provide pointers to those who may be potentially more disturbed by, and less able to adjust to, life transitions. These individuals can then be targeted for more help and support.

Eysenck's factors are three in number: stability–instability (often called neuroticism), extraversion–introversion, and psychotism–normalcy. The stability/instability continuum is concerned with emotional stability. Anxious, moody people are at the low end of the scale while calm, even-tempered individuals score at the high end. Neurotic (or anxious) people have a highly reactive sympathetic

**Table 7 Cattell's sixteen personality factors**

| Low score description | Trait or factor | High score description |
| --- | --- | --- |
| Reserved, detached, critical, aloof | A | Outgoing, warm-hearted, easygoing |
| Less intelligent, concrete thinking | B | More intelligent, abstract thinking |
| Affected by feelings, easily upset | C | Emotionally stable, calm, mature |
| Humble, mild, conforming | E | Assertive, competitive |
| Sober, prudent, taciturn | F | Happy-go-lucky, enthusiastic |
| Expedient, disregards rules | G | Conscientious, moralistic |
| Shy, timid | H | Socially bold |
| Tough-minded, realistic | I | Tender-minded, sensitive |
| Trusting, adaptable | L | Suspicious, hard to fool |
| Practical, careful | M | Imaginative, careless |
| Forthright, natural | N | Shrewd, calculating |
| Self-assured, confident | O | Apprehensive, troubled |
| Conservative, respects established ideas | Q1 | Experimenting, radical |
| Group dependent, good 'follower' | Q2 | Self-sufficient, resourceful |
| Undisciplined, self-conflict | Q3 | Controlled, socially precise |
| Relaxed, tranquil | Q4 | Tense, frustrated |

nervous system. The sympathetic nervous system is the one which prepares the body for coping with stress, e.g. increases the heart rate. Thus people at the neurotic end of the continuum react quickly and strongly to stress and worries. They are more likely to be upset in conditions of stress than colleagues whose scores locate them towards the stable end of the continuum. Those scoring towards the neurotic end on Eysenck's scale tend to report more pain, more psychosomatic illness, and less tolerance of uncertainty than those towards the stable end. The anxious, reactive personality is a cause of additional stress because the reaction to a stressful event is self-perpetuating; the anxiety caused by the event becomes a stressor in itself, creating still more anxiety and stress. It is an anxiety feedback loop.

The extraversion/introversion continuum is a measure of sociability and impulsiveness. People at the extraversion end of the scale are highly sociable, impulsive, excitable, active, carefree and outgoing; they are stimulus seekers. Those at the introversion end tend to be withdrawn, reserved, quiet, bookish and careful; they are stimulus avoiders.

Psychotism is mainly the concern of clinical psychologists, as it relates to degree of mental illness.

A lot of research shows that introverts and extraverts prefer to be in different situations and perform differently under different conditions. Extraverts work better where there is plenty of activity and do poorly, for example, in jobs involving repetitive tasks. Introverts are less easily bored with repetitive tasks.

Both unstable introverts and unstable extraverts have problems in adjustment. Moody, quiet introverts will ruminate negatively over their fate and the problems that beset them. The extreme pessimism and anxiety of unstable introverts may lead to stress-related illness and behaviour, total withdrawal, depression and, for some, suicide. The touchy, aggressive, changeable, impulsive nature of the unstable extravert can affect life transitions, with angry outbursts directed at those believed responsible or at scapegoats like children and spouses. Irresponsible behaviour marks the extreme unstable extravert—such people form a large proportion of the violent part of the prison population. Research has shown that Cattell's sixteen factors can be clumped together to form several overarching ones which resemble Eysenck's factors.

## Summary

This section has presented a number of personal factors that affect the coping behaviour of individuals in a context of change. Stress cannot be avoided and every event, whether subjectively perceived as positive or negative, creates some degree of stress. Stress can have serious effects on physical, mental and emotional health. The work context is a potent source of stressors such as poor environmental conditions, job overload, role conflict, performance pressures, anxiety about job security and organisational change.

A positive self-concept enables people to cope better with everyday challenges and events. It makes them less anxious, more willing to try new things, more confident, more resilient in the face of difficulty, more resourceful, and more able to maximise their strengths, maintain productive relationships with others, and adopt a self-validating belief in their ability to control their life. All these attributes are vitally important in a rapidly changing world where jobs are scarce, qualifications and work skills are increasingly necessary, and new work horizons open up daily.

Those with high self-esteem also tend to demonstrate an internal locus of control and believe they have a fair degree of control over their lives. Those with an external locus of control will tend to feel that no matter how hard they try they cannot influence the course of their lives very much; for them, luck and the decisions of others are the deciding factors.

A person with a Type B personality tends to cope much better with the pressures of change than one with a Type A personality. The latter react much more quickly and strongly to frustration, with anger and an increased risk of cardiovascular illness. Unstable introverts and unstable extraverts also react badly to stress: the former withdraw and blame themselves while the latter may actively engage in irresponsible, antisocial behaviour.

Self-assessment will hopefully have provided some insight into the areas that you will need to work on using the activities that follow in Chapters 5 and 6. The personal factors seen most frequently in both managers and employees suffering from the stress of change are:

- low self-esteem
- type A behaviour
- heavy smoking
- excessive alcohol consumption
- external locus of control.

These factors are precipitating agents which increase susceptibility to stress, with consequent health and emotional problems. If you can identify some of these factors in yourself from the above self-assessments, then you must take extra steps to manage them by practising the relevant activities in Chapters 5 and 6.

# 4
# Coping with change
## *The human response*
## *Interpersonal strategies*

### Transactional analysis

Transactional analysis, or TA is a personality theory which focuses on the interactions between people. It was developed by Eric Berne. Berne claims that the personality consists of three major parts, or ego states: the Child, the Parent, the Adult. Berne argues that our interactions with parents in the first few years of life are never forgotten. The memories of these interactions, our responses to them, and our experiences and feelings associated with them constitute the Child ego state. Feelings associated with childhood may be happiness, guilt, rebellion and so on.

The basic structure of the personality is often illustrated by three adjacent circles, as in Figure 9. The Parent and the Child are subdivided into three components which indicate the different ways in which the Child can feel and the Parent can control.

*The Child*

In each of us there is a child made up of the residues of childhood ways of thinking and feeling. The Natural Child is spontaneous, creative and fantasising, lovable and friendly; expresses feelings and engages in activities for the fun of it. The Rebellious Child is selfish, manipulative and demanding; the Adapted or Conforming Child is compliant, polite and restrained.

*The Parent*

The Parent ego state is made up of the attitudes and behaviours each of us has seen in our parents and other influential grown-ups when

**Figure 9  The figure TA states**

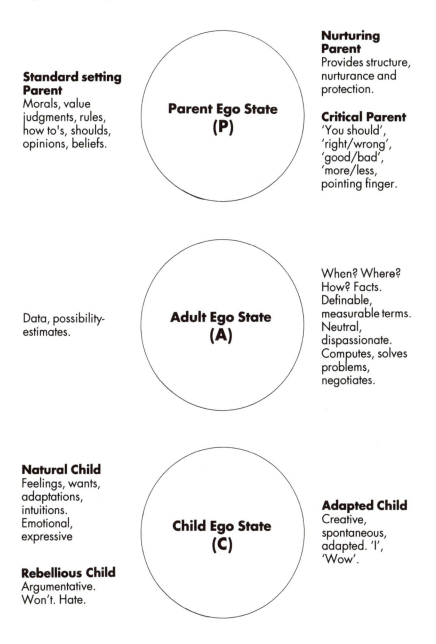

**Standard setting Parent**
Morals, value judgments, rules, how to's, shoulds, opinions, beliefs.

**Parent Ego State (P)**

**Nurturing Parent**
Provides structure, nurturance and protection.

**Critical Parent**
'You should', 'right/wrong', 'good/bad', 'more/less, pointing finger.

Data, possibility-estimates.

**Adult Ego State (A)**

When? Where? How? Facts. Definable, measurable terms. Neutral, dispassionate. Computes, solves problems, negotiates.

**Natural Child**
Feelings, wants, adaptations, intuitions. Emotional, expressive

**Rebellious Child**
Argumentative. Won't. Hate.

**Child Ego State (C)**

**Adapted Child**
Creative, spontaneous, adapted. 'I', 'Wow'.

we were small. Words, voice tone, gestures are all replayed when we find ourselves in similar situations later in life. The Critical Parent sets standards, makes rules, is arbitrary and authoritarian. The Nurturing Parent has the function of comforting, caring for, and being concerned about others. There is open expression of caring. Managers and trainers may spend more time than they should in the Critical and Nurturing Parent roles.

*The Adult*

The Adult deals with facts and reality; it measures alternatives and makes decisions; it stays on track with the problem at hand.

Each ego state is desirable or undesirable only insofar as it is relevant to the situation at hand. The Critical Parent is vital to enable us to know what is right and wrong and to give us a moral code to live by. However, too much reliance on this state will interfere with effective communication. An authoritarian, rigid management style with a lack of feeling for the needs of others is not helpful in encouraging proactive, creative behaviour in others. Similarly, an excess of Nurturing Parent behaviour in a manager will smother and block the psychological growth of others, producing over-reliance and dependence.

The balance between the three ego states varies from individual to individual. We all have preferred ego states which we can move between. Some of these states are effective for improving interpersonal relationships but others are ineffective and destroy relationships (Table 8).

*Transactions*

A transaction is a basic unit of behaviour, involving an interaction, verbal or behavioural, between people. I may say something to you or I shake my fist—both are transactions. Each transaction is indicative of the ego state prompting it, and can be identified by content and the way in which it is said. In addition, every transaction is targeted at a particular ego state in the other person. The sender is hoping that the receiver will respond from the targeted ego state. This may not always occur. Many Critical Parent transactions initiated by the manager are targeted at the Compliant or Adapted Child state in the other person. Managers often use the former, hoping to hook into the Compliant Child in the employee. However, the employee's reaction may stem from the Rebellious Child state so that a 'Who do you think you are' type of response is forthcoming rather than the Compliant Child's 'I'm sorry, I won't do it that way again'. Sometimes a veiled Rebellious Child utterance is produced, e.g. 'With respect ...'

**Table 8  Features of the effective ego states**

| Ego state | Description | Examples |
|---|---|---|
| Nurturing parent | A caring, nurturing, empathetic function that leads to a healthy relationship with self and others. Provides permission to be, think, feel and act in a natural manner. Looks for and invites out the best in others and self. | Offers help. 'Fantastic!' 'Congratulations!' 'Would you like a hand?' A comforting arm around your shoulders. A warm smile. 'They're lucky to have you.' |
| Standard-setting parent | Stores decisions about ourselves and others, values and principles. This is stored as firm guide-lines rather than rigid rules. Gives clear information about how to succeed, what is expected and limits. Willpower and self-confidence, security come from the good use of this ego state. | 'You need to be here by 9am.' 'Hold on—stick to the issue here.' 'This needs correcting—let me have it by 3pm.' 'Right—let's get back to it!' Delegates. 'Here's how it's to be done.' 'What will you do about it?' (in a firm tone). |
| Adult | Evaluates and analyses information in a logical and objective manner. Makes decisions to be stored for later use. Reasoned and predictable ego state leading to effective problem-solving. Makes sense and acts on it. | 'What are the facts?' 'What is the problem?!' 'How did it happen?' 'When will it be ready?' '9am.' 'I don't agree with that—here's how I see it.' 'When you do that I feel angry.' |
| Natural child | Is natural and spontaneous. Is what s/he says s/he is. Expresses emotions appropriate to the situation. Is aware, here and now. Creates, constructs, visualises. See what we see, feel what we feel and say what we mean from this ego state. | 'Yuk!' A belly laugh. Grief. Humour. 'I've got it!' Piss off! Wow! I don't want to! I wonder what would happen if . . .! I can't wait! Enjoys. Dreams—I could own this company one day! Invents. |
| Rescuing parent | Being over-protective of self or others and usually insincere in relationships with others. Restricts and discounts or confines the thinking feeling or behaving abilities of others. Guilt is stored here. | 'I've organised for Ron to help you' (without consulting you). Oh, I'll do it—you go. Overworks. 'You poor thing, never mind.' 'Here, I'll do it for you.' 'You need help.' |

**Table 8 (Cont.)**

| Ego state | Description | Examples |
|---|---|---|
| Critical parent | Stores decisions about ourselves and others, values and principles in a rigid manner. Uses absolutes and believes that everything should be exact and flawless. Frustration is stored here. | Why on earth did you do that!? I have TOLD you before. You should KNOW—I shouldn't have to tell you! I don't care—you have to. Your attitude's wrong—improve it or get out! |
| Compliant child | An almost automatic reaction or action resulting from fear or an excessive desire to comply to rigid rules. Tries to live up to others expectations even by behaving in a manner that we believe others want us to behave. Ignores true feelings. | All right. OK. I'm sorry. Um . . . I don't know. Sort of. I'll try harder. Sighs. Stays quiet even when s/he wants to speak. Anxious, shy. Depressed. Feels helpless. I can't. |
| Rebellious child | Imagines self to be under attack or restraint from being self. Imagines the ways we can't succeed because of situations and others. Images are usually negative. Vengeful at times. | I'll show them! I'll get even! Leave me alone! Lay off me! You're/They're always picking on me. Sarcastic. It's not MY fault! I don't want to. I won't. Huh! No way. Get . . . . . d! |

**Crossed, complementary and ulterior transactions**

In a *complementary* transaction the initial statement is successful in hooking the appropriate ego state in the other person and elicits a response from it.

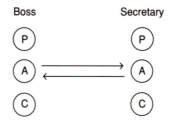

Boss: Have you seen my keys?
Secretary: Yes, they are on the top of the filing cabinet.

The Adult to Adult complementary transaction is concerned with information exchange and rational decision-making. This type of transaction is likely to achieve worthwhile results.

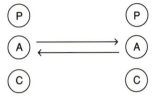

General manager      Personnel manager

General manager: Have you interviewed Smith yet about his proposed voluntary redundancy?

Personnel Manager: Yes, I spent two hours with him this morning. He is clear about the issues involved. My report will be on your desk later today.

A common complementary transaction is the Compliant Child to the Nurturing Parent, in which the former seeks help. A subordinate may use this towards the manager in order to gain attention deceitfully or obtain needed support and advice.

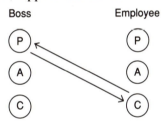

Boss      Employee

Employee: I'm sorry to bother you but could you look at these plans I've drawn; what should I do next?

Boss: Yes they look accurate and clear. I would annotate them here and here. Don't worry about asking, I'd rather you did that than make a mess of things.

Another common complementary transaction in the work situation is the Critical Parent to the Critical Parent, where for example, two or more employees in the lunch break or on a training course criticise, attack or denigrate their bosses, their employer, the course etc.

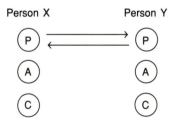

Person X      Person Y

Person X:  This firm never considers its workers.
Person Y:  I know, my boss never told me my promotion had been refused.

This transaction may help to relieve tension but it does not produce effective change or amelioration of the situation.

The Child–Child complementary transaction is often a temper tantrum, or a boasting, or a wishful fantasy type of conversation.

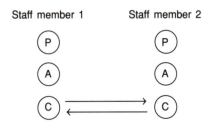

Staff member 1:  I'm just not going to do it.
Staff member 2:  I feel like handing in my resignation, and in front of you know who.
Staff member 1:  That would show him.
Staff member 2:  Wouldn't it be lovely to see his face.

In a *crossed* transaction, the transaction does not hook the appropriate ego state and will cease, whereas in the complementary transaction it continues.

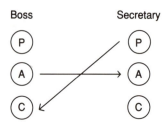

Boss:  Have you seen my keys?
Secretary:  They are where you left them!
or
Boss:  There are some mistakes in this report.
Secretary:  Could you do it better?

An *ulterior* transaction occurs when the transaction is being carried out at two levels, i.e. saying one thing but meaning something else.

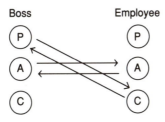

Boss          Employee

Boss:     I've got another job for you to do.
          (You are not doing the one you've got properly; I don't think
          even you could make a mess of this one.)
Employee: Good, I'll enjoy the change.
          (Always chopping and changing; how does he expect
          me ever to finish what I'm supposed to do?)

Managers need to be careful to distinguish what the real message
and agenda is. Is the employee in difficulty or just 'crawling'? Is there
an ulterior transaction around?

*Games*

Games are ulterior transactions used to attain control of an interaction. They are destructive to the person playing them and to the
others involved. The problem with games is that they do not allow
honest relationships to develop and often result in bad feeling. In the
game *Kick Me*, the initiator does or says something that provokes
others to criticise or punish him in some way. Negative attention is
better than no attention at all. In *Blemish*, the Critical Parent finds
some minor fault no matter how well the job is performed in order
to gain a feeling of superiority. In *If It Weren't For You*, the player
complains endlessly that if it were not for the boss or stupid work-
mates they could do the job much better/faster/cheaper.

## Activity 27   Ego states

All the organisation's managers and assistant managers are meeting to consider the implications of the introduction of a new piece
of production technology. Alan jumps up from the table, throws his
chair back and starts to leave the room, saying, 'I don't think any-
body here really cares about our employees and how they feel.'
Can you identify which ego state Alan is using? All the others at the
meeting respond to this outburst. Can you identify the ego states
used by each?

a.   Jane asks, 'What evidence have you for that?'
b.   Jim mutters uncomfortably, 'I hope he doesn't start on me.'

c. Maria thinks to herself, 'This guy is really frustrated. I wonder what is really wrong. I'll pop in and see him this afternoon when he has cooled down.'

d. Phil retorts, 'This is the first time I've known you to show concern for the employees.'

e. Lena smiles and shakes her head. 'He's off on some hobby horse again.'

f. Ian says, 'This matter sounds very important to you.'

g. John says, 'I feel personally insulted by what you claim. We have all put in a lot of work to involve and communicate with our staff. So lay off.'

h. Peter says, 'Hold on, Alan. Don't leave. This sounds like an issue we must resolve. Can you tell us quietly what it is that you feel we are not doing and how we might rectify it.'

Which of these ego states are likely to lead to a successful resolution of this conflict?

## Activity 28   More ego states

Which ego states are being used in these transactions?

a. 'What do you think about my plan to robotise the entire production line?'
   Response: 'If it were left to you we would all be out of a job!'

b. 'You have been criticising me behind my back.'
   Response 1: 'Get lost?'
   Response 2: 'I'm sorry if you think that. I have never done it intentionally. Perhaps there is some misunderstanding with your informant. Let's try and sort it out.'
   Response 3: 'Well, now you know how it feels.'

## Activity 29   Recognising ego states

In response to someone saying to you, 'I've lost my job because of your restructuring of the accounts system,' how would you respond from the following states: Adult; Critical Parent; Nurturing Parent; Rebellious Child; Conforming Child; Natural Child.

*Improving transactions*

TA can be employed to improve personal interactions in the workplace and ease problems. The first step in gaining better control over personal interactions is learning to recognise the ego state that is initiating the interaction. Next, it is necessary to identify which ego state it is intended to hook, especially if it is the Child, as therein lies

**Table 9    Non-verbal and verbal characteristics of ego states**

|  | Expressions | Attitudes | Voice | Words |
|---|---|---|---|---|
| Critical parent | frowning, pointing | judging, authoritarian | critical, condescending | never, don't, do, should |
| Nurturing parent | accepting, smiling | caring, understanding | encouraging, sympathetic well done | careful, let me |
| Adult | interested, thoughtful | open, evaluative | confident, inquiring | what? why? |
| Free child | uninhibited, spontaneous | curious, changeable | excited, free | where?, wow!, hi, great, let's go |
| Adapted child | helpless (c) sorry (c) sullen(r) won't (r) | agreeing (c) rebellious (r) | apologetic (c) defiant (r) | |

Compliant (c), Rebellious (r)

the source of feelings. If you do not want the transaction to continue, create a crossed transaction. If you can do this to the Adult ego state of the other person, he has to follow you or cease the transaction.

The source state of the transaction can be recognised in a number of ways. The tone of voice and the words used are a major indicator. Nonverbal cues and gestures will provide another clue. Table 9 provides a list of some common indicators.

*Being OK*

Being OK means very much the same in TA as it does in everyday language. OK and not-OK postures are feelings of security and self-esteem or of inferiority and doubt. If someone is OK then they are seen as of value, worthwhile, genuine and competent and their opinions are taken seriously. Those who are not OK are the opposite. They are perceived as incompetent, of little worth, and to be paid little attention. Being OK or not OK can be applied to self as well as others. There are four possible combinations when viewing self and others from the OK-not-OK perspective.

**I'm OK; you are not OK**   Here you regard the other person as not counting. It is the hire-and-fire managerial approach. There is no help offered, no counselling, no consideration of the possible problems that the other may be experiencing. In fact there may be nothing wrong with the other at all; you may be using the 'not-OK' assessment simply to defend yourself against a possible usurper of your position. When things go wrong it must be the other person's fault. This is the Critical Parent, when the boss is blaming, or the Rebellious Child, when the employee blames the management.

**I'm not OK; you are not OK**   Here no-one is regarded as coping or in control or as knowing what is going on. It is a recipe for interpersonal and organisational disaster. These mutual not-OK perceptions can arise all too easily in a context of sudden and poorly prepared-for change. The phrases 'You don't have to be insane to work here but it helps' and 'You think I'm strange; wait till you see my boss' encapsulate this situation.

**I'm not OK; you are OK**   'I'm the only one not coping' is the predominant message: 'I'm the one who is going to get the push.' Often a letter of resignation will be written to preclude an anticipated sacking. Another approach is to keep a low profile to prevent others realising that you don't feel all that competent. This is a common feeling during the first few weeks in a new position or when coping with changed work practices.

**I'm OK; you are OK**   Here both parties perceive each other as competent and are able to work together in harmony. No-one is a threat to anyone else. There may be disagreements but these can be discussed and mutually agreeable solutions worked out that do not cause either party to feel demeaned or inferior. Motivation is high and self-esteem is not compromised. Psychological health is apparent and promoted, enabling change to be coped with in an effective way by self in collaboration with others. The only way to interact effectively with others and thereby facilitate their and the organisation's development is to stay OK about self and others. Table 10 summarises the way OK positions influence a range of behaviour.

## Defence mechanisms

In order to control stress, people use defence mechanisms in their relationships with others. Freud was the psychologist who introduced the world to defence mechanisms. He proposed that mankind was governed by powerful instinctual impulses (id) which if allowed full reign would place man at an animal level; social life would not exist in conditions of 'nature red in tooth and claw'. The development of ego or 'I' provides an intermediary between the external world and the internal instincts, permitting society to function. The ego is able, using reality as its basis, to put off instinctive demands until an appropriate time and place. Additionally, the development of the superego internalises the influence of parents and acts as a conscience, checking the id impulses through guilt feelings.

According to Freud, the id, ego and superego are in constant

**Table 10 How life position influences behaviour**

| client person An employee when his life position is; | Communicates | Accepts delegation | Develops | Handles disagreement | Solves problems | Spends time | Is moved to act | Feels to others |
|---|---|---|---|---|---|---|---|---|
| I'm OK— You're OK | Openly | Readily | Independently, learns willingly | By seeking clarification and mutual resolution | By consulting others, trusting himself | Taking necessary action and producing | On assignment or initiative | Equal |
| I'm not OK— You're OK | Defensively, self-deprecatingly | Timidly | Slowly: needs reassurance and coaching | By perceiving differences of opinion as evidence of inadequacy | By relying almost completely on others | Brooding or overcompensating in constant activity | By praise or admonition | Inferior |
| I'm OK— You're not OK | Defensively, aggressively | By procrastinating, bickering and bargaining | With difficulty, learning is blocked | By placing blame on others | By unilaterally rejecting others' ideas | Boasting, provoking others, playing persecutor | When forced, may demand official instructions | Superior |
| I'm not OK— You're not OK | Hostilely, abruptly | By trying to beg off, Delegating upward, Unwillingly accepts resposibility | With difficulty, withdraws and repeats errors | By escalating the conflict: involving a third party | By succumbing to problems | Withdrawing; playing a variety of games | By reprimands or threats | Despondent, alienated |

conflict. The id impulses demand instant gratification while the ego and superego try to constrain them. This pressure creates anxiety, a fear of not being able to control the id and of guilt and remorse for even having bad id impulses. In order to reduce this tension the individual adopts defence mechanisms which in various ways deny, distort or disguise the underlying motives which would be unacceptable to themselves and to others. There are many defence mechanisms. Here are a few that are common in periods of change and life transitions within organisations.

*Repression*

This is a form of selective forgetting. 'I can never remember his name —he's the one who always has the highest sales figure in the group.' Knowledge, ideas, beliefs, experiences which are threatening can all be pushed out of the conscious mind into the deep recesses of the id. A manager who continues long-term planning to ensure higher production levels or increased sales even though the closure of the company has been announced is repressing the knowledge that redundancy is round the corner by carrying on as if nothing will happen. The repression occurs because the redundancy and its effects are too painful to contemplate or recognise. A person who appears to ignore future events, does not discuss them, and fails to take action, may be repressing.

*Projection*

In projection we tend to attribute to others things we cannot accept about ourselves. Projection is a basis for prejudice. We often hear employees muttering about the Asian immigrants who take their jobs, or managers criticising their employer for bringing in a young graduate over their heads. It does not matter whether these things are true or not. If an individual believes that something is the case then his behaviour will reflect that belief. The fact that employees may be losing their jobs due to restructuring or recession is forgotten. It is better for self-esteem to claim that immigrants are willing to work for lower wages than to accept that your own lack of work skills for the new technology have caused the redundancy. Paranoia is a form of projection whereby, instead of accepting that you cannot get on with other colleagues, you twist the facts and claim that it is they who hate you.

Another form of projection is the 'bad workman blaming his tools' attitude, e.g. 'I cannot give you the monthly sales figures as the computer keeps going down.' This sort of excuse may on occasion hide an inability to carry out the tasks required in the given time. The charge of poor performance on the job, leading potentially to demotion or sacking, can be deflected from self by blaming the equipment, the work practices, other workers, the management etc. 'How do they expect me to produce fault-free items when the machine is twenty years old?'; 'How can you soar with the eagles when you work with crows?' Placing the blame on others just might ensure that some of them get the push rather than you.

Projection is 'justifiable' retaliation which requires a scapegoat—the unacceptable problem or difficulty is offloaded onto another person or thing. The scapegoat, of course, has to be a safe goat which is unlikely to fight back. Bad luck and fate can be overworked targets of projection, as we have already seen for the person with an external locus of control. Other scapegoats that are 'safe' to use are equipment failures and subordinates.

*Rationalisation*

'But doesn't everyone use the company car occasionally on private business?' This is where a plausible excuse is given for doing or not doing something. An employee may take a longer tea break than allowed on the grounds that 'Everyone else does it'. Petty theft from factories and the taking of regular 'sickies' are often justified in the same way. Without too much effort, most people can think up good excuses for not turning up for work, for not maintaining the required output, for losing their job. Many excuses for having done something that should not have been done or for not doing something that should have been done are rationalisations. A rationalisation therefore enables the person to protect self-esteem and reputation, and prevent guilt feelings. A rationalisation is likely if the other person seems to be hunting around for reasons to justify his behaviour and gets emotional (angry, guarded etc) when the reasons are questioned.

*Reaction formation*

Here the opposite line to that expected is taken. 'I'm glad I have been retrenched, I've always wanted to retire early.' Many employees faced with redundancy or lack of promotion will either produce a plausible rationalisation such as 'Bad management is to blame' (see above) or display the opposite reaction to the one normally expected. In both these approaches there is an attempt to deny reality, a refusal to face up to what has or is to occur. It is a 'pretend' situation: 'I don't care, so what!' An air of bravado appears to hide feelings of inadequacy and worry. Essential to a sound plan of action for the future and wise decision-making are a realistic appraisal of what has happened and what might happen and an evaluation of the options. Denial, distortion and disguising the events by defence mechanisms preclude realistic action and problem-solving.

*Conversion hysteria*

'I'm sorry I can't turn up today for that interview. I've had a tummy upset for several days now.' In this defence mechanism, physical symptoms develop to protect the person from situations in which they might feel inadequate, unable to cope and highly stressed. The headache, tummy upset, asthma, even limb paralysis, deafness and blindness provide excuses for not turning up for work, not coping with the job, not retraining/reskilling, not listening to or seeing what is going on around one. For example, the employee who through age becomes less deft in manipulating the equipment may not want the management to know, so he develops a paralysis. This gives a valid excuse for being moved to another job or for early retirement—an excuse which leaves no stain on his record and may even gain sympathy. The same can hold in a retraining context. The illness is less of an ordeal than the situation from which it allows an escape. Many of these symptoms are termed psychosomatic; there is no conscious pretense on the part of the sufferer because the 'illness', while not physical in origin, is 'real' to the sufferer. Conversion hysteria is an extreme form of defence requiring treatment by a psychiatrist or psychologist. There is often no medical cause for these psychosomatic illnesses.

*Compensation*

Compensation is an attempt to disguise the existence of a weak or undesirable characteristic by emphasising a more positive one. A physically handicapped person may attempt to overcome the handicap by extra effort and persistence. However, the defence may take less desirable forms such as when an employee who feels inferior becomes the workshop bully or braggart; or when the incompetent secretary dresses to kill in the office, hoping glamour will offset poor keyboard skills. The employee who feels threatened in retaining his job may try to compensate through other activities, such as becoming indispensable as the company's football coach. A manager with low self-esteem or feelings of incompetence might become authoritarian, protecting himself behind the presumed status of his role.

*Displacement*

This is a shift of emotion away from the person or object to whom it is really directed and towards a more neutral person or object. For example, a junior manager upbraided by the senior manager will not direct his anger towards the latter but later release a torrent of abuse onto employees or his wife and children. The phrase 'kicking the cat' encapsulates displacement. An object may also become the target, such as when the office door is slammed, a tool is thrown or equipment is damaged. Displacement results in a failure to recognise the real object of the emotion and a loss of ability to resolve anger more directly by talking it through. It must be remembered that it is appropriate to be angry at times and this anger should in turn be expressed appropriately by telling the other person frankly that you feel angry about his behaviour or about what he has said. On the whole one is psychologically better off when one learns to express and discuss feelings with the person at whom the feelings were directed in the first place. This means that the relationship between the two people must be positive to begin with. All the defence mechanisms indicate that where positive relationships exist there is little need to fall back on such attempts to deny or distort reality.

Understanding some of these common defence mechanisms enables managers to understand many of their own and their subordinates' responses to change and life transitions.

## Nonverbal communication or body language

We may speak with our tongues but we communicate with our whole bodies. In other words, actions, gestures, facial expressions, body movements and positions speak louder than words. Nonverbal communication is very potent, and we do not for most of the time realise that we are revealing ourselves through it. Nonverbal communication has several functions. It can confirm or emphasise the verbal message. It can contradict the verbal message and convey the 'real' message. It is easy to lie to someone verbally but our body language can give us away. We can tell a friend that she is not being considered for retrenchment but our inability to look her in the eye, the shuffling of our feet and the hesitancy of our voice suggest otherwise.

Here is a list of some features of nonverbal communication.

### *Eye contact*

Effective eye contact consists of looking directly at the other person when listening or talking to them. It should be spontaneous, with short periods of noncontact to prevent staring the other out. Ineffective eye contact consists of not looking at the other, looking down or away, or staring blankly. There is more eye contact between people who like each other than between those who do not. A person may avoid eye contact because he is embarrassed, depressed or just shy. There should be less eye contact when the other person is physically close since it can become uncomfortable (except for lovers!). That is why everyone looks at the floor in a crowded lift.

*Body posture*

Effective body posture is relaxed and attentive with a slight forward lean if sitting. Occasional fluid hand and arm movements can be used to emphasise important points. Ineffective body posture includes arms across chest, body turned sideways from the other, and slouching backwards in a chair. The closed posture (Figure 10) indicates that social interaction is unwanted. The open posture is an invitation to interact.

*Head and facial movements*

Effective movements include occasional affirmative head nods, appropriate smiling, and expressions that match those of the other. Ineffective movements include constant nodding, rigid facial expression, head down, no smiling.

*Vocal quality*

Effective vocal qualities are a pleasant, interested intonation, moderate rate of speech, simple, precise language, a natural conversational style. Ineffective vocal qualities are a monotonous tone, too loud a voice, rapid rate of speech, speech disruptions with hesitancies.

*Personal habits*

Ineffective habits are distracting ones such as tapping with the fingers, fiddling with a pen, twisting the hair, rattling money in the pocket.

*Bodily contact*

Effective bodily contact must be appropriate. For example, shaking hands or putting an arm round someone's shoulder both convey a meaning. Bodily contact usually implies caring and support but it can easily be misconstrued, for touching another person is surrounded by 'rules' dictated by cultural behaviour and taboos. It is essential to be aware of the 'rules' and how the touching will be interpreted.

*Proximity*

Different messages are conveyed by how close you are to someone. People do vary in the amount of 'personal space' they prefer. Some feel uncomfortable when another comes too close. Do you prefer to sit on a bus or at a library desk by yourself? Observe how close people stand to one another at work. Among managers and employees, who stand closest together and furthest apart? There are

**Figure 10**

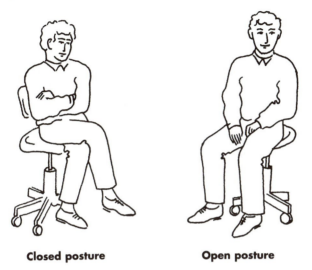

**Closed posture**          **Open posture**

cultural differences to note, too. People from the Middle East and from Latin cultures tend to stand closer than Europeans.

*Orientation*

Orientation is how individuals position themselves in relation to other people. Messages are conveyed by the layout of a room. For a discussion with staff, placing the chairs in a circle will evoke more participation than placing the chairs in rows facing the manager, which implies that the manager will do all the talking and the audience is there only to listen. In one-to-one conversation it is preferable to sit at 90 degrees to each other rather than directly facing. Sitting opposite someone can be interpreted as confrontational or competitive. The 90-degree position is perceived as inviting cooperation and contribution. The worst scenario is the manager sitting behind a desk; here the implication is that the other person is inferior and about to be given orders or told off. Communication is more comfortable if both parties are on the same level. Not inviting someone to sit down when they enter an office conveys the message that they are not welcome and ought to leave quickly.

*Dress*

Communication can be impaired if appearance and dress make either party uncomfortable. Hairstyle, earrings, nose studs are among a range of features that might cause a manager to react differently to an employee than he might otherwise do. The appearance of an employee at an interview can easily affect the outcome of the interview when other variables such as skill and qualifications should bear the weight of the assessment.

## Activity 30   Messages

Imagine the following situations and work out what messages they send to others:

a. one person sitting in a high chair talking to a person on a low chair
b. one person sitting behind a desk talking to another standing in front of the desk
c. one person writing at a desk while talking to another person
d. a meeting with one person in front facing the others who are seated in rows
e. a meeting with people seated around a table
f. a person sitting with arms folded and legs crossed
g. a person leaning back on chair with hands behind head
h. a person pacing up and down while talking to others
i. a person sitting on the edge of their chair
j. a person fiddling with their keys while talking

*Active listening*

Nonverbal communication helps to facilitate communication by indicating whose turn it is to speak during a conversation and the listener's interest. When a speaker is coming to the end of what they are saying, they look more intently at the listener, indicating 'It is your turn now.' A person who wants to start speaking signals that intention by looking away meaning 'It is my turn now.' This orchestration, using the eyes as conductors, aids communication if the parties are aware of it. Interest is shown by maintaining eye contact ('Keep talking; I'm not going to interrupt'), nodding at appropriate times ('I understand what you are saying'), making 'Mmm' or 'UhUh' noises at the end of important statements, and mirroring the emotions displayed by the other person as they speak.

   In a training, advisory, interviewing or counselling context, even though the helper may express concern in words, if the client feels the helper is uninterested he is also likely to feel the helper is unconcerned and of little help. A manager, human resource person or change agent who looks away, interrupts, reduces eye contact, who seems restless, in a hurry, whose voice is hesitant, and who smiles

**Table 11  Nonverbal communication**

| Depressed, worried, anxious | Angry, aggressive | Positive self-esteem, emotionally stable |
|---|---|---|
| **Posture** | | |
| slumped<br>shoulders forward<br>shifting often<br>chin down<br>sitting: legs entwined | erect, tense, rigid<br>shoulders back<br>jerky shifts or planted in place<br>chin up or thrust forward<br>sitting: heels on desk, hands behind head or tensely leaning foward | erect but relaxed<br>shoulders straight<br>few shifts, comfortable<br>head straight or slight tilt<br>sitting: legs together or crossed |
| **Gestures** | | |
| fluttering hands<br>twisting motions<br>shoulder shrugs<br>frequent head nodding | chopping or jabbing with hands<br>clenched hands or pointing<br>sweeping arms<br>sharp, quick nods | casual hand movements<br>relaxed hands<br>hands open, palms out<br>occasional head nodding |
| **Facial expression** | | |
| lifted eyebrows, pleading look, wide-eyed rapid blinking<br>nervous or guilty smile<br>chewing lower lip<br>shows anger with averted eyes, blushing, guilty look | furrowed brow, tight jaw<br>tense look, unblinking<br>glare<br>patronizing or sarcastic smile<br>tight lips<br>shows anger with disapproving scowl, very firm mouth or bared teeth, extreme flush | relaxed, thoughtful caring or concerned look, few blinks<br>genuine smile<br>relaxed mouth<br>shows anger with flashing eyes, serious look, slight flush of color |
| **Voice** | | |
| quiet, soft, higher pitch<br>uhs, ahs, hesitations<br>stopping in 'midstream'<br>nervous laughter<br>statements sound like questions with voice tone rising at the end | steely quiet or loud, harsh<br>'biting off' words, precise<br>measured delivery<br>sarcastic laughter<br>statements sound like orders or pronouncements | resonant, firm, pleasant<br>smooth, even-flowing<br>comfortable delivery<br>laughter only with humor<br>voice tones stay even when making statement |

inappropriately will not be perceived as trustworthy, accepting or caring. No-one seeking help could relax and discuss personal concerns with such a person. So we must be very careful to ensure that verbal and nonverbal communication are congruent when we are interacting with colleagues and employees, particularly in a context of potential or actual change where support, caring and empathy need to be the matrix within which the interaction occurs.

It is important for the manager not only to convey the correct nonverbal cues but also to recognise nonverbal signals from others, since these signals communicate how others feel and think. Greater awareness of nonverbal communication certainly assists any manager or adviser to better understand others. Table 11 provides some important signals to look out for.

## Activity 31   Nonverbal expectations

Can you report any occasions of nonverbal expectations that have influenced you?

*Judging others*

This chapter has so far focused on the reactions of others to change, life transitions and stress. However, it has assumed that the manager is capable of detecting and judging the reactions of others correctly. Research suggests that judging others is rather an unreliable activity, as there is considerable bias involved.

**Context**
As we have seen, behaviour is an interaction between the person and the environment/situation. However, we tend to ignore the situation when assessing or evaluating the behaviour of others. A worker who is often late for work will explain his lateness in terms of the train being cancelled or late or the alarm clock failing to go off. If an outsider tried to explain the lateness they would tend to use personality characteristics, e.g. the worker is not a punctual or reliable person. In other words, we make external attributions for our own behaviour but internal ones for the behaviour of others. We tend to ignore the situation when judging others. An effective manager should always look for a possible situational explanation for a worker's behaviour and not just focus on the worker.

**Consistency**
Behaviour varies depending on time and place. We all have off days and most people tend to be ratty if tired or not well. It is therefore important not to make a snap judgment about a worker's suitability or reaction to change on the basis of one observation. A number of observations at various times and in various places are needed to produce valid and reliable judgments.

**First impressions**
These are a problem in interviews, for the first impression is a strong one. We make a hypothesis on first meeting a person, then look for confirmatory evidence, ignoring non-confirmatory evidence.

**Recency effect**
We tend to remember best what has just occurred, so that our strongest impressions of a person are the most recent ones.

**Attractiveness**
There is a wealth of evidence to suggest that people have more positive expectations of attractive persons. Judging workers on attractiveness (of physical appearance, skin colour, gender, dress, personality etc)

can lead to gross errors of judgment. A positive appearance may belie gross incompetency, lack of skills and stressed behaviour; a negative appearance may overwhelm high motivation, portable skills and a stable disposition. This bias is often based on stereotyping and labelling.

If we are to observe behaviour objectively, we have to take the subjectiveness out of our observations. To achieve objectivity we should avoid two types of words and phrases: those which describe the other person's inner qualities (honest, intelligent, ambitious, sincere), and those which describe our own reactions, feelings and judgments about a person (likeable, nice, confusing, he bugs me). The words and phrases we use to decribe someone objectively are those which describe what he is actually saying or doing, such as loud voice, direct eye contact, shuffling feet, slow speech, frequent absences, meets production targets.

The conclusion to all this is: don't make hasty judgments about people, about their reactions, about their potential and competency without a sound basis.

## Summary

This chapter has attempted to provide some information on interpersonal strategies that managers will find useful in their relationships with their staff. Transactional analysis enables us to understand the real meanings behind the verbal interactions we are involved in. Knowing how others habitually respond, whether as Adult, Child or Parent, can help us adapt what we say to them. Each ego state and the transactions that follow from it can impede or facilitate relationships and the resolution of issues. An understanding of TA will improve personal interaction in the work place.

People use ego defence mechanisms to prevent themselves and others really knowing what they feel and think. Defence mechanisms distort, deny and disguise unacceptable motives, providing plausible and spurious justifications for doing or not doing certain things.

Nonverbal communication is very powerful and can inform others how we really feel and think about them even though verbally we may be able to lie convincingly. Eye contact, body posture, proximity and orientation are major features of nonverbal communication and are vitally important in interview and counselling contexts.

In judging others, we must take care not to be too much influenced by first impressions, physical attractiveness or most recent behaviour. Hasty judgments about the potential and competency of a person are never sound.

# 5
# Positive self-management

*If you think you are beaten, you are;*
*If you think you dare not, you don't*
*If you like to win but think you can't*
*It's almost a cinch you won't.*

*If you think you'll lose you're lost,*
*For out in the world we find*
*Success begins with a person's will,*
*It's all in the state of mind.*

*If you think you are outclassed, you are*
*You have to think high to rise,*
*You have to be sure of yourself*
*To win a prize.*

*Life's battles don't always go*
*To the stronger or faster man,*
*But sooner or later the one who wins*
*Is the ONE who THINKS he can.*

Anon.

*The more a person accepts himself, the less is he threatened by the*
*experience of being known by others.*

Jourard (1971) p. 76

*Argue for your limitations and sure enough they will be yours.*

Bach

## Stress management

Stress management in work settings has generally focused on employees as the target of change. Interventions aimed at modifying stressful aspects of the work environment are rare. Programs have usually been offered to white-collar rather than blue collar workers and have included such topics as relaxation, positive thinking, self-concept enhancement, relationship/communication skills, time management and decision-making.

Evaluation of the outcomes of such programs tends to show that stress management is associated with significant reductions in anxiety, depression, sleep disturbances, muscle tension and blood pressure, and in more positive proactive behaviour, increased job satisfaction, greater feelings of control, and decreased absenteeism. However, long-term follow-up reveals, in some cases, a regression to original levels mainly because (i) participants fail to continue practising taught techniques and skills, (ii) stress derived from the way the organisation functions has not been addressed, and (iii) the organisation has failed to involve employees in changes emanating from current economic conditions and kept them in the dark. It is not surprising that stress management may achieve poorer than expected results when it is countered by inadequate management techniques. It is somewhat ambitious to expect that increasing a worker's coping capabilities will act as a panacea for all organisational problems. However, stress management is still a very effective tool to help people cope with organisational change where some stressors can not be eliminated, e.g. the lack of promotion, the fear of redundancy, the lack of new job skills. It can help many to cope and to experience a much reduced stress reaction.

### Relaxation techniques

Some people try to relieve stress by smoking, drinking, overeating, denial and other inappropriate behaviours. They are inappropriate because while they may relieve tension for a short time, providing temporary relief, they do nothing positive to solve the problem in the long term. They do not elicit positive thinking, or promote wise solutions and decisions.

A most important technique in managing stress is acquiring the ability to elicit the relaxation response. Learning to relax has short-term and long-term consequences. In the long term, continued use of relaxation techniques makes life more satisfying for ourselves and those around us. In the short term, relaxation increases our ability to manage current problems, generates pleasant feelings of well-being, and frequently produces increased creativity and motivation.

The relaxation response involves specific bodily changes including decreased heart rate, lower metabolism and lower breathing rate, all of which bring the body into healthier balance. Tension disappears rapidly, leaving the relaxed individual able to deal constructively with the current or future problem. Most methods of relaxation follow the approach of Jacobson, who developed a method of progressive physical relaxation training involving muscle tensing followed by a gradual release to a state of no tension. His method has been refined over the years to provide a relaxation technique that is fairly simple, easy to use and easy to teach to others.

Relaxation techniques are recommended for reducing stress because:

a.  relaxation may be approached as a physical skill which can be learnt in similar ways to other skills
b.  there are no mystical connotations to put beginners off
c.  it can be successfully learnt in a few short sessions
d.  side-effects like hallucinations do not occur
e.  it does not involve drugs and costs nothing.

So anyone can learn relaxation, and apply it as they go about their daily activities. Mastering relaxation can usually bring about the following benefits:

a.  Relaxation decreases feelings of stress.
As we read in Chapter 3, stress is increasingly being identified as incompatible with good health. For those who want to cope without recourse to medication and drugs, relaxation is the prime strategy. In relaxation there is a reduction in muscle tension and more efficient abdominal breathing. Through this the physiological effects of tension are countered and the degree of mental arousal lowered to an optimum level.
b.  Fatigue is diminished through relaxation.
With less tension in the body, less energy is used up.
c.  The sense of pain is decreased through relaxation.
Decreasing muscle tension makes headache, backache, writer's cramp, RSI etc less likely. Relaxation techniques also increase pain threshold.
d.  Personal relationships are improved by relaxation.
It is far easier to get along with people if you are relaxed than if you are tense. Through nonverbal and verbal cues, others can sense how you feel and a sense of tension does not promote sound interpersonal relationships.
e.  Relaxation can promote sleep.
A calm mind and body allows peaceful sleep with less tossing and turning. A restful night in turn helps one to maintain a relaxed state the next day.

f.  Self-esteem is enhanced by relaxation.
When self-control is available, self-confidence is improved and with
it self-esteem. You feel good about your competencies to cope.

*Learning the relaxation response*

## Activity 32    The relaxation exercise

Figure 11 supplies the instructions for learning the relaxation
response.

## Activity 33    Several quick relaxation methods

As you develop skill at relaxing, there are some quick relaxation
techniques that you may find quite effective as supplementary
methods. These quick methods can be used, for example, while
you are sitting in a traffic jam in the car, as you sit in the car before
you leave for work or as you arrive home, in the rest room at
tea-break, waiting for an appointment etc. For all these methods,
remember to sit as comfortably as possible, focus on your breathing
as a natural easy process, and remain passive, just letting whatever
thoughts come to mind happen.

a.  Spot focusing. Pick a spot to focus on. Count five breaths,
working backwards from five to one. With each breath close your
eyes gradually until on breath one, your eyes are fully closed. Focus
on the feeling of relaxation.
b.  Clouds. Imagine the air you breathe as a cloud. Focus on your
breathing and imagine the air cloud filling you and then flowing out
from your mouth as you exhale. There may be a colour to the cloud
that you can imagine. Keep focusing on the image of the cloud as
you breathe slowly and easily.
c.  Tensing the body. Hold the whole body tense for as long as you
can. Begin to release the tension slowly. Feel it leave your body.
Repeat this several times.
d.  Take a good deep breath. Breathe slowly and deeply. Let your
shoulders droop and sag. Unclench your teeth by opening your
mouth. Allow the wrinkles in your forehead to unwrinkle.

*Some general problems with relaxation*

• You can have difficulty finding a time and a comfortable place
  where no interruption is likely.
• Deep silence is offputting, so quiet background music is helpful.
• Feelings of guilt can arise about 'sitting doing nothing'. Relaxation is not a waste of time.

**Figure 11   Instructions for the relaxation exercise**

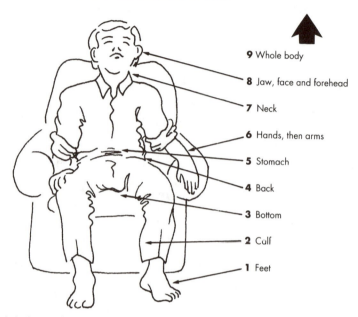

**9** Whole body

**8** Jaw, face and forehead

**7** Neck

**6** Hands, then arms

**5** Stomach

**4** Back

**3** Bottom

**2** Calf

**1** Feet

Start with the feet: work up to the head, then repeat the routine another two times . . .

Practise this exercise as often as you can, preferably once a day for about ten minutes. Many people find relaxation can help them get to sleep.

**Stage 1**—Getting prepared—takes about two minutes.
1  Find a quiet place—if you like, have some soothing music playing . . .
2  Sit in a comfortable chair . . . (or lie flat on your back or stomach).
3  Close your eyes, arms at your sides, legs uncrossed . . .
4  Breathe deeply in and out . . .
5  Let your body go loose and floppy

**Stage 2**—Muscle relaxation—for major muscle groups . . . Breathe **in** . . . **tense** muscles . . . breathe **out** . . . **relax** muscles for each muscle group.

**Stage 3**— Do your routine, but while you are doing it, try to think of some nice relaxing scene of your choice.

Draw a favourite relaxing scene of yours here

- Do not try to relax too soon after eating or after physical exercise. The former may result in indigestion, and a cooling-down period is needed after exercise for breathing rate and heartbeat to return to normal.

## Activity 34  Putting change in perspective

Another way to handle stress from change is to try and put the change into perspective.

a. Draw a vertical line about 15cm long. Place 0 at the bottom and 100 at the top. This is the catastrophe scale with 100 the worst catastrophe you can think of and 0 the least.
b. Think of a change at work that is stressing you now. Where do you rate it on this scale? Write it in with a number beside it to represent the degree of catastrophe.
c. Imagine the three most catastrophic things that could happen to you and place these on the scale too.
d. Imagine two things that would be moderately bad and rate them on the scale.
e. Now think of something that you would consider only a very minor catastrophe and place that on the scale.
f. Finally, re-rate the change you are currently dealing with. Where would you place it now?
    It is usual for the change's rating to be lowered as you realise that it probably isn't as awful as you first thought.

*Diet, exercise and sleep*

Adopting healthy living habits can help you to manage stress. In Chapter 3, it was noted that stress tends to result in ill-health and encourage behaviours, such as alcohol abuse, which impede healthy living. If behaviours that promote good health can be maintained or developed then the deleterious effects of stress can be thwarted and the stress managed. The important good health habits are generally common-sense ones which can all too easily be dropped when pressures arise. The seven important ones appear to be:

Do not smoke
Moderate your drinking (0–2 drinks per day)
Sleep 6–7 hours a day
Eat regular meals without in-between snacks
Eat a regular, balanced breakfast
Exercise regularly
Maintain your recommended weight

**Diet**

Food is essential for survival but a poor diet can increase susceptibility to heart disease, strokes and cancer. These degenerative diseases weaken the body and make it more susceptible to the increased adrenalin secretions and raised blood pressure which are central features of the stress reaction. Inadequate, irregular or excessive eating habits can cause extra stress to the body, making it less able to cope with the stress of daily activities.

Excessive weight also debilitates the body. Regular mealtimes are essential to get the body used to the ebb and flow of blood sugar, rising after meals and falling slowly between meals. When we do not respect the rhythms of the body we put a strain on the system. When we eat more balanced meals at regular times the body is more able to withstand stress. Being fat generates additional stress because it affects emotional as well as physical well-being. Fat people tend to be unhappy about their weight and hold a negative self-concept.

When we are under stress, the stress reaction in our bodies makes fats harder to process. When we are under stress we are likely to skip meals, or replace regular meals with high-fat convenience foods. Our health and stress levels would be better if we ate more balanced meals and natural rather than processed foods.

The removal from the diet of coffee, tea, cola drinks and chocolate will help to reduce the stimulants in the body that create a highly alert and over-active state and thus increase stress. Vitamin depletion occurs during times of stress and higher levels of vitamin C and B-complex are required to maintain a properly functioning nervous and endocrine system. Salt should be reduced in the diet as it adds to the risk of high blood pressure, which can occur in stress reactions.

**Exercise**

Exercise is a good stress reduction technique, even though exercise itself places the body under stress. When you are exercising you are using a stressful activity to combat the ravages of distress. Exercise has two major benefits. Vigorous activity properly conducted increases cardiovascular fitness; and relaxation is inevitable after exercise.

Ironically, the more regular exercise you do the more energy you will have for other activities such as coping with work. If you have trouble keeping pace at work because you are tired the answer may be more exercise rather than more sleep. Exercise also makes people feel better about themselves. A positive outlook is a powerful mediator of stress. When you feel good about yourself, things don't seem quite so difficult or out of your control. Most people who involve themselves in physical leisure activities have more self-confidence and possess a positive self-image.

One of the reasons for this positive self feeling and the reduction of stress, anxiety and depression is that when you exercise vigorously for at least half an hour, your brain releases more *endorphins*, opiate-like chemicals which make you feel happy and exhilarated. The problem is that people who suffer from stress tend to say they cannot spend the time to exercise. This suggests that time management is one of the causes of their stress (p. 140). What they do not realise is that they cannot afford not to create time for relaxation. An interesting and demanding recreation is a tension saver for many overburdened workers at all levels. Whatever recreational pursuit you choose should be personally enjoyable, invigorating and work plenty of muscles. Keeping muscles in good tone and developing good posture and muscle control will ensure the body is not under strain in any other activity in the home or at work. You are giving your body its best working capacity and promoting your health. This is the right preparation for 'coping'. Alternatively, the right preparation for *not* coping is poor chest expansion with insuffient oxygen intake, tensed muscles in neck and back, all of which place the body under tension, lower its vitality and reduce mental alertness.

A successful exercise program must be:

- capable of being sustained for at least 30 minutes
- performed vigorously enough to keep the heart working at between 70 per cent and 85 per cent of its capacity for the entire exercise period, and
- participated in at least three times a week.

Swimming, cycling, brisk walking, and rope-skipping all fit the bill and can be done by most people.

Some European and American organisations have introduced keep-fit programs for their staff. In one program for 1125 managers, absenteeism declined by 22 per cent and productivity rose by 3 per cent. The managers involved reported that they felt more positive about themselves, developed better relationships with their subordinates, and felt less stressed. Another company organised relaxation training for its employees during work breaks. Attendance was voluntary. Volunteers were compared with those not taking part. The results showed not only that this relaxation break was feasible during the working day but that participants' blood pressure readings, general health, well-being and job performance all improved. Such initiatives, while not removing the actual redundancy or lack of job promotion, can help employees and managers cope better with potential stress.

Of course it goes without saying that no-one should undertake an exercise program without having a medical check-up first. Moreover, the exercise program should be arranged and supervised by someone with expertise in the field.

**Sleep**
Sleep helps to restore the depleted resources of the mind and body
and can be an important help in relieving and reducing feelings of
stress and tension. Insomnia itself is a powerful stressor. A sequence
of hectic days followed by sleepless nights means that you will not
be in any shape to cope with work each day. This creates more
stress and a vicious cycle is established which is hard to break. The
hormones produced during stress are, of course, meant to keep you
alert!

Sleep and relaxation superficially appear to be similar. They are
both states of rest but they are very different in physiological terms.
In relaxation, there is a quicker and more marked decrease in oxygen intake and therefore a faster drop in metabolic activity. Oxygen
consumption may fall by 12 per cent in three minutes, and returns to
normal very quickly after relaxation stops. In sleep there is a gradual
decrease in metabolic activity over five hours, while oxygen consumption falls by only 8 per cent. Heart rate, breathing rate and
blood pressure are lower after relaxation than after a night's sleep.

**Take control of your stress**
While there are no easy solutions to the problem of stress, using the
relaxation techniques provided above will help you manage it. Other
things you can do to improve your management of stress include:

• manage your time effectively, establish personal and professional
  priorities; set target dates and anticipate possible crises and deadlines (this chapter)
• set reasonable goals for yourself (Chapter 6)
• establish the emotional support of family and friends; make an
  effort to create rewarding, pleasant and cooperative relationships
  (Chapter 6)
• possibly change direction and course if necessary but never give
  up
• maintain good health habits
• learn to feel positive about your performance and potential (see
  below)
• determine the causes of some of your stress and find ways to
  eliminate or reduce the causes
• apply a decision-making process to find solutions to problems
  (Chapter 6)
• communicate with others in a rewarding and positive way (Chapter
  6)
• unite staff through involvement and a 'we' approach (Chapter 6)
• use some quick relaxing methods; instead of six seconds to pop a
  valium try six seconds relaxing for free
• take a walk for five minutes

- try visiting a lunchtime hideaway several times a week, e.g. a museum, a health club, a seat by the river.

All these methods will assist in creating and maintaining a low-conflict, low-stress climate.

## Activity 35  Stressors at work

List some sources of stress in your work and/or home situation. These could include physical conditions (cramped office), role issues (expectations, work load, promotion), social status, emotional elements (competency judgments, friendships), organisational factors (time pressure, lines of authority), and environmental conditions (noise). Choose one or several stressors that affect you and decide how you might tackle them so that stress is reduced. What skills can you bring to bear on the problem? Who else may you have to involve? Who will you need to negotiate with? What support group can you count upon?

## Self-concept enhancement

The origin of much personal stress lies within our concepts of ourselves. The possibility or actual existence of such demeaning situations as being made redundant, losing a promotion opportunity, being offered early retirement and not possessing the new skills required can summon up feelings of rejection, failure, and incompetency. There is evidence that people of low self-esteem behave in ways that permit them to play out the negative self-evaluations they have given themselves; this in turn contributes to the circular pattern of inadequate performance and low self-esteem. This pattern of self-induced outcomes has to be broken. To create positive outcomes, you must start with positive expectations. Therefore, by improving self-esteem and feelings of self-worth, stress can be reduced. Many activities can be used to enhance self-esteem and a variety of these can be found below. Basically, the activities attempt to encourage people to think more positively about themselves, have more positive expectations about themselves, and recognise their good points while accepting their weak points. You must start to see yourself being successful, feel confident, hear your voice strong and steady, and experience the satisfaction of feeling successful. Self-concept enhancement is usually conducted through counselling and individual activities, or in workshop situations.

## Activity 36   What I like about myself

The aim of this activity is to establish the importance of having a positive self-concept and recognise that it is not wrong or boastful to express a positive view of oneself when that is appropriate and correct. Why should you hide your light under a bushel or constantly downgrade yourself? Everyone has some positive points; what are yours? Write down five sentences starting 'I feel good about myself because . . .' or complete the checklist below. Practise saying these statements to yourself first aloud and then in thought, beginning, 'I FEEL GOOD ABOUT MYSELF BECAUSE . . .'

Speaking and thinking positively about yourself in areas where you have the right to do so will enable you to improve the way you feel about yourself.

## Checklist

| Questions | My answers |
|---|---|
| Any skill I have | |
| Anything I have done, written or said recently | |
| Anything I do regularly to help others | |
| Anything I have done at work | |
| Anything I have achieved recently | |
| Any special relationship I have developed | |
| Any spare-time hobby/activity | |
| Any physical feature | |
| Any aspect of my personality | |
| Any artistic accomplishment | |
| Any sporting achievement | |
| Anything I have won | |
| Any way in which I have changed | |
| Any way in which I maintained my values/beliefs | |
| Anything I have done to improve/maintain my health | |
| Any fears I have overcome | |
| Any time I have been positive rather than negative | |
| Anything I have done to protect the environment | |
| Anything I have done to support the less fortunate | |
| Any award I have received | |
| Any strengths/qualities I have | |

## Activity 37 Awareness of weaknesses and strengths

This activity helps you to realise that you can learn from failure and gain something positive from it. Write out an account of an event/ situation in your life that you regard as a failure. Reflect on what you have written and see what you have learned from that failure, how it has benefited you.

## Activity 38 Positive strokes

Make a 'New Year resolution' with yourself or among your staff that you will avoid putting each other down for the next week and relate to each other as positively as possible, supporting, encouraging, helping and praising. Review the effects at the end of the week. Try to keep this behaviour going in the future.

Counsellors must assess self-esteem before any career or personal counselling is done. If self-esteem is low, the first task in counselling should be to improve the client's self-evaluation. It is difficult to discuss abilities, competencies, alternative career options, new role conceptions with a person with low self-esteem, as he will have beliefs about self that lead to misjudgments of personal and work-related competencies.

Eliminating negative thinking about self, others and one's problems requires not only the use of counselling techniques but also the use of positive thinking techniques. It will be obvious from the discussion on the self-concept in Chapter 2 that thinking negatively about self and events can cause considerable stress. Thus a focus of treatment must be to help the client restructure irrational beliefs and dysfunctional self-attitudes. There are several ways to do this such as using affirmations or cognitive restructuring.

Generally, to improve self-esteem in yourself and others you must concentrate on the following:

- Get to know your abilities and use them. This will bring feelings of success and confidence.
- Set realistic standards for yourself. If you set standards too high you will fail, judge yourself a failure and lose confidence.
- Always think of your strengths. Develop these and don't daydream about the ones you wish you had.
- Develop your interests. You become a more interesting and fulfilled person with other strings to your bow.
- Don't compare yourself unfavourably to others. They have weak points too where you may have strengths.

- Be positive in your relationships with others. Give help, acceptance and support; don't boast or criticise. Others will then be
  more positive to you, giving you lots of positive feedback. This
  helps you to be even more positive, creating a 'ring of confidence'
  with others.

## Affirmations and positive thinking

An affirmation is a positive statement about self. To affirm means to
make firm. Most of us are aware that we conduct a nearly continuous
dialogue with ourselves, keeping up an endless commentary about
life, the world, our feelings, our problems, other people. This mental
commentary colours our feelings and perceptions about what is going on in our lives. It becomes a tape-recording directing or program-
ming our behaviour. The practice of making affirmations allows us to
begin replacing some of our stale, distorted, automatic negative mind
chatter with more positive thoughts about self and environment. This
transforms our attitudes, expectations and behaviour—a self-creative
exercise. If we can make ourselves think negatively, we can surely
make ourselves think positively.

A person is composed of many different aspects, roles and beings.
For example, everyone has a physical self, an emotional self, a social
self, a spiritual self, an intellectual self, a sexual self and so on. These
should be recognised as different from the vocational self and as
alternative sources of self-esteem. Clients need to be made aware of
these different facets of the self-concept and come, through counselling, to recognise their self-worth in a variety of these areas. Too
often, self-concept assessment is located only in the occupational
arena, with job role and job performance. One technique is to get the
client to represent himself as a complex array of small 'i's rather than
as one big 'I', with each 'i' representing one aspect of his being.
When the self is viewed this way, one component may be less than
desirable but that does not mean the totality is less than desirable. A
useful analogy is that of a tree, with each root or limb representing
one component of the self-concept. If any one limb is too large, the
tree becomes off-balance. If work-related self-concept has dominated
the picture, the self-concept has been similarly skewed.

Thus the client becomes more aware that he is more than his
occupation. He is not a production manager, a bank teller, a welder
but a person who does those things as an element of his life. Then
if problems occur in the work context, the whole person does not
have to be viewed negatively; only one component of the person has
developed problems. 'If I fail it does not make me a failure, only a
person who has failed at something.' As a corollary, the counsellor
can also place more emphasis on non-work-related aspects of the

client's life which may provide satisfaction and meaning. This may involve consideration of hobbies, sports, volunteer activities, home-related activities, the quality of the client's relationships. These may well provide other avenues of affirming self-worth if the vocational avenue is blocked.

Another strategy is to reframe the work situation so that setbacks there need not impact on the whole person and be projected as total life failure. The aim is to substitute the words setback or loss for failure. Those who have participated in sport know full well that one can recover from a setback or a loss and reach a winning position. Sometimes you win, sometimes you lose; but changes can be made to reduce the possibility of losing next time.

Affirmations and positive thinking enable negative self-talk to be changed to positive self-talk. This then changes the self-concept. In Chapter 3 the role of negative self-talk in lowering self-esteem and impairing one's own performance and that of others was stressed. We need to be very careful how we talk to ourselves. Many times with our self-talk we establish a ceiling that has no relation to our true potential. If we perform below our level of expectation or if we anticipate a poor performance, we may use such self-talk as:

'How could I be so stupid?'
'There I go again'
'I can't do anything right'
'Why can't I do as well as . . .'
'It's another of those days'
'I'll never manage this'
'I'm no good at technical things'
'What's the point—it will be changed again next week.'

These statements only help to perpetuate poor performance, by reinforcing the failure picture and ensuring a negative self-concept. As Eleanor Roosevelt said, 'No-one makes you feel inferior without your consent.'

## Activity 39   Change and opportunity

Some people always think of problems first and hardly ever of opportunities. Can you give personal examples of changes that have led to opportunities for you or your staff? What opportunities might spread from any current changes?

We must create success talk and thoughts so that our picture of ourselves alters. When actual or expected performance is below par, instead of belittling ourselves we must teach ourselves and others to affirm:

'That's not like me, next time I will . . .'
'I know I can manage this, I've succeeded in the past'
'I intend to make a new start on this'
'Maybe they will change it next week but at least I'll have learned
a new skill.'

Statements like these give positive feedback and trigger a picture
of the acceptable and competent performance and performer. The
key to coping with change is to reinforce an already positive self
image or produce positive self talk indicating what you want your
performance to be like. Stop picturing what you do not want or want
to avoid. When your performance pleases you and you feel good
about yourself, use positive self-talk to reinforce this picture. Affirm
to yourself:

'I did that well'
'That was a good result'
'That's more like me'
'I am pleased with the way that went.'

These sorts of phrases deliberately lock out the negative, devalu-
ing 'put-downs' we use on ourselves and that other people may try
to make us accept. Below are some activities to help you develop
and use affirmations to enhance self-concept and promote positive
thinking.

## Activity 40   Write your own affirmations

An affirmation is a positive, personal statement written in the present
tense as though the goal had already been achieved. Examples
are:

'I am a supportive manager'
'I respect myself'
'I expect to achieve my goals'
'I am positive in my approach to life'
'I cope with setbacks and enjoy new challenges'
'I communicate clearly and effectively.'

The easiest way to write out an affirmation is to select a change
item, then get a clear picture in your mind of how you will act in
keeping with the new image. Next write down a description of your
picture in one sentence. This is your affirmation. Writing each affirmation on a small index card is useful, as the cards can be carried
in the pocket and pulled out to read on any suitable occasion. Write
out at least three affirmations in this way.
Repetition of the affirmation is essential. Read each card several
times when in a relaxed condition—hear the words, believe them

and let them sink into your relaxed mind. As you are verbalising the affirmation you should be vividly visualising yourself having accomplished the change.

Affirmations can be spoken aloud, sung, or made silently. Ten minutes several times each day of repeating positive affirmations can counterbalance years of old restrictive thoughts and attitudes. Each affirmation can be read with the accompanying visualisation several times each day at a time when you are able to relax, e.g. just before rising in the morning, during a work break, before going to sleep at night. Some people have done this activity while travelling on the bus or train to work, while sitting in the lounge apparently watching TV, in their car before driving off in the morning and even while on the toilet. Linking this affirmation technique with the relaxation exercise is very beneficial.

By this means you are displacing old negative self-images with new positive words and pictures of how you want to be, feel and act. You are creating expectations of yourself, and very quickly you should begin to move easily and naturally into the new behaviour. We act like the person we see ourselves to be.

If you are counselling others, you should get them to write out about five affirmations applicable to their problem. For each affirmation, they should visualise themselves doing or being as their affirmation states.

Affirmations can also be written by teams. Examples of team affirmations are:

'We bring out the best in all our employees'
'We care for our staff'
'We are efficient and organised'
'We keep abreast of change so we can anticipate the problems.'

## Activity 41   Anti-anxiety affirmations

Choose an event/activity/behaviour about which you are anxious. Develop an affirmation to help you build a positive feeling. Complete some of the items below to help you isolate the features of the situation.

Event/behaviour/activity ................................................................
Who ........................................................................................
Where ......................................................................................
When ........................................................................................
What I want to achieve ................................................................
How I want to perform ................................................................
Now design an affirmation with appropriate imagery that will trigger the sorts of positive, successful feelings that will lead to the desired outcome.

## Cognitive restructuring

We have seen that the way people perceive themselves and the events they are involved in affects their emotional behaviour and stress levels. Some of this perception and thinking involves illogical, distorted, inaccurate and irrational ideas and views, such as when someone sees himself as an overall failure because someone else once made an unkind remark about his competency at a particular task. This leads to the self-fulfilling prophecy discussed in Chapter 2. Such mistaken beliefs can lead to maladaptive behaviour. People trap themselves and experience unnecessary misery by viewing situations, themselves and the future in a particular way. As well as adopting the counselling techniques outlined earlier, the counsellor can, when faced with such irrational beliefs, act as a counterpropagandist by questioning and querying these beliefs.

So the counselling of irrational beliefs consists of verbal persuasion and challenging with reinterpretation of disturbing events. Repeated cognitive rehearsal aimed at substituting rational, positive self-statements for previous distorted perceptions is used. Some examples of inaccurate perceptions and thoughts are given below.

### Selective abstraction

This involves focusing on one detail taken out of context. The whole experience or event is interpreted on the basis of this one point. For example, an employee might receive negative feedback from a job-search trainer on one item in the résumé she wrote as part of the training course. Ignoring the positive feedback about the rest of the résumé, the employee assumes the whole of the résumé and activity is worthless.

### Arbitrary inference

This involves drawing a conclusion in the absence of supportive data; often a negative inference is drawn when there is nothing to substantiate it. For example, an employee is promoted to a more responsible position with a substantial wage increase. The employee thinks this means she is going to be fired. To support this claim she refers to her predecessor, who was fired after occupying the position for only a few months.

### Catastrophising

This entails exaggerating the importance of things. For example, an employee does not receive an expected promotion and concludes he is a complete failure. This interpretation not only affects his self-esteem but leads to a variety of self-defeating behaviours. This cycle of faulty thinking results in severe depression.

*Overgeneralisation*

This involves drawing conclusions on the basis of more or less isolated incidents. For example an employee who is to be made redundant decides to look for work as a salesman. He applies for one position but is not offered the job. He concludes that being a salesman is not a viable option and stops applying for jobs in this field.

*Should and must statements*

These reflect unrealistic demands on the self. Deeply ingrained beliefs become moral imperatives. For example, beliefs like 'I must have a job', 'I should provide for my family', cause considerable emotional distress when someone loses their job through no fault of their own.

*All-or-none thinking*

This is the tendency to see things in black-and-white terms. For example, 'Management is always trying to screw the worker,' or 'Union officials are covert communists trying to subvert the country.'

*Dysfunctional attitudes*

These are attitudes that prevent employees fulfilling their potential, or influence the goals they set, their relationship to work and the degree to which they will be active agents in their career development. Examples of such attitudes are: 'Success at work is due to luck'; 'Most people are dissatisfied with their job'; 'Work is drudgery'; 'There are mainly men (women) in that job'.

To help clients with these distorted ideas it is necessary to question and challenge them so that the thoughts become testable hypotheses that can be rejected. The questioning should help them to investigate the validity and utility of their beliefs. This leads to a more flexible, mature, adaptive view of self and of the events and encourages the development of other approaches to the situation. Questions that ask for data, evidence or proof, and probes such as 'Tell me more about it'; 'What do you mean?'; 'What evidence do you have?'; 'I'm not sure I understand'; 'What aspects of the situation do you think you are neglecting?'; 'Are causal relationships that simple?'; 'How do you know that will happen?' can facilitate self-exploration and reframe faulty thinking as the client is forced to explain.

For example, 'I have never applied myself,' says the client. The

**Figure 12   Counselling sequence within a cognitive restructuring framework**

*CO:* Do you see a common thread running through those statements you made to yourself?
*CL:* It almost sounds as if I don't believe I'm competent.
*CO:* Sort of like, 'I'm not competent.' How did those thoughts affect you?
*CL:* Well, I started to feel hopeless about getting a job.
*CO:* And so what did you do?
*CL:* Nothing. I stopped doing everything related to my job search. I even began to read classified ads, looking for all the ways my qualifications came up short.
*CO:* Now, what kind of feedback have you received from others about your résumé?
*CL:* Generally favourable. In fact, a few people have said they were really impressed with it.
*CO:* Is it reasonable to expect everyone to react positvely in the same way to a résumé?
*CL:* No. I guess not.
*CO:* Why not?
*CL:* Because everybody has different opinions and there's no one right way to do a résumé.
*CO:* That's right. So how did you permit one person's opinion to affect your life for a week?
*CL:* By forgetting it was just an opinion and by not remembering the positive comments.
*CO:* How else?
*CL:* By getting carried away with my negative thinking.
*CO:* Especially. 'I'm not competent'?
*CL:* Yeah.
*CO:* What proof do you have that you're incompetent?
*CL:* Well . . . none. Sometimes it just feels that way.
*CO:* Why is that a bad term to use?
*CL:* Obviously because I'm competent at many things.
*CO:* So how much confidence do you *really* have in the validity of the belief 'I'm not competent'?
*CL:* None. I guess it's pretty silly, isn't it? (*laughing*)
*CO:* Yes. Is there anything that makes you so different from other people that precludes the possibility of your finding rewarding work?
*CL:* No.

*CO* = Counsellor
*CL* = Client

counsellor focuses on the word 'never'—'You have *never* applied yourself' with a great deal of credulity. In dealing with a client who catastrophises everything, we can ask, 'What is the worst that could happen?'; 'How might that be helpful to you in the long run?'; 'Can you think of good things that can happen if X occurs?'; 'This is your version of the situation, can you think of other versions?'.

It is rare that a single question will lead to insight but a strategic string of questions will start the ball rolling. Figure 12 is an artificial counselling sequence aimed at removing an irrational belief and improving self-confidence.

Asking clients to keep a diary of their dysfunctional thoughts can help them recognise those thoughts and substitute more rational/ coping thoughts. Figure 13 illustrates the form such a diary could take.

## Activity 42   Cognitive restructuring

a. Think of a situation in which your performance is lowered by your negative thoughts or unrealistic standards.
b. For a week keep a log of these thoughts that occur before, during and after the situation.
c. Analyse the log. Which of your unrealistic or negative thoughts are self-defeating, not based on fact, occur before, during, after?
d. Construct some coping, realistic thoughts with vivid imagery as you imagine yourself operating successfully in the situation. Practise and rehearse repeatedly.
e. As you feel comfortable with the new thoughts and images, apply them to the real situation. You can apply thought stopping (below) to stop the self-defeating thoughts, and cognitive restucturing to replace them with coping thoughts.

## Thought stopping

Another way to remove dysfunctional beliefs that prevent you from functioning fully is thought stopping. When a negative thought occurs, e.g. 'I am the only one not coping', say '*stop*' and start making and visualising one of your relevant affirmations. Some people find that imagining an open book being closed with a bang helps, as the closure is the shutting out of the negative thought. This needs to be practised until it can be used effectively immediately any negative thought occurs.

## Activity 43   Thought stopping

a. Identify some non-productive negative thinking in which you sometimes engage.
b. Commence thinking along these negative lines.
c. Shout '*stop*' to yourself and clap your hands at the same time.
d. Continue to do this and on further practices think and imagine the word '*stop*'. Eventually '*stop*' will come into your mind automatically whenever you start to think that particular negative thought.

**Figure 13 Diary of hopeless thoughts (Modified Beck's Dysfunctional Thought Form)**

| What happened | Feelings/ emotions | Automatic thoughts/hopeless thoughts | Rational response/coping thoughts | Behaviour changes | Changes |
|---|---|---|---|---|---|
| 1 What made you upset? | 1 Be precise about what you are feeling, sad/ anxious/angry. | 1 Write down the thoughts that came immediately before these feelings. | 1 Write down your rational/coping thoughts in response to automatic thoughts. | 1 What plan of action will I now make? | 1 How much do you believe your automatic thoughts now? 1–100 |
| 2 Stream of thoughts or daydreams leading to upset. | 2 How much do you feel it? 1–100 | 2 How much do you believe in these automatic thoughts? 1–100 | 2 How much do you believe in these thoughts? 1–100 | | 2 What emotion do you feel now? How much? 1–100 |

| Situation | Emotion | Automatic thoughts | Rational response | Action | Outcome |
|---|---|---|---|---|---|
| Asked wife a question, she ignored me. | 1 Rejected<br>2 Sad 80 per cent | 1 She never listens to me. No one listens to me. I'm so boring, and uninteresting. No wonder I'm unemployed. I'll never achieve anything. I'm a failure<br>2 98 per cent | 1 She was in the kitchen busy cooking. Maybe she didn't hear me. When I used to meet my friends they seemed to find me interesting and amusing. I doubt whether that's the reason I'm unemployed. The unemployed figures are so high. It's probably very little to do with me. Achievement isn't the only road to happiness although I want to do something with my life<br>2 80 per cent | 1 Make sure when I talk to my wife she is in the room and not busy. Make more effort to go and meet my friends. Go and badger careers advice and Job Centre again. Look in the newspaper more regularly. | 1 30 per cent<br>2 Sad 20 per cent Rejected 10 per cent |

*Note*
Cognitive Errors
never—
generalisation
no-one—
magnification—'I'm a failure.'

## Behavioural rehearsal and modelling

An adjunct to the techniques of cognitive restructuring and thought stopping to overcome negative thinking is the rehearsal and modelling of appropriate behaviour. This 'rehearsal' approach is very valuable in overcoming stress that might impede performance. Many managers use rehearsal when they have to give a presentation or talk. They stand in front of a mirror and give the talk several times until they are confident of their manner and content. Another area where rehearsal or modelling is useful is preparing for an interview or rebuking an employee for not following established procedures. A modelling session with an employee who has asked for help at a job interview might go something like this:

'Now, John, watch me and remember each point as I go through it slowly. Knock firmly on the door like this. When you hear 'Come in', stand up straight, open the door and step into the room. Look straight at the interviewer, smile and greet the interviewer with a pleasant 'Good morning' and a firm handshake. Have you got all that? I'll go through it again while you watch, then we will go through it together. After that you can do this entry section by yourself while I watch.' Effective rehearsal and modelling involves:

- isolating parts of a behaviour sequence for observation, demonstration and practice
- repeated practice with observer feedback
- rehearsal until a smooth, natural performance is achieved.


## Activity 44   Rehearsal and modelling

With a partner who can observe/ play the other person if necessary, plan modelling sessions by breaking up each of the following events into several segments. Consider every detail—appearance, timing, posture, words, tone, facial expression. Get each segment working well before putting the whole event together. Your partner can give you feedback.

- Rebuking an employee for turning up for work late on a regular basis
- Making a complaint to a supplier about faulty goods
- Entering the managing director's office to discuss your application for promotion
- Meeting a tough union negotiator for the first time.

## Systematic desensitisation

This technique is useful for removing fears and anxiety. Some people find themselves in the grip of extremely strong—even disabling—but irrational fears of such things as being in a closed room, crowds, travel, elevators, going outside, cats and so on. There are hundreds of such phobias but they too can be removed with systematic desensitisation. It is impossible to do a good day's work if any of the following such as traveling to work on a crowded train, the elevator to your 20th floor office, the warehouse cat, your enclosed office, even leaving the house, cause such anxiety you believe you may faint, or collapse.

The technique is as follows:

a.  Ask the person to make a list of all the situations in which the anxiety arises and arrange these in order from those which produce the least fear to those which produce the most
b.  Teach the person how to relax (see p. 117)
c.  Once the person has relaxed, ask him to consider the situation that produces the least level of anxiety and either imagine realistic scenes with concrete detail or put himself into the actual situation. Since anxiety is incompatible with relaxation, the person should soon be able to think about or experience the situation without the anxiety reaction
d.  As each situation is dealt with, tackle the next situation on the hierarchy of fear until the fear is completely eradicated.

Here is an example of an anxiety hierarchy for giving a presentation. It lists the stages by which a speech-anxious person becomes progressively more nervous about the task ahead.

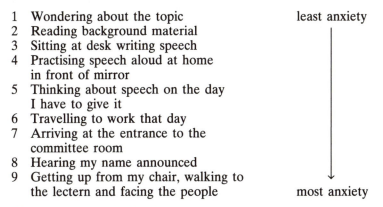

1  Wondering about the topic                     least anxiety
2  Reading background material
3  Sitting at desk writing speech
4  Practising speech aloud at home
   in front of mirror
5  Thinking about speech on the day
   I have to give it
6  Travelling to work that day
7  Arriving at the entrance to the
   committee room
8  Hearing my name announced
9  Getting up from my chair, walking to
   the lectern and facing the people         most anxiety

Here is an example for fear of going out:

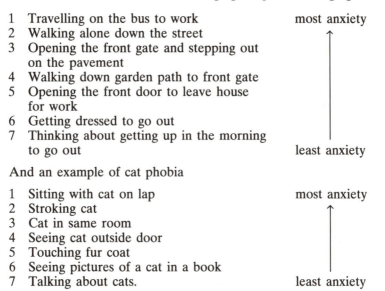

1  Travelling on the bus to work                    most anxiety
2  Walking alone down the street
3  Opening the front gate and stepping out
   on the pavement
4  Walking down garden path to front gate
5  Opening the front door to leave house
   for work
6  Getting dressed to go out
7  Thinking about getting up in the morning
   to go out                                        least anxiety

And an example of cat phobia

1  Sitting with cat on lap                          most anxiety
2  Stroking cat
3  Cat in same room
4  Seeing cat outside door
5  Touching fur coat
6  Seeing pictures of a cat in a book
7  Talking about cats.                              least anxiety

Systematic desensitisation works particularly well if linked with rehearsal and modelling i.e. if each stage is practised and rehearsed as it is reached in a state of relaxation and often with a supportive person present.

## Activity 45   Systematic desensitisation

If there is a situation or object that causes you anxiety, write out a personal hierarchy of scenes. Practise the relaxation response over a few days until you have mastered it. Then, after getting into the relaxation response, take the lowest item on the hierarchy and, either using vivid imagery or actually undertaking the behaviour, try to eliminate your anxiety at this lowest level. Only move to the next level when you have eliminated the current one. Remember to make the scenes realistic and vivid as you bring them to mind in your relaxation state, or to act out the scene in the real situation by rehearsing your positive, non-anxious behaviour there.

## Modifying Type A behaviour

As we read in Chapter 3, Type A people are more prone to stress and Type A behaviour has been shown in a number of studies to precede the development of coronary heart disease in between 72 per cent and 85 per cent of men tested. Cultural influences make important contributions to the development of Type A behaviour. The underlying values of our culture promote hard work and achievement. Thus Type A people view their behaviour as rewarding, positive and reinforced. But as this is mainly a learned pattern of behaviour, it can be unlearned, or at least modified by stress-reducing techniques. It won't happen overnight but practice and effort plus a desire to change will help considerably. A Type A person was not born that way but has learned that his behavioural traits are effective and has repeated them so many times that they become a habit. What we must do is pick up new habits to replace the old ones by practising Type B habits. These eventually become your habitual way of responding. Once we begin to adopt Type B behaviour it becomes easier and easier to continue, because we start to look at stressful situations in a different way.

Here are some Type B behaviour exercises. They must be practised because the physical act of doing something is a much more powerful conditioner than just thinking about it. After doing some of these exercises you will be able to think up others relevant to your situation.

## Activity 46 Type B behaviour conditioning

Determine what activities bring out Type A behaviour in you and perform them using Type B behaviour. For example, standing in a long, slow-moving queue or in a traffic jam may generate considerable irritation and tension. The next time you stand in line or land in a traffic hold-up try consciously not to get irritated. Think about what you are going to do at the weekend, about the comedy you saw on TV last night, about anything pleasant. Pretty soon you will start doing this pleasant thinking naturally whenever there is a hold-up in what you are doing.

At mealtime, put down your knife and fork between bites. This will force you to eat more slowly and leave more room for conversation and interaction with others. It will help digestion too. Try slowing down other habits by building short breaks into them.

Involve yourself in more recreational activities. When at home, put down job-related books and journals. Read some good recreational books instead. Take up a former hobby again or find a new one. Enjoy a walk each evening. Go to the theatre, cinema, club on a regular basis. These are only a few of the ways you can slow yourself down and start to enjoy life.

Spend an entire day without your watch on at weekends. Clock-watching and a sense of time urgency are major components of Type A behaviour. Make a real effort to forget time and just enjoy the day without being rushed. You will look at your wrist a few times but as there is nothing there, this behaviour will decrease. When you finally realise that time isn't an important part of that day you will relax and settle back more. Eventually clock-watching will become less important to you.

Stand in front of a mirror and practise positive expressions such as smiling. Every time you notice yourself starting to tense up, put a smile on. The tension cannot compete. After a week or two, a negative facial expression will trigger a reaction to smile that will relieve facial tension.

Talk positively to yourself (see affirmations and self-esteem above). Use expressions like stay calm, slow down, relax, easy does it, don't rush, you can cope. Say them aloud if necessary as a very forceful self-instruction. This enhances the conditioning process and makes practising more effective. Your brain is getting the message loud and clear. Eventually you will automatically give yourself these instructions.

Start rewarding yourself for exhibiting Type B behaviour. After showing patience in a queue or reading a book for enjoyment, give yourself a reward of something you enjoy.

Schedule one thing at a time by developing good time-management skills (see below). By planning things in advance, and building relaxation/leisure time and adequate meal breaks into your day, you will find that the important things get done.

Through activities such as the above you can turn off Type A characteristics. Since you have had a lifetime of learning and practising Type A behaviours, you cannot lose them in a day. But the same principle of habit formation can enable you to learn Type B behaviour by doing Type B things. You substitute one for the other by practice and conditioning.

## Time management

With reductions in staffing, many employees and managers are having to increase their workload. This adds pressure and contributes to stress. Poor time management creates stress because without time we lose the freedom to do what needs to be done, to be who we want to be and to enjoy the things we want to do. By structuring your time in ways that facilitate the completion of tasks and provide time out for recreation, you can meet your professional and personal goals without increasing stress levels.

Many people under stress claim that they haven't time to do everything they need to. They are pressured because everything is dictated by the clock or calendar. In a panic, they do nothing well. The reasons for inability to manage time are improper behaviour patterns. The first step is to recognise those behaviours that cause time-related problems in self and in others. The following questionnaire will help identify trouble spots and guide you towards becoming a more successful time manager.

## Activity 47   How well do you manage time?

Read each statement and circle the most appropriate number for you.

Always = 1; Usually = 2; Sometimes = 3; Rarely = 4

- I find I have enough time to do the things
  I want to do                                       1   2   3   4
- I am aware of deadlines and schedule my
  work to meet them                                  1   2   3   4
- I set priorities in order of importance            1   2   3   4
- I say no when I am pressed for time                 1   2   3   4
- I make a daily 'to do' list                         1   2   3   4
- I make out a weekly/monthly timetable              1   2   3   4
- I feel in control of time at work and at
  home                                               1   2   3   4
- I use a diary for appointments, deadlines
  and things to do                                   1   2   3   4
- I write down specific objectives in order to
  work towards goals                                 1   2   3   4
- I schedule time for leisure and recreation         1   2   3   4
- I find it easy to keep up with changes
  that affect my schedule or workload                1   2   3   4
- I schedule blocks of time for something
  extra that has to be fitted in                     1   2   3   4
- I eliminate unnecessary paperwork                  1   2   3   4
- I shift my priorities as soon as they
  change                                             1   2   3   4
- I delegate responsibilities to others to
  make more time for myself                          1   2   3   4
- I organise my desk and work area to
  eliminate clutter                                  1   2   3   4
- I reschedule low-priority items                     1   2   3   4
- I try to do things in a way that cuts down
  on duplicated effort                               1   2   3   4
- I find that doing everything myself is very
  inefficient                                        1   2   3   4
- My meetings are well organised                      1   2   3   4
- I try to schedule most of my difficult work
  during my most productive time                     1   2   3   4
- I finish one job before going on to the
  next                                               1   2   3   4
- I try to get the most pertinent information
  before making a decision rather than

trying to get as much imformation as
possible                                              1 2 3 4
• I get things done on time                           1 2 3 4

Your score:

24–40     excellent time manager
41–54     average time manager
55–96     poor time manager

Now go back to your responses to the questionnaire and identify
those areas where you scored 3's and 4's. These are the problem
areas.

The common problem areas are:

not prioritising tasks
not scheduling daily, weekly, monthly activities
not delegating responsibility
not giving up total control
not shifting priorities
not reducing unnecessary paperwork/clutter.

It is impossible to practise good time management without first
knowing what it is that makes us poor at accomplishing a certain
amount of work in a given time. Once we have put our finger on the
problems we can adjust our behaviour to eliminate the bad practices
and substitute more effective ones.

The next task is to become clear on what is really important to
you, what is less important and what is of no importance at all. Are
your employees clear too? If you and/or they are not clear it is easy
to hop from one task to another without ever finishing one properly.
If you can place things including leisure into a system of priorities by
setting aims for yourself you will have more control over your life.
With more control, there will be less stress and less sense of failure.
It is not what you plan but how you plan.

Everyone needs to set priorities, both long-term and short-term. It
is easy to slide into doing what is easiest, what others would have you
do, or what is habitual. You can let others spend your time for you
or you can plan to spend it in ways that bring best returns for you.
In teaching yourself and others how to manage time, the first task is
to work out how you and they actually spend your time.

## Activity 48   Keeping a diary

Keep a diary of how you spend your time for a week. Sort the
activities into appropriate categories, e.g. sleep, answering memos,

supervision and inspection of production operations, interviewing staff, leisure etc. Calculate as a percentage what proportion of the week you devoted to each type of activity. Make a pie chart to display this information. This indicates clearly how the week was spent.

Looking at both the diary and the pie chart, does the way you spent your time surprise you? Are there any changes you would like to make? Did you waste any time? Did you meet all your deadlines? Did you put off anything you should have done?

## Activity 49 Making timetables

You need to make daily and weekly timetables or lists. Calendars, appointment books, diaries and pocket-size computerised diaries are useful here. Work out your priorities not only in terms of what has to be done now or tomorrow, but also in terms of hobbies, family commitments and so on. Having listed and prioritised all these tasks and activities, draw up a daily and a weekly timetable. Plan for 'time out' to carry out the relaxation and affirmation activities already discussed. The list can be colour-coded for (i) things that *must* be done today, (ii) things that would be useful to do today, and (iii) things that can be safely left to tomorrow. Other matters can be built into the list as they surface. At the end of each day, cross off every task completed. It is very rewarding to see a set of items crossed off in this way. Planning should help you relax more and allow more time for relaxation.

Every one needs to plan time for relaxation or 'time out'. During short periods each day such as when travelling to or from work, or at meal breaks, time scheduled for relaxation enables relaxation exercises to be performed on a regular basis. Such time out must become a regular part of your life. For example, at the end of the workday just sit quietly for a couple of minutes relaxing; or find a scenic route home if possible and avoid the mad commuter rush; or after arriving home, sit in the car in the driveway and relax for a couple of minutes.

Remember five things: prioritise, schedule, delegate, eliminate unnecessary activities and leave 20 per cent of your daily schedule open for emergencies.

## Activity 50 Planning time for relaxation

Work out for your own particular routine/arrangements short periods when you can regularly carry out relaxation exercises.

## Summary

This chapter has introduced a variety of methods for positive self-management. Relaxation techniques will help to reduce tension, as will an adequate diet, regular exercise and sound sleep. Developing more positive feelings about oneself will build confidence and resilience to cope with whatever may lie round the corner, while affirmations can provide a more positive self-picture which then gains from self-validation.

Cognitive restructuring, too, can remove negative, self-defeating thoughts. Anxieties and fears can be removed by the use of systematic desensitisation. The development of adequate time-management skills will aid considerably the reduction of stress, and improve the chances of building into one's schedule time for relaxation and recreation or exercise.

A combination of these techniques will ensure that a manager is in the best of psychological health to deal with his own life transitions and those of the people he deals with.

A useful practical guide to managing stress and thinking positively is *10 Skills for Working With Stress* by R. Burns published by Business and Professional Publishing, PO Box 5065, West Chatswood NSW 2057

# 6
# Humanising the organisation
## *Supporting, networking, involving and counselling*

*No man is an Iland, intire of itselfe; every man is a peece of the Continent, a part of the maine ...*

John Donne, *Devotions* 17

In the previous chapters, we discussed a range of behaviours and symptoms that may occur before, during or after change. This chapter will concern itself (i) with methods and techniques of counselling that managers can use to help prevent such symptoms and behaviours in themselves and others, and alleviate them if they have already occurred, and (ii) with humanising the organisation to encourage the involvement of staff at all levels in the decision-making process.

## Humanising the organisation

This is more than just a slogan. A humanistic organisation has definite characteristics.

- Its members generally express satisfaction with their jobs and feel that the organisation values them
- Within and between levels, there are positive, supportive, accepting relationships and communication
- Members feel part of the organisation through involvement and contribution to managing change
- Members of management are visible and approachable.

The extent of the current economic and structural changes in industry means that many managers and employees are likely to respond with immature and ineffective coping styles such as defence mechanisms, low self-esteem and emotional outbursts. When a large number of people in an organisation show this, the organisation needs humanising. This may not be the only thing it needs but without it, solutions to other problems will not be as effective. Supporting and developing people, rather than treating them as things to be used, is not only the right thing to do from a humanistic point of view but makes sense economically and operationally. Some managers may feel that 'Stress is none of our business', or 'They must learn to cope', or 'Our responsibility is to make profits for the shareholders'. But even if an organisation doubts the merits of caring for employees, it should see the cost-saving argument. Failure to care for employees results in lost work days, absenteeism, poor performance, high staff turnover and the need for retraining. Programs for helping staff to cope with their working context are known as 'wellness programs', 'lifestyle change programs' or, more usually, Employee Assistance Programs or EAPs.

*EAPs*

EAPs vary widely, but all share some essential ingredients:

- commitment and support from top management
- clear explanation to all staff about procedures, policies and operations
- cooperation and support of unions
- education of employees about EAP services
- buying-in of outside expertise as required
- training of in-house counsellors, trainers and other support personnel in problem identification, in counselling and in running workshops
- a primary prevention component to anticipate problems
- the availability of continued care
- an explicit policy on confidentiality
- program evaluation.

Such programs in the United States and Britain are saving companies millions by helping employees at all levels manage their problems with less stress and ill-health (e.g. the New York Telephone Company saved $2.7 million in one year). The Post Office in Britain has since 1986 employed in-house counsellors. The provision of individual counselling to employees who are experiencing high levels of stress appears to result in substantial and long-lasting improvements in psychological well-being. Stress management training and counselling are the two main interventions applied to occupational and organisational problems. The former is typically offered to employees as a group activity while the latter is offered to those who refer themselves or are referred by a supervisor. Both approaches help to reduce individual distress, encourage positive thinking and action and enable staff to cope with the problems facing them at work and at home.

However, it is naive to think that such interventions will do any more than this. They are not designed to enable managers and other employees to comply with unreasonable demands on their services, nor to solve organisational problems which may require job redesign or increased participation in decision-making. So for a total approach an organisation needs to ally its psychological intervention strategies with organisational changes.

While we can never prevent some employees being retired early, losing promotion chances, being forced to relocate, or having to return to training to develop new skills, doing any of these is less stressful within a humanised context.

Improving the quality of work life within an EAP has four steps.

## 1 Assessment
This involves all the diagnostic activities that may reveal the psychological health of the organisation: employee attitude surveys, health surveys, assessment of the quality of manager–employee relations and union-management relations, analysis/evaluation of current planning and methods of introducing change, and analysis/prediction of the likely effects of technological, structural and economic change.

## 2 Planning
This involves finding key opportunities for substantial improvement in the quality of the work experience by involving employees at all levels and getting support for whatever changes are judged by the teams as necessary, feasible and economically sound.

## 3 Action
This puts the results of the planning process into operation. Given the complexities of organisational life and the tendency to resist change, there could be a gap between objectives and initial results. The best results are achieved by simple programs of change that everyone understands and that almost everyone can support. The changes must be attractive and sold to employees via their fellow workers who have been involved in the planning.

## 4 Follow-up
Initial enthusiasm may stir great hopes and expectations that gloss over the disappointments and disadvantages that accompany every change. All change has both positive and negative aspects. Attention to how the changes are proceeding and analysis of unforeseen snags and difficulties will obviate much disillusionment and cynicism before such attitudes take hold. Feedback is essential from all levels of the workforce. Revision in collaboration with the planning team to take account of feedback information should be an ongoing activity.

Interventions to reduce stress at work and the outcomes of such interventions can be classified into three levels: those focusing on the individual, on the individual–organisation interface, and on the organisation. Interventions aimed at the individual try to reduce physical and emotional reactions to stress by means of individual counselling and relaxation techniques, or to alter the way people see themselves and structure their lives by teaching them self-concept enhancement, positive thinking, communication/relationship skills, decision-making skills and time management. Interventions at the interface between the individual and the organisation are not well developed, but involve developing strategies that enable employees at all levels to participate in and contribute to the planning of work procedures, changes in job content, job skills and reskilling, and to develop an understanding of the changes that are to occur in their working lives. Interventions that are aimed at the organisation tend to focus on physical conditions such as improving health and safety factors or reducing noise and pollution.

A comprehensive EAP to assist staff to cope with current and future changes in the world of work must address at least the first two levels. Restricting a program to the first level only implies that the individual needs to adjust, ignoring the fact that interaction between the person and his context is important to the harmony and viability of both parties.

## Networking

Networks are systems, paths or channels by which individuals and organisations support each other and pass on information. No man is an island; we all need networks or support systems in our personal, work and community lives. An important way to improve the emotional, social and physical health of lonely and stressed people is to help them develop or enter new personal and social networks. The business organisation is a network. Information flows between its parts; each part supports other parts; individuals in each part are all part of the team; complex work and/or friendship relationships exist.

Figure 14 shows the business and personal network of a sales manager. Only the main elements have been included. If we got down to detail, many more individuals and groups could be added, creating a complex network and set of interrelationships. This entire network provides a basis of potential support in times of change.

## Activity 51   Networks

Draw your business and personal network.

Were you aware of the large number of people and groups with whom you interact, whom you support in a variety of ways and who

**Figure 14  A personal network**

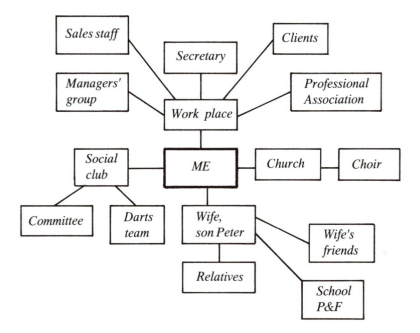

also support you? These relationships help to satisfy your need to belong, to achieve, to attain acceptance, to gain self-esteem. They also help satisfy the needs of the other people in the network. All parties should gain satisfaction, mutual support and the sharing of troubles and advice. A business cannot function as a set of individuals; it must be a network of mutually supportive people all with approximately the same objectives for the organisation and themselves.

A business network may also provide mutual aid in a crisis through 'mateship', protect the group's interests, keep everyone properly informed, defend individuals from discriminatory practices, encourage cooperation rather than competition, promote participation rather than imposition, and encourage commitment rather than a sense of being duty-bound. A network in these circumstances is a support system.

## Your support system

To cope with stressful conditions, people need physical and emotional networks to provide contact with others as well as relaxation techniques and counselling. A person's network of relationships has an important influence on his reactions to stress. A 1991 American study which compared death rates in people with weak and strong social networks found that developing good social support systems enhanced health as much as giving up smoking and improved the chances of surviving health challenges such as heart attacks. Laboratory experiments have shown that the same threatening stimulus evokes a milder physical and psychological response if it is experienced in the presence of others rather than alone. The effect of another's presence is enhanced if the other is able to empathise and provide warm, unconditional acceptance—the hallmarks of an effective counsellor.

Support from or access to helpful, caring and sympathetic individuals at work, at home and in the neighbourhood reduces potential stress and facilitates recovery in those who suffer from stress. Emotional and social support plays an important role in maintaining emotional balance and the development of a rounded, stable personality. This support starts in infancy, when it is given by caring parents. Later, friends, peer-group members, colleagues, spouses, personnel officers, counsellors and the like also lend support. When disaster of any sort strikes at work or in our private life, stress is easier to tolerate and better managed when it can be shared with others who are supportive, empathetic and helpful. We are well aware that major community disasters such as floods, fire, earthquakes, wars, hurricanes often bring out the best in people as individual anxieties and conflicts are forgotten as everyone works together against a common enemy or towards a common goal. During the intensive bombing of London in the Second World War there was a marked decline in the number of people seeking help for emotional reasons. In Australia, the Anzac spirit of mateship, for both men and women would go a long way to helping each other through the crises of technological and occupational change.

Supporting others does not mean giving blind assurances such as 'Everything will be all right'. Realistically supportive statements and behaviours are far better: 'We are in a mess, but let us work today on a way of improving the immediate problem and then we can start to tackle the long-term solution tomorrow. It is not going to be easy but if we can keep working together we should sort it out.' Supporting each other in the problems of the workplace, together with counselling and open discussion and planning, enables all those affected to realise they are not alone, and that they can talk profitably to someone whatever the immediate conditions may look like.

Employees who participate in planning, initiating and monitoring change that affects them have less stress, lower rates of absenteeism, and greater commitment to and acceptance of change. Participation is a major element of social support. It is reasonable to conclude that support acts as a buffer to stress.

Social support can come from the family, within which members can talk about their experiences, hopes, needs and fears without losing face. Other family members can offer alternative interpretations and plans of action, and provide emotional support and a context in which individuals can succeed in non-work roles. The family is the major provider of positive feedback, enhancing members' self-esteem with verbal and nonverbal reinforcement. People can also draw on their families for practical help, such as financial aid, helping with children, and care during illness, without losing self-esteem or feeling like a burden.

The work group is less able to act as a support group than the family because it is usually larger and less intimate and because most people believe work is not the place to deal with emotional and personal problems. But this is not to write off the work context as a source of support. If a more humanitarian, caring ethos pervades the workplace, more mutual support will occur as employees face the problems of change together rather than as rivals. It is up to management to try to create this more caring atmosphere.

*External or internal support in organisations*

Organisations can provide support for their members by buying in an external expert such as a counsellor, psychologist or occupational health specialist. The external-expert strategy is fine for a sudden crisis which the organisation lacks the resources to handle, but is less well suited for longer-term caring and development. Experts tend to come in, complete their contract, then go. Neither the expert nor the organisation has a commitment to the other beyond the immediate task. Once the expert is recruited, the organisation can comfortably pass on to him the responsibility for dealing with the problem. Bringing in an expert to do, for example, the counselling or stress management training is often an inoculation approach, training employees to cope with difficult work environments which remain unchanged. The value of such a temporary buy-in is further decreased by the lack of post-training maintenance after the expert leaves. Experts are also distanced from employees by their status and by their implied links with management.

On the other hand, experts can be valuable in working alongside management to devise the programs and approaches needed in particular circumstances. They can also train volunteers in the specific counselling techniques already outlined, thereby leaving in-house support in place when they leave.

The best support comes from within the organisation. It is therefore always present, and intimately aware of the issues and problems. Small organisations cannot afford to bring in experts, so they must develop in-house skills among management and selected employees

**Table 12  External and internal support systems**

|  | Cognitive | Emotional | Behavioural |
|---|---|---|---|
| External support by specialists on contract | Advice by experts:<br><br>Doctors<br>Counsellors<br>Consultants<br>Superiors | Support provided by experts:<br>Counsellors<br>Occupational health nurses<br>Welfare officers<br>Supervisors (rarely) | Take person off job or change job<br>Find someone else to solve problem<br><br>Give early retirement<br>Take responsibility from person |
|  | Person is largely a recipient | | |
| Internal support and self-help | Pooling problem-solving resources by widening information network which may include 'experts' known personally to group members | Support spontaneously marshalled by the group. If given is more likely to be felt as genuine by the recipient | Help person to do the job<br>Share responsibility with person<br>Provide training to improve skills<br>Counselling for redundancy early retirement well in advance |
|  | Person may be both giver and receiver | | |

to create a supportive environment. Training selected staff in lay counselling is worthwhile in all organisations. Table 12 summarises the contrast between external and internal support systems.

For personal work crises such as involuntary relocation, enforced early retirement, redundancy and so on, counselling help is not generally available. Yet a person's access to sympathetic and helpful support may be an important factor in how they cope with and adapt to such major life transitions. Managers need to think about what support systems are available for them and for those they know to be in distress.

## Activity 52  Support systems

1  Consider some crises that have been experienced by people you know. What support systems were available to help them? What support systems were needed? Have any such systems been developed since?

2   What different types of support systems do you think could be organised to assist some of the following:
A person forced to retire early
A person with a preschool-aged child forced to relocate
A person moved from fulltime to part-time work
A person who can no longer pay her mortgage
A young mother who has to work
An unemployed school leaver
An unemployed single parent
A spouse whose partner has to work away
Elderly parents whose children have left the area
An employee who is abusing drugs or alcohol

3   You might consider ways you could provide an active support-group system, either individually or collectively, for other people who are experiencing a crisis.

## Activity 53   Potential support systems

Opportunities for mutual support and networking in the community help to lower stress, improve self-esteem, make one feel wanted and valuable and may be a useful support system should troubles such as redundancy occur. Make a list of the activities in your community that you could share in, e.g. a choir; a holiday play scheme; offering help to the elderly as a volunteer.

## Activity 54   Your support system

Have you problems where you need support? Do you know who can provide such support? For each of the situations below, try and think of someone who might provide the help you need.

Someone who will listen to me          _____
Someone who makes me feel
   wanted                              _____
Someone who is fun to be with          _____
Someone who can cope in an
   emergency/crisis                    _____
Someone who makes me feel good
   about myself                        _____
Someone I can talk to                  _____
Someone who is honest/open with me     _____
Someone who cheers me up               _____
Someone who cares about me             _____

Did your list of names surprise you?
Have you any situations where you could think of no-one?

Support people do not all have to be your friends. You may have an acquaintance who is marvellous in a crisis. Even people who annoy you by asking awkward and pointed questions, or demanding that you consider a variety of courses of action, may help by making you think of consequences and alternatives.

If particular individuals' names crop up constantly, you run the risk of having all your eggs in one basket. What happens if one of these crucial people moves away? You should try to develop a wider range of support people.

If there are gaps in your group of helpers, the first step is to be aware of them. The next step is to look around for suitable people to fill those gaps. The third step is to create a relationship with those people. The characteristics you should look for in finding support are:

• They are people who generally offer help to others
• They are prepared to spend time with you
• You are likely to know them
• They may have gone through a similar experience
• You can trust them to keep confidential anything you reveal to them
• You believe that talking to them can make a difference
• You believe that they won't laugh at you.

Everyone has a right to ask for help, and most of us are prepared to give help to others if they need it. It is not a sign of weakness to ask for help. Rather it is a sign of maturity and strength to accept that we need help to cope with and resolve a problem, and to be confident enough to share difficulties with other people.

## Counselling

Counselling is important in the work context for both humanitarian and practical reasons. It is humanitarian to recognise that the changing pattern of working life is bringing real pressures and hardship to some and it is practical to realise that counselling may be an economical means of improving performance. Man is a social animal; mutual cooperation and interdependence is the basis of the survival of the species whether the threat is physical or psychological. Counselling is trouble-sharing using a variety of verbal and nonverbal communicative techniques which can range from a sympathetic smile through individual and group discussion to relaxation exercises.

All human relationships are potentially therapeutic, allowing the relief of distress in an atmosphere of support, acceptance and understanding. Informal counselling is often given without those involved being aware of it: by bartenders to drunks, by ministers of religion to parishioners, by neighbours across the back fence, by colleagues to each other. When a problem is revealed and shared in an accepting context, it can be faced and dealt with. Informal counselling is part of good neighbourliness and good listening. But there is a difference between being a qualified counsellor and using counselling skills. Counselling skills can be taught to a person who is willing to use them. Lay or non-professional counsellors (often managers, supervisors, workers) can be trained and encouraged to use their skills in any organisation. Such people are best placed to spot employees and colleagues with potential or actual problems and do something to help them. A timely or early intervention can often prevent a situation requiring more intensive professional help.

A counsellor is someone who assists individuals to change the way they feel, increase understanding of self and environment, and make and implement decisions. Counselling is a process of interaction between a counsellor and the person being counselled. In the work context, the counsellor's role is to help limit the impact of change on individuals and to help them anticipate the impact of change in an overall context of social responsibility. This helps individuals to create their own guiding images of personal, social, home, and employment options, and thus to become stakeholders in a more meaningful future. But counselling cannot be seen as the answer to organisational problems.

Some people are not willing to learn the skills or don the mantle of lay counsellor. They are reluctant for a number of reasons: they don't think they have time, they don't think it is part of their job, they believe a show of sympathy will be exploited, and so on. For those who are resistant or doubtful the best advice is not to attempt counselling. For those who do want to help, what follows is a basic outline of the main skills. Like making love, counselling is something we all do naturally but which not all of us do very well. These skills will assist in any relationship or communication, therapeutic or otherwise.

Counselling is a set of techniques, skills and attitudes to help people manage their own problems using their own resources. We say manage rather than solve because some problems cannot be solved. The only acceptable solution for the employee with a redundancy notice would be to have it revoked. That is not going to happen, but a supervisor can help the employee manage the problem. The employee should do this as far as possible using his own resources. The counsellor must not jump in and try to fix things for him. What people need is help in clearing their muddled thinking, and encouragement in dealing with their own problems. People need counselling when they:

are tense, troubled or anxious
engage in self-defeating behaviour
are not coping with or adjusting to their environment
are not making necessary decisions
have low motivation
exhibit a noticeable change in behaviour.

The general aim of counselling is psychological growth so that clients can satisfy their need for acceptance, recognition, positive self-feeling and mastery of the environment.

Work problems also impinge on the home and vice versa. Traditional counselling has often simply focused on the individual and his problem in the context of that problem. Work and family are closely related. Changes at work may create pressures at home, sometimes requiring families to redefine their relationships and the roles of members. This implies that in some cases effective counselling must involve other family members too, so that each is able to understand and support the other psychologically. Particular problems in the current context of change are the difficulties family members have in adjusting to redefinitions and blendings of traditional male and female roles at work and in the home. Many employers are starting to recognise the importance of restructuring the workplace in ways that support the family, such as providing child care, parental leave, and flexible hours. In addition, workers may need counselling to help them accept new roles and redefine what constitutes a competent father/husband or mother/wife. Lowered of expectations in one area may be countered by increased feelings of self-worth in another, as role negotiation and reassignment of responsibilities occurs within the family. Essentially the counsellor aims at clarifying and redefining the client's view of success and sources of life satisfaction in response to the changing interactions between work and family roles.

*The therapeutic relationship*

A therapeutic relationship may exist in any human interaction. However counselling is different from lay help in that the former is guided by prescribed techniques and theoretical rationales. The personality of the counsellor is paramount in the counselling relationship since it determines the client's attitudes to the relationship, and the likelihood of a successful outcome. In counselling, the desire to help and care for others is not enough to ensure effectiveness. It is rather like the *Peanuts* cartoon in which Charlie Brown cannot understand why his baseball team never wins a game when its members are so sincere. Three basic qualities mark the effective counsellor:

1 Empathy—being with the other person.
2 Warm acceptance—providing a safe, non-threatening ethos with

**Table 13  Relationship skills in counselling**

| Relationship-building skills | | |
|---|---|---|
| Respect | Empathy | Genuineness |
| **This behaviour** conveys to the other person that they are valuable, worthwhile, and important to you | informs the other person that you understand how they see the world, how they experience it | shows the other person that you are trustworthy and open, not deceitful and phony in your relationships |
| **It is shown by** actively listening and attending to the other person; giving up your time; asking questions; not interrupting or criticising; remembering a name; showing concern; not criticising | sharing similar experiences of your own; showing you are in tune with their feelings—'You sound angry'; by understanding; by mirroring their nonverbal behaviour | being natural; not trying to act a role; not being on the defensive; appropriate nonverbal behaviour that matches verbal behaviour |

These three behaviours must be shown to the other person in a recognisable way. The recognisable ways are (i) by what you say, and (ii) by how you convey what you say with body language or nonverbal behaviour.

unconditional acceptance and love. It is the ability to accept another without condition as a worthwhile human being.
3  Genuineness—being interested, real, authentic, nondefensive, sincere. Counsellors must be genuine to themselves before they can help others to be that way.

Those seeking help respond favourably where these three essential qualities are present in the counsellor and respond unfavourably in their absence.

Effective counselling, then, is dependent on the counsellor, on the kind of person he is, and on his ability to establish a warm, trusting relationship with the other person. These three therapeutic ingredients are not unique to counselling; they are qualities of universal human experience that are present or lacking in varying degrees in virtually all relationships (Table 13). The two characteristics of the client that contribute to effective counselling encounters are:

1  a high degree of expectancy of personal improvement, and
2  the ability to engage in extensive self-exploration.

In other words, the client must be willing to be involved in the counselling process.

Some companies employ a professional psychologist to counsel from time to time. However the prevalence of problems caused by current economic and structural change makes it preferable for organisations to acknowledge the existence of problems requiring counselling help and establish a counselling service. While a professional is the ideal person to organise such a service, lay, even peer, counselling can achieve a great deal. Employees are often more willing to talk to and work things out with a person whom they know, trust and respect, who may have been there before them, who understands the particular circumstances of the organisation. The lay counsellor has the advantage of being able to establish a peer-like relationship with the counsellee and empathise more effectively with their problems and way of life.

*The counselling or helping process*

The counselling or helping process consists of three main phases. Clients may not produce all their problems at once. Thus the three phases may have to be recycled as new behaviours produce new feelings which in turn produce new problems for exploration and understanding. Table 14 shows the sequence of the three phases.

**Phase 1   Getting involved**
If this phase fails then no adequate counselling is possible. Only if the  counsellor has the required qualities of *attentive listening, conveying respect, empathy and acceptance, reinforcement* and *creating an ethos of trust*  are clients able to voice their concerns and problems, and enter into a counselling relationship. This phase of getting the client involved is based on relationship-building skills. It is essential to emphasise to the counsellee that whatever is said or occurs in a counselling session is confidential.

These skills are not only important in the first phase; they are essential in all phases. However, if they are lacking at the outset the counselling will fail, be damaging, or will hardly begin.

*Attending* involves being an active listener—using the 'third ear' and being sensitive to verbal and nonverbal communications. Reread Chapter 4 if you cannot remember what meanings the various nonverbal signals may convey. Remember too that the client is noting your verbal and nonverbal signals.

*Respect* is signalled by treating each person as a unique human being and accepting them unconditionally. *Genuineness* exists in a relationship when you are spontaneous, open, non-defensive and honest, and willing to share yourself and your experiences if this is perceived as helpful.

*Empathy* is shown by appropriate responses to both content and feeling in the message. Empathy is not sympathy but an ability to put

**Table 14    The counselling process**

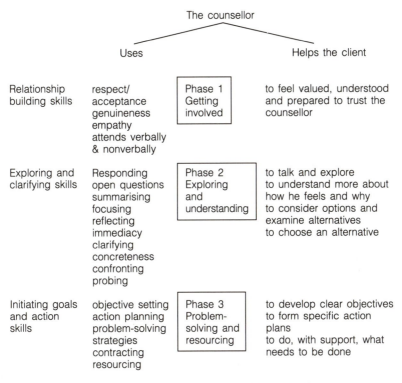

The counsellor

Uses                                                    Helps the client

| Relationship building skills | respect/ acceptance genuineness empathy attends verbally & nonverbally | Phase 1 Getting involved | to feel valued, understood and prepared to trust the counsellor |
|---|---|---|---|
| Exploring and clarifying skills | Responding open questions summarising focusing reflecting immediacy clarifying concreteness confronting probing | Phase 2 Exploring and understanding | to talk and explore to understand more about how he feels and why to consider options and examine alternatives to choose an alternative |
| Initiating goals and action skills | objective setting action planning problem-solving strategies contracting resourcing | Phase 3 Problem-solving and resourcing | to develop clear objectives to form specific action plans to do, with support, what needs to be done |

Counselling is helping people to help themselves

yourself into the shoes of the other person and see things from their point of view. The other person usually realises that you can take their perspective from your accurate reflection of their feelings. To be empathetic you must listen to feelings, reflect those feelings back and clarify anything you don't understand by asking.

*Acceptance* is the ability to accept people as they are, with an unconditional, non-possessive warmth and regard, offering a safe space in which they are free to be themselves without fear of judgment or criticism. *Reinforcement* encourages a client to say more. You reinforce a client by verbal encouragers such as 'Go on', 'I see', 'Yes', 'Can you tell me more' together with nonverbal encouragers such as eye contact and nods. Reinforcement can also be given by 'parroting', or repeating to the client the last phrase he said. 'You say you were worried when the job evaluation scheme was announced.'

Listening is not simply hearing, for we can hear without listening. A counsellor must never be a glassy-eyed listener who looks at his client but has his mind on other things. Just as we can tell whether or not a person is interested in us, so too can the person being counselled. We must attend to both content and feeling, for the words are not the whole message. Never jump to conclusions, and avoid personal prejudices and blocks that hinder understanding of what the other person is really saying. Take time to listen and give time for the other person to finish.

Counselling is not judgmental, nor does it involve moralising, warning or condemning: it is a supportive relationship that enables the other person to express his problem, come to understand it and begin to recognise an acceptable solution. Table 15 lists a number of blocks to communication in the counselling situation. Managers may find it difficult not to indulge in 'red flag' listening, in which words like 'trade union', 'sickie', 'strike' evoke an automatic negative reaction. This reaction must be avoided in a counselling context in order to maintain the other person's feelings of trust and acceptance. Not only is practice at the skills of listening and conveying acceptance and empathy of vital importance in counselling employees but it will also improve communication and relationship skills generally. Economic and structural problems may not go away but we can certainly learn to handle them more sensitively at an interpersonal level.

The following activities will help you develop your communication and relationship making skills for Phase 1.

## Activity 55   Experiencing non-attending

a. You will need a partner. You should talk for two minutes to your partner about your future goals or some other similar topic. Your partner should violate the rules of attending, with no eye contact, no smiling, no nodding, fiddling with a pen or book.
b. Swap the roles around so you fail to attend while your partner talks for two minutes.
c. Now discuss how you both felt. What impact did non-attending have?

## Activity 56   Impact of visible behaviour

a. Sit back-to-back with a partner. Carry out a conversation.
b. After two minutes stop and discuss the difficulties experienced with non-visual communication. What were you missing in terms of visual feedback?

## Activity 57   Nonverbal role play

Using a mirror, role play by gesture and facial expression the following characteristics: caring, confused, hostile, unconcerned,

**Table 15   Roadblocks to communication**

a.  *Solution messages* (the hidden message is 'You're too dumb, here's the answer').
1   *Ordering, directing, commanding*
    'You must . . .', 'You have to . . .', 'You will . . .'
    can produce fear, submissiveness
    invites 'testing' to see if you really mean it
    promotes rebellious behaviour, retaliation
2   *Warning, threatening*
    'If you don't then . . .', 'You'd better, or . . .'
    can produce fear, submissiveness
    invites 'testing' of threatened consequences
    can cause resentment, anger, rebellion
3   *Moralising, preaching*
    'You should . . .', 'You ought to . . .' 'It is your responsibility . . .'
    creates 'obligation' or guilt feelings
    can cause person to 'dig in' and defend his or her position
    communicates lack of trust in person's sense of responsibility
4   *Advising, giving solutions or suggestions*
    'What I would do is . . .', 'Why don't you . . .', 'Let me suggest . . .'
    can imply person is not able to solve their problem
    prevents person from thinking through the problem, considering
    alternatives and trying them out for reality
    can cause dependency or resistance
5   *Persuading with logic, arguing, lecturing*
    'What I would do is . . .', 'The facts are . . .', 'Yes, but . . .'
    provokes defensive position and counter arguments
    often causes person to 'turn you off', to quit listening to you
    can cause person to feel inferior, inadequate
b.  *Judgmental messages* (The hidden message is a put-down—'There's
    something wrong with you')
6   *Judging, criticising, blaming*
    'You are not thinking maturely . . .', 'You are lazy . . .'
    implies incompetency, stupidity, poor judgment
    cuts off communication from the person for fear of negative judgments
    person often accepts the judgment as true (e.g. 'I'm bad') or retaliates
    (e.g. 'You're not so great yourself')
7   *Praising, agreeing*
    'Well, I think you're doing a great job!', 'You're right that person sounds
    terrible!'
    implies high expectations as well as supervision of the other person's
    behaviour
    can be seen as patronising or as a manipulative effort to encourage
    desired behaviour
    can cause anxiety when person's perception of self doesn't match your
    praise
8   *Name-calling, ridiculing*
    'Cry-baby', 'Okay, Mr Smarty . . .'
    cause person to feel unworthy, uncared for
    can have devastating effect on self-image
    often provokes verbal retaliation
9   *Analysing, diagnosing*
    'What's wrong with you is . . .', 'You're just tired', 'You don't really mean
    that'

**Table 15   (Cont.)**

---

can be threatening and frustrating
person can feel either trapped, exposed or not believed
stops person from communicating for fear of distortion or exposure
10  *Reassuring, sympathising*
'Don't worry', 'You'll feel better', 'Oh, cheer up!'
causes person to feel misunderstood
evokes strong feelings of hostility (That's easy for you to say!')
person often picks up a message of 'It's not all right for you to feel that way'
c.  *Avoiding messages* (The hidden message says 'I don't want to deal with this')
11  *Diverting, sarcasm, withdrawal*
'Let's talk about pleasant things . . .', 'Why don't you try running the world', remaining silent, turning away.
implies that life's difficulties are to be avoided rather than dealt with
can imply person's problems are unimportant, petty or invalid
stops openness from person when they are experiencing a difficulty

---

interested, welcoming, doubtful, upset, enthusiastic, at ease. When you are interviewing or counselling, remember how you looked in these various roles and focus on the positive ones.

## Activity 58   Seating and body position

The following exercises will help you to learn the most appropriate seating and body positions for helping the other person relax and feel accepted and listened to. You will need a partner for these exercises.
a.  Distance. You and your partner sit facing each other. Start about two metres apart, then move in gradually until your partner feels at a comfortable distance for counselling. What is the comfortable distance?
b.  Height. Your partner talks and you listen while you sit in (i) a lower chair, (ii) a higher chair, (iii) a chair of the same height as his. Reverse roles and discuss how you each felt in the various situations.
c.  Angle. Your partner talks and you listen while (i) sitting facing him squarely on, (ii) sitting at 90 degrees to him, (iii) sitting side by side. Then move your chair round until your partner indicates that this is the comfortable angle for being counselled.
d.  Posture. Both seated, your partner talks and you listen while you (i) have arms and legs tightly crossed, (ii) sprawl loosely, (iii) sit with a slight lean forward.

## Activity 59   Encouragers and mirroring

Good television interviewers or chat-show hosts are skilled in making remarks or minimal encouragers that demonstrate attentiveness and enable the conversation to continue but do not take it over. In the counselling context such minimal encouragers might be, 'Could you tell me how you see your situation?'; 'Where would you like to start today?'; 'Can you tell me in your own words what is concerning you?'; 'Really'; 'I see'; 'Can you tell me more?'; 'Go on'; 'Um-hum'; 'Yes'; 'Ah'; 'Then'. The message contained in all these statements is 'Go on, I'm with you, I'm listening and following you.' This encourages the client to speak.

Mirroring, or restating what the client has just said, is another way of confirming that you are listening attentively, e.g. 'You say that you have difficulty understanding the instructions given by your supervisor'; 'You want to resign'; 'You would like to know what your future is with this company'. This again encourages the client to elaborate further.

## Activity 60   Minimal encouragers

You will need a partner who will discuss some topic of interest. You must use a variety of minimal encouragers.
Avoid too-frequent repetition of the same encourager.

## Activity 61   Mirroring and repetition

Get your partner to describe a real or fictitious problem in one or two sentences. Try to remember exactly what has been said. This forces you to pay attention! Then repeat what the partner said, only changing 'I' to 'you', 'my' to 'your', etc. Try this several times with different statements. Try to reflect the partner's tone of voice and intensity of feeling in your mirroring.

## Activity 62   Mirroring and repetition 2

Have a partner read out the statements below. After each one, write down the mirroring response. At the end, compare your statements with the originals.

a.  I feel awkward talking to people at work. I feel that they are going to laugh at what I say.
b.  I was the last person taken on in the workshop. I am worried that I will be the first to be made redundant.

c. I feel slighted being passed over for promotion. Doesn't my work count here?
d. I'm worried about being made foreman. I can do the job all alright but my mates will make life hell for me.
e. My wife is objecting to me working overtime and never being at home. Is overtime compulsory?

Opening the interview

a. Set interviewee at ease—welcome—thank for coming
b. Set self at ease—open posture
c. Get interviewee to start talking about anything—use minimal encouragers and nonverbal signals
d. Ask about current concern and continue with minimal encouragers and mirroring as appropriate.

**Phase 2 Reflecting, exploring, understanding and challenging**
As the client responds to someone he recognises as clearly wanting to help him, he starts to understand more about himself and his problems, eventually exploring and personalising feelings, problems and goals. Helping the client restate the problem in a way that permits a solution to be found is a major aim of the second phase. The skills the counsellor uses now in addition to the skills of the first phase include *paraphrasing, summarising, clarifying, reflecting* and *questioning.*

*Paraphrasing* is the restating of the other's message in brief, in your own words, and without interpretation. It often captures only the last phrase, e.g. 'I'll have to take some time off; the pressure has really been building up' is paraphrased: 'The pressure has really been building up'. *Summarising* is like paraphrasing but involves expressing the essence of the problem in your own words.

*Clarifying* is a means of increasing the accuracy of your understanding of the client's message. Typical phrases used in a clarifying response include 'Are you saying . . .'; 'Does that include . . .'; 'Would this be an example . . .'; 'It seems to me that . . .'

*Reflecting* is like paraphrasing but feelings are paraphrased rather than content. The emphasis of the previous techniques has been on the content of the messages, i.e. what the speaker is saying. But the content is usually laden with feeling, as feelings are at the heart of most problems. Reflection brings feelings out into the open by identifying and verbalising them. For example, the client says: 'The other receptionist I work with has turned her back on me; I don't know why. I think she is trying to criticise me behind my back. Damn!' The counsellor might reply: 'You feel quite angry about this.' The counsellor thus demonstrates empathy. Once the counsellor has reflected the feelings and brought them into the open, it is easier for the client to acknowledge the feelings and admit to them.

Let silences occur without feeling you have to fill them. Silence allows time for reflection and thinking. Don't interrupt a silence unnecessarily.

*Questioning* needs to be used sparingly, or the client may feel threatened, especially if you question facts or content. Questioning can be useful to help clients define or evaluate their value system—'Is that really important to you?'—or to examine consequences or alternatives—'What would happen if you did x?'. Open-ended questions rather than closed questions should be used, e.g. 'How do you feel about it?' rather than 'Do you want to hit your boss when he says that to you?', which only requires a yes or no response. *Probing* is a form of questioning in which you select a word or phrase and restate it in a questioning manner, e.g. 'I don't know which training course to apply for. It's all confusing to me.' Reply: 'Confusing?'

The end of Phase 2 comes when the client can say, 'I think I can do something about it now; I need to look at some of the options.' Having been nudged in the right direction, the client is able to start moving ahead. Here are a few activities that provide practice in some of the skills of Phase 2.

## Activity 63   Paraphrasing and summarising

Write a paraphrase and a summary for each of the statements below.

a.   I don't respect the supervisor I report to. He is unable to do the tasks we are expected to do.
b.   I give all my energy to work and I've none left when I get home.
c.   I have worked here five years and all I get is the routine stuff. Doesn't anyone trust me?
d.   As you get older you start looking forward to retirement but I never expected it to come so suddenly, out of the blue.
e.   I've been made redundant. My life seems purposeless now.
f.   Who the hell does the production manager think he is, pushing us around like that?
g.   I don't really know what my boss wants. He says I'm doing fine, then he blows up over nothing. I don't know what is going on— he is so inconsistent. I wonder whether I am in the right job.
i.   Sometimes I think I am living a lie. I've no real interest in the job. But I'm settled in the community and I don't know that I could cope with a change of job or location.
j.   It's not a big thing but it is the third time this month that I have been asked to change hours with her. It certainly shows who is

more important—why has it always got to be me who defers to her?

## Activity 64    Reflection of feelings

Use the statements in Activity 63. For each one write several statements expressing the feelings that the interviewee could be experiencing. Try to avoid 'You feel . . .' on every occasion. Genuineness requires that you respond to other people naturally, using your own style. e.g. 'I had a hard time coming back in to work today. I didn't know whether my job would still be here or what sort of excuse I could make for being away again.' To this you might reply: 'You've been asking yourself how you will be received. It's not easy for you at this present moment' rather than 'You felt uneasy about what might happen when you came in today.'

## Activity 65    Open questions and probes

Read each statement, then write an open question (can't be answered by a simple yes/no) and a probe.

a. I dislike my supervisor. I'm afraid I'll get fired if I say anything. Yet if I don't I feel I'll go crazy.
b. Being unemployed has made me feel beneath everyone else. I have thought seriously of suicide.
c. This new automatic machine is difficult to control. I don't think I have the skill.
d. I am unhappy being relocated to this country town. I know my old branch was not doing too well but I feel very lonely.

### Phase 3    Problem solving strategies and resourcing
On the basis of this new understanding, action is initiated to solve the problem and attain new goals, with the counsellor giving, guiding, directing the client to whatever resources he needs to effect the solution and manage the problem. Decision-making skills come into play and the model of decision-making skills presented later in this chapter will provide for this phase. One other skill the interviewee needs is knowing how to set goals to aim for which will solve the problem.

### Goal setting
A goal must be specific, measurable and realistically attainable. It is no use simply saying, 'I want an accountancy qualification.' You need to know which qualification, where you plan to obtain it, whether you will do so by part-time or fulltime study and so on. The goal may

thus become to gain a Diploma in Accountancy from the local TAFE by evening part-time study over six years. Once the goal is established, sub-goals or steps must be developed. The first step might be to write to various academic institutions asking for brochures and information on the accountancy courses they offer. Further steps are planned out in collaboration with the counsellor if necessary. The essential feature of each step is that it is attainable, so that progress to the final goal is in an appropriate sequence, manageable and within a reasonable time frame.

A major element of Phase 3 is evaluating options and trying out the most feasible. The counsellor should be prepared to let the client take more charge and eventually to drop out of the scene, but should always be ready to come back in if needed. In some cases the counsellor may refer the client on to other experts who can provide specific resources.

## Activity 66   Setting goals

Assess and analyse a problem drawn from your life. Write out your end goal and then write out the sub-goals or steps that will take you there. Remember to state your goals in specific, realistic and measurable terms.

### The balance sheet
The balance sheet is a decision-making aid. It helps counsellees to examine the consequences of different lines of action in the light of their values (Can I live with this course of action?) and usefulness (Will this course of action get me to where I want to go?). It also helps counsellees consider benefits and losses not just for themselves but also for significant others in their lives. Figure 15 is an example. A newly married man has been offered promotion within the company provided he move to the other side of the continent. He is trying to decide between moving or staying in a less well-paid, dead-end job.

## Activity 67   The balance sheet

Use the Balance Sheet as practice to help resolve any dilemma you now have.

Here is a summary example of the three stages of counselling.

*Phase 1*   Distressed client entering counselling: 'I have no future in this company now we are automating.'
*Phase 2*   Insight into problem: 'Yes, I really do need to learn some skills in using the new equipment.'

**Figure 15   Promotion with relocation**

| Gain for self:<br>Promotion more money | Acceptable to me<br>because:<br>I want to get on in my<br>career and earn more | Not acceptable to me<br>because:<br>Other more local jobs<br>might turn up |
|---|---|---|
| Losses for self:<br>See parents family<br>upset at losing friends | Acceptable to me<br>because:<br>Can afford to visit<br>parent & friends | Not acceptable to me<br>because:<br>Children will miss their<br>grandparents |
| Gains for significant<br>others:<br>Better house, holidays<br>etc for family | Acceptable to me<br>because:<br>I want to provide the<br>good things in life for<br>them | Not acceptable to me<br>because:<br>Money isn't everything—<br>family support is<br>important |
| Losses for significant<br>others:<br>Spouse loses support<br>groups<br>Children change school | Acceptable to me<br>because:<br>All are fairly adaptable | Not acceptable to me<br>because:<br>Cause stress to rest of<br>family |
| Gains for social setting:<br>Could afford golf club | Acceptable to me<br>because:<br>I must meet<br>professional clients | Not acceptable to me<br>because:<br>Time away from wife<br>and family |
| Losses for social<br>setting:<br>Lose friends—have to<br>find new ones | Acceptable to me<br>because:<br>I am a sociable person<br>and won't have difficulty | Not acceptable to me<br>because:<br>My current friends are a<br>great set. |

*Phase 3*   Resourcing: 'The local TAFE prospectus you gave me to look at had some part-time courses in the skills I need. I am going to apply.'

In group counselling, six to eight clients are counselled by the one counsellor at the same time for about one hour a session. There are obvious economies to this format. All the counsellees must want to be members of the group and be willing to contribute to the open discussions. The benefits are that employees realise they have common problems, develop insight into the problems and associated feelings, realise they are accepted by others and not alone, and recognise that they are capable of helping, understanding and accepting each other. There are disadvantages, in that some individuals feel threatened by the group context and the counsellor's interaction with each individual is limited.

## Participation in decision-making

Decision-making has traditionally been vested in the upper echelons of organisations. Scientific management theory held that the hierarchical concentration of power was the most efficient, enabling managers to manage and obviating the need for workers to be distracted from their duties by having to make decisions. However, research shows that lack of participation or opportunity to contribute, particularly in times of change, is associated with negative emotional states, stress reactions, declining health and increased absenteeism.

Among other things, increased participation serves to increase information available to employees so they don't function on and react to unsubstantiated rumour about what changes are to be made and how they will be affected. Workers feel that they have an influence; this gives them a sense of control over a bigger part of their lives and improves self-esteem. They thus manifest less emotional distress over events which may not initially be favourable to them.

In surveys about what workers most want out of a job the top place nearly always goes to 'Having work that is meaningful and gives a feeling of accomplishment'. It does not seem to matter how much money is on offer, how much free time they get or how many hours they have to work—if workers have a feeling of accomplishment in their work and are recognised for it, their job stress is low and job satisfaction high. We all have a need to be thought worthwhile and to be rewarded, if only verbally, for what we do. Successful managers and companies try to satisfy these human needs and create a rewarding work environment even under conditions of change. Several methods can be used to do this and thereby reduce stress in the changing workplace. They are all to do with sensitive company–employee relationships.

1 Employees need to be involved in decision-making that affects them even if it is on a small scale. This can remove some anger and hostility as reasonable awareness of the potential changes replaces disconcerting rumour. Employees can plan, organise and think about their future with more certainty and acceptance. Job satisfaction and motivation are more likely to remain high.
2 Improved manager–employee relationships help to reduce tension, dissatisfaction and hostility. Involving employees as above is part of this improvement but managers also need to avoid being abrasive, abusive, intimidatory, arrogant, cold or aloof.
3 Sensitivity to working conditions is essential. Being insensitive to working conditions, to the effects on employees of changes in work practices and of future planning causes alienation, resentment,

anxiety and dissatisfaction, which eventually manifest as illness and/or absenteeism.

4  Give positive feedback wherever possible, recognise achievement, and provide warm support. Employees need to know that they are appreciated and that the work they are doing is valued. This enhances self-concept, enabling them to be more confident in their handling of change.

5  Avoid placing employees in role-conflict situations. Ensure that all know what they are expected to do and how they are to do it. Anxiety, lowered self-esteem and lowered self-confidence can result from difficulties in balancing role conflicts. In changing situations in the workplace, employees need to know how they are expected to operate in the new circumstances.

We cannot eliminate stress in the context of change but we can foster the conditions that will reduce it by responding to employee needs and establishing policies and procedures that reflect those needs. Small changes in attitudes, behaviour, and treatment of employees have a big impact on the health and well-being of everyone in the organisation including managers, whose own stress levels are closely tied those of their employees. Instead of saying, What is good for the company is good for everybody, we must say, What is good for everybody is good for the company.

## Decision-making

The changes in the world of work are making wise decision-making essential for managers and workers as career and life opportunities decrease. Having to make a decision can cause stress. How do we ever know we made the right one? How long can we delay making the decision? What will be the impact not just on ourselves but on others who have had no part to play in the decision? These and other questions cause decision-making to be fraught with anxiety.

A decision is a choice between a number of possible solutions to a problem. We often think of decisions as being something momentous in our lives but in fact we make decisions all day long, for example, should I get up immediately the alarm clock rings or should I have a few more minutes in bed; should I take an umbrella with me this morning? Being able to make decisions gives a person confidence. But as society becomes increasingly complex, more and more decisions have to be made and more of those decisions appear to be made on our behalf by other people. This causes us frustration and stress as we lose control of what happens to us, and also enables us to avoid making decisions. Then, when we have to make a decision, we are poorly prepared to do so.

Negative self-talk often gets in the way of making decisions, e.g. 'I

**Figure 16   The 'Decide' model**

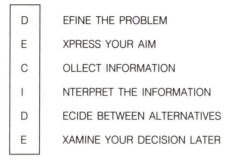

| D | EFINE THE PROBLEM |
| E | XPRESS YOUR AIM |
| C | OLLECT INFORMATION |
| I | NTERPRET THE INFORMATION |
| D | ECIDE BETWEEN ALTERNATIVES |
| E | XAMINE YOUR DECISION LATER |

don't know what I should do'; 'I don't think I could manage to . . .'. By constraining ourselves, we miss valuable opportunities. For most things in life you do have a choice. Similar lack of confidence and doubts about personal effectiveness are also displayed by those who have poor self-concepts or those who have an external locus of control.

Decisions aways contain risks; the problem is to choose the option with the best possible payoff and the highest probability that the payoff will come about. Decisions also occur in sequence. Later decisions may be constrained by the consequences of earlier decisions. This interdependence makes present decisions more important and in a sense more risky, because you cannot know all the ways in which a decision may affect your future range of choices.

*A decision-making model*

The six stages of making a decision are shown in Figure 16. The stages are easy to introduce to other people in a group teaching situation.

**1   Define the problem/determine the aim**
For some people, this step is the hardest; these people require counselling to help them recognise their problem. You will remember that the aim of Phase 2 in the counselling process was to enable the client to recognise the problem. The necessary first step in any kind of personal problem is to recognise that you have it. Once delineated, the problem or goal should be stated in clear, precise terms. Stating the problem as 'I want promotion' is too general. You will have a better chance of deciding on the best way to go if you state your problem or aim with specific goals in mind. For example, 'I want to move from being a bookkeeper to being an accountant within twelve months', or 'After two years as assistant sales manager I shall apply for sales manager posts in companies in the same field as my present post'. Decisions can then be made about, for example, further pro-

fessional training, which follow logically from the initial statement of the goal.

## 2 Express the aim or options

Options become obvious if the problem or goal is stated clearly. The options for further professional training in the example above might be part-time attendance while still maintaining a job, fulltime attendance, or a correspondence course.

## 3 Collect information

Gather information on each of the options. In the example, the relative financial costs of each option are of concern, as are the availability of student places in particular institutions, the time each option takes and the support of the employer for particular options. The more important the decision and the more impact the decision has on your future, the more important and worthwhile it is to collect as much information as possible.

## 4 Interpret the information

This is the stage where the information gathered on each option is weighed and sorted, and the options are evaluated.

## 5 Decide

One option or a combination of options is chosen as a result of the preceding evaluation and information-gathering. Unfortunately, one option may not stand out as the best, since one alternative might be better in some ways while another is better in other ways. Sometimes no alternative is better than any other. So conflict may still be present when you are trying to make a decision. At least this model will help to reduce the possibility of conflict.

## 6 Examine your decision later

Examining the actual consequences of a decision makes a lot of sense. It is never too late to change. Although certain options may be ruled out because of earlier decisions, there is usually something that can be done to improve a bad situation. The sooner you evaluate the consequences, the sooner you can get back on track. Minor adjustments made early to the course of a space mission can make a big difference to the final destination!

## Activity 68   Decision-making

Select one of the major decisions you are currently making or will have to make with reference to your career, work situation or work practice. Use the scheme outlined above and work through the first five stages.

# Summary

Humanising an organisation helps its members to cope with change. It involves developing support networks, encouraging staff at all levels to be involved in planning and initiating change in the workplace, and introducing Employee Assistance Programs. Counselling is an accepting, empathetic relationship that helps people manage their own problems. Lay counselling by peers can be extremely effective. Counselling skills can be learned. There are three phases in the counselling process: (i) getting a counselling relationship established by means of attentive listening, empathy, respect, genuineness, reinforcement (verbal and nonverbal) and acceptance; (ii) exploring and understanding by means of paraphrasing, reflecting and probing; (iii) using problem-solving strategies and resourcing. The use of all these skills makes clients feel valued, cared about and accepted and feel that what they are saying is important. People cope better if they are well supported by those around them.

Participation in decision-making requires some skill in learning how to make decisions. A model of decision-making is offered. By humanising the organisation and including workers at all levels in this decision-making process it should be possible to develop and promote a vision of the organisation and its mission that is acceptable to all staff.

# 7
# Special issues

*Today is the first day of the rest of your life*

We have considered the general problems managers and employees face in the current context of change and the human responses to those problems. However, two particular problems deserve more intensive consideration, namely involuntary relocation and involuntary job loss (unemployment/redundancy/enforced early retirement).

## Involuntary job loss

This is increasingly common today. Individual or large-scale lay-offs, plant closure, restructuring and rightsizing all result in redundancy or enforced early retirement for some. While some workers may initially be pleased to be offered early retirement or redundancy with a nice pay-out package, many have no real choice.

Work fulfils a variety of human needs besides the obvious one of money. It can provide:

- a sense of achievement
- a sense of responsibility
- intrinsic pleasure
- a time structure to the day, week and year
- opportunities for social interaction
- opportunities for the development of self-esteem and identity
- opportunities for regularly shared experiences with family and friends
- links to goals and purposes that transcend those of the individual—participation in a collective effort.

Involuntary disengagement from the workforce is thus a complex transition, involving loss of work role, loss of income, change in social interactions, change in identity, change in residence, change in daily schedule, change in health status. The person concerned may have a strong attachment to work or a weak one, a fulfilled work career or an unfulfilled one, a spouse who is also stopping work or one who will go on working. Different combinations of these factors act to a different extent on different people, so the individual response cannot be clearly predicted. Which particular response is due to which particular factor is uncertain.

Employees who seize the chance to retire early tend to be those in jobs of lower status or skill level who carry out tasks of low quality in mechanised line operations or do heavy, fatiguing jobs. Perceptions of declining health and reduced ability to keep up with physical job demands are also involved.

Those who take voluntary or planned retirement tend to show no decline in health status and to have positive attitudes to retirement. These attitudes stem from deliberate planning for retirement, and the development of interests outside work with support-group activities. All this leads to speedy adjustment to the new lifestyle. The general conclusion is that a planned transition from work to disengagement does not generally lead to poorer physical or mental health. Those on the other hand who are forced into early retirement or redundancy have trouble adjusting, develop health problems and report low levels of satisfaction about disengagement. This is mainly due to the sharp drop in income, the loss of a meaningful role, and missing the companionship of mates at work. The outcome of disengagement depends to a large extent on a person's attitude to it. This in turn is influenced by whether the disengagement was forced or voluntary, the person's self-concept, the meaningfulness of the work role, the existence of social and leisure interests, and the financial implications.

Most surveys and case studies reveal a similar pattern of physical, psychological and social effects for enforced job loss. Of course those forced to leave the workforce are not a homogeneous group who will all respond alike. They differ not only in work role and status but in health and psychological make-up. The way each individual experiences unemployment depends on his own unique circumstances. After the initial shock has disappeared, up to 20 per cent may come to regard unemployment as a liberating, constructive experience which forces them to reconsider their previous ways of life and challenges them to find more fulfilling ones. But this is still a small minority.

Studies carried out in other countries during times of rising unemployment reveal a strong correlation between increases in unemployment and the rates of suicide, admissions to mental hospitals, cirrhosis of the liver, and deaths due to cardiovascular disease. There are also reports of increased susceptibility to influenza, colds, asthma and the like. Ian Webster, the Professor of Public Health at the University of New South Wales, suggests that unemployment is a major public health issue. According to Derek Silove, Professor of Psychiatry at Liverpool Hospital in Sydney, unemployment is responsible for a hidden epidemic of emotional disorders, particularly depression. There is no specific funding to meet this current epidemic which will become an added burden to an already underfunded health service.

After studying longevity in a number of cultures, a team of physicians at Harvard University concluded that people who no longer have a necessary role to play in the social and economic life of their society generally deteriorate rapidly. In a similar vein, Phillip Lynch, a researcher on heart disease, concluded in his book *The Broken Heart* that a major factor in heart disorders and deaths due to heart disease is loneliness. And that what often causes such loneliness is people's failure to take on roles that place them in ongoing intimate relationships with others, or the loss of such roles. While retirement can be satisfying, there is no doubt that it is a tremendous upheaval if not prepared for.

The most recalcitrant problem of becoming unemployed arises from those aspects of work which meet the basic human need for structure in both the physical and social environment. It is a problem of not being in work rather than of not being employed. At a physical level there is lassitude, a slowing of movement, a loss of muscle tone; at a psychological level there is boredom, depression, resignation; socially there is withdrawal. Time not only hangs heavy but the sense of time breaks down and actions seem purposeless. Unemployed people commonly relate a pattern of life like this: 'I sleep in until midday, then sit around eating, watch movies until midnight.' The boredom, frustration and crushing loss of self-confidence that set in make the job search harder and the routine of doing nothing eventually overrides any thought of looking for work.

Studies of unemployment in the United States and in Britain correlate peak unemployment rates with peak mortality rates. A study of men in Edinburgh from 1968 to 1981 found that the rate of attempted suicide throughout that period was ten times higher among unemployed men than among those with jobs. A 1981 survey of unemployed men in Canberra found that 50 per cent had a psychiatric disorder after five months of unemployment. A 1986 study in Adelaide found higher levels of stress-related symptoms, surgical interventions and long-term health problems among unemployed middle-aged men.

It is widely assumed that these destructive effects will largely disappear as the concept of being 'unemployed' loses its stigma, as the unemployed come to share more equitably in the wealth of the community and as more resources are provided for leisure. But it is not that simple. Work gives life a structure by specifying time, place and social relationship patterns, whereas leisure pursuits are often individualistic or conducted in parallel rather than interdependently. So unemployed people will still lack the structure work provides. To be unemployed is to feel different, ineffective, looked down upon, excluded from the normal patterns of life of 'normal' people. In losing work, people lose not only occupational but social identity. The outcome is a syndrome of retreatism in which they withdraw from much of their former social network. The significance of becoming unemployed is that it invalidates many of the basic expectations they had of themselves. These unmet needs account for the deep frustration that the majority of enforced job losers feel.

Enforced removal from the workforce, if sudden, cannot be planned for, and it is the lack of preparation for disengagement that causes most personal problems. A turmoil of negative feeling can dominate the thinking and behaviour of employees who lose their job through no fault of their own.

First, there is the feeling of rejection: someone has apparently made a judgment that one cannot carry out the work required or that one is unwanted in that role for other reasons. Second, one may feel anger towards others, perhaps unknown others, who have decided one's fate, and anger and suspicion towards colleagues who may have not suffered the same fate. Third, there is self-blame and guilt as anger is turned inwards and as a sense of failure as worker, spouse, parent and breadwinner permeates all one's thinking about the situation. There is usually worry over financial loss, and a void to fill in place of paid employment. The self-concept changes to take account of the new feelings and role. Common attitudes of early retirees that reflect a poor self-concept are:

- Demanding attention from others simply because you are retired rather than earning attention through your own courteous behaviour.
- Looking as though you have no self-respect by dressing untidily, taking little care over appearance.
- Complaining constantly.
- Walking dejectedly.
- Commenting negatively about younger people.

All these behaviours occur when one feels left out of the community. If you are in pain over the loss of a job, don't get bogged down with unexpressed emotions but share your thoughts, fears and frustrations in a sensible way with family and friends. Once you have expressed these fears, it is likely you will feel rid of excess baggage and more positive about yourself and your new role.

Two theories have been propounded to explain how some people do take positive steps to combat the disillusion of unemployment. *Activity theory* says that you are most likely to maintain a positive self-image by replacing former satisfying activities with new forms of participation. We have seen in earlier chapters that self-esteem is often dependent on roles and status and that life can seem empty without such roles. In this sense it is a positive move to find replacement roles to maintain satisfaction in life. However, it is not necessary to be active to be a successful early retirer. *Disengagement theory* views 'successful' unemployment as a mutual disengagement of individual and society. This means that after retirement some people become more passive, more introverted and less interested in achieving than when they were younger. But disengagement can be dangerous if it leads to intense self-reflection and/or the feeling that society does not want you any more. Disengagement must be done by choice and must revolve around the enjoyment of a less competitive, more leisurely life doing what you enjoy doing. This is to be seen as one of the rewards of retirement.

Retirement only means leaving paid work behind. It does not mean leaving reality behind. Although you may lose support systems, a continuing income and daily contact with work colleagues, it's up to you to take charge of your life. Avoid making excuses for not doing things, e.g. poor health, no money. These may be true but rarely is health so bad or finances so strapped that some activity isn't possible. Set goals to achieve certain things at different times in the future. Simply surviving in retirement is not enough. Early retirement has to be seen as a new phase in life when a new lifestyle is created, when time is used imaginatively and when you make things happen.

Companies could help former employees for whom they currently have no work by developing self-help groups which would deal with job-search and interviewing skills and maintaining self-esteem and psychological well-being, and would offer leisure pursuits, free health advice and counselling, and opportunities for retraining and meeting together. The ex-employees would be in better physical and psychological shape to re-enter the workforce and the organisation would have a stock of skilled people ready and willing to work for it again. Setting one room aside with a coffee bar in which ex employees could meet and make use of such services would cost little yet provide a back-up workforce for when the economy turns around.

## Activity 69   Retirement activities

Create a list of activities you and perhaps your family might start or get involved in within the informal economy and local community. For example, toy-making; bee-keeping for honey; bicycle repair or hire. Plan how you might start up each activity should you become redundant.

*Changing concepts of career, work, job and leisure*

In considering the adjustment problems of those about to become unemployed, four particular concepts need to be thought about clearly by those engaged in designing training programs. The terms career, work, job and leisure are changing in meaning and implication, and both managers and employees will need to adjust their perceptions of these terms. Retention of traditional perceptions will retard general adjustment to the changes and impede the acceptability of their implications for life transitions.

**Work and job are not the same**
Work is not synonymous with a job. A job is conventional employment. Work is useful activity which may or may not be performed for money. There is plenty of work for everyone even though there may not be jobs for everyone. All the trends noted in the opening chapter suggest that the conception of these terms is slowly changing. There was a time when 'the job' was the central organising principle of life. Living arrangements, income, voting pattern, possessions, family size, hours worked, everything, in fact, was determined in large measure by the nature of the job. Satisfaction in one's work contributes significantly to one's emotional balance. Work helps satisfy not only a person's economic needs but also personal needs for acceptance, companionship, self-esteem and the esteem of others. Work enables us to gain fulfilment and satisfaction. It gives us our principal basis for mattering. It provides a role, a purpose, enables us to contribute and earn respect. Work is not solely about money but also about identity. This explains why changes in work practices, or in whether you work at all, can lead to demoralisation, loss of self-esteem, and alienation.

In Toffler's technological and information society, the entire present occupational structure of society will be disturbed. In the past children knew what occupations would be available for them when they grew up. Yet in a generation, the notion of having a single occupation for one's entire life will seem quaintly antique. The job will no longer serve as people's anchor and organising principle, providing psychological and social identity. Some jobs will simply disappear; others as yet unthought-of will spring up. This will affect the texture of life for millions of workers and their families. On current figures from the United States, most workers can expect to change occupations four times in their working life.

The hidden or black economy meets these needs without formal employment. By do-it-yourself jobs, neighbourly help, and other private commercial activities not only income but life structure, self-esteem and social contacts are maintained. Employees who have identified too closely with their jobs create an identity dependence. When they cut the umbilical cord connecting them to their job placenta, they must learn to breathe on their own.

We need to recognise that work, income, and self-esteem need not come from one source, employment, as in the past. We need to develop individuals whose self-esteem and identity are not dependent on a job, who can find work possibilities for themselves other than a paid job and derive income from sources other than job-linked wages. It is a matter of teaching people not only how to find a job but also how to live without a job. There may be more people than jobs in the formal economy, but there is more work than people available if you know how to find it. Job creation will come not from big business as it invests in technology but from one-person operations which have the potential for growth. The share of total employment accounted for by small enterprises of around twenty employees appears to be increasing (Leadbeater and Lloyd 1987). As E.F. Schumacher (1974) said, 'small is beautiful'. So when jobs are not plentiful we must try to ensure that people alter their conception of work so that self-esteem, the sense of being needed, self-respect and acceptance are byproducts of whatever they may turn their hands to, even if it is not a conventional job.

**Leisure**
Leisure is not necessarily the opposite of work. Many people already, and more in future, will work at their leisure pursuit. Leisure is not simply non-activity, recovery time, relaxation or even plain self-indulgence; it may be all these but it is also, and will become more so, a form of personal and family development where interests and hobbies may form the basis of a satisfying activity or another career. This is a far cry from the Protestant work ethic which held that work was our ticket to Heaven. A life with a lot of time for leisure is not necessarily an idle or purposeless life. It depends what you do with the time. The extension of leisure is the corollary of the shrinking role of the job. The working week has been cut by 50 per cent since the turn of the century and by the year 2000 it will have been reduced again. We cannot shrug the implications aside.

Paid employment is a major factor in defining the time parameters of, and giving structure to, an individual's life. Unemployment and involuntary early retirement place the individual outside this taken-for-granted system. Work, even boring work, is a source of money, a chance to be with friends and an alternative to the boredom of unemployment. This is revealed in the complaints of workers who have lost their jobs: 'Not having anything to look forward to when you get up in the morning'; 'Getting on everyone's nerves just sitting around'; 'You can't go out with your mates when they are working';

'There is no difference between the weekend and the rest of the week'; 'It's only leisure when your mates get off work'.

Periods of unproductive job searching and prolonged periods of boredom accumulate into a structureless, confused time state and a sense of general debility, leaving people unmotivated and unprepared to take advantage of any recreational and educational opportunities that may be available. Unlimited and unstructured time is not leisure but a heavy burden.

If you have no work, the concept of leisure as relaxation is insulting. Doing something that matters in leisure should be the aim, whether as an individual or family activity. If we can define work and leisure in much broader ways, the stigmas of redundancy, retirement and unemployment will fade. In any case, these terms only make sense in a world where it is assumed that everyone is employed for a wage by someone else. Self-employed people have never been able to become unemployed or redundant. Neither do housewives retire; they do less housework more slowly as age progresses. In the future, people will have more flexible work commitments, which they will tailor to suit themselves, sometimes working for others; sometimes working for themselves using leisure skills and talents; sometimes working with others in an entrepreneurial cooperative venture. The possibilities are many.

What will we do or feel like when the job no longer fills the day? How will the role of the father be transformed when he is no longer the family provider? How will people determine their self-esteem and their esteem for each other when work is less central to their lives? We must prepare for this.

One of the major challenges for those without a job is to find functional roles which are meaningful and satisfying and which can replace the social loss brought about by job loss. Recreation must not be simply a filling in of time but must have a purpose—personal fulfilment. In a practical sense, leisure means being able to choose from a variety of pleasures such as reading, walking, bridge, gardening, talking with friends etc. Where the strategy comes in is being able to schedule these activities so they continue to be enjoyable. Another trick is to have a broad range of interests so that you can:

alternate between physical activities (swimming, walking) and mental ones (reading, bridge, studying)
alternate between activities that can be done alone (craft, reading, music) and social activities (dancing, card games, golf)
try out an activity you have never indulged in.

Another valuable activity is returning to education. This can open the doors to a variety of other activities, and potential jobs. Formal education is no longer just for the young.

The development of hobbies and skills through leisure and a return to education can also provide a source of earning power and self-employment. Offering a service to other people such as fix-it jobs, babysitting, gardening, delivery service, teaching a craft, not only brings in money but provides social contact. Seasonal and part-time jobs are often available and can use existing work skills. For those who do not need to earn money, volunteer work with hospitals, Meals on Wheels, family support, home help, driving and escorting can bring considerable happiness and contentment.

**Career**
The 'one career for life' approach of career guidance is finished, as is the notion of fitting a person to a career. Career has formerly implied identity with a lifelong endeavour. Continuous and increasing occupational obsolescence has made one's occupation an unsuitable, even dangerous anchor for identity. Identity needs to be anchored instead to transferable skills, rocks that can hold fast over a lifetime. We should no longer ask 'What is your occupation?' but 'What skills do you have?' A variety of skills and a highly adaptable personality will be needed in the future. Success in the world of work will be based on the ability to adapt to a changing labour market by using a range of portable or general skills.

This scenario suggests a drastic rethinking of career guidance, from a simple process of matching personal abilities to job requirements leading to a once-and-for-all decision, to a process of developing resourceful, flexible individuals who can see opportunity in change and who have alternative sources of identity and self-esteem outside the work role. Vertical career progression, controlled by level of skill, qualification, age, experience, ambition and even influence, will be replaced for many people by discontinuous, horizontal and circular career patterns. These will require flexibility and a willingness to retrain at intervals, and will demand that individuals consider lateral development or new starts as acceptable and attractive as promotion used to be.

Recurrent education and training, shorter working weeks, job sharing, short-term contracts, cooperative self-help ventures, self-employment, sabbaticals and early retirement will be some of the building blocks of individually designed and constructed working lives. We need to make a virtue of diversity, encouraging initiative and flexibility in career thinking, producing adaptable, confident and resourceful workers. Such people can find work even if they cannot find jobs.

The people we should aim to develop for the world of tomorrow are very much like Abraham Maslow's self-actualised person. They can stand confidently, participate fully and learn continually in their world. They possess the independence, the freedom, and the skills to approach their world as a series of surmountable problems over which they have some control. They have the ability to recognise and choose from a variety of options and to accept fully the consequences of and responsibility for their actions. They have the ability to adapt to changing conditions. They recognise that truth is evolutionary and unstable. Thus they act in the knowledge that learning and change are continuous lifetime processes.

**What can you do to prepare for a retirement that might come at any time?**
Promote alternative aspects of your life aside from work, so that if someone asks you what you do you can reply without mentioning work, i.e. refer to your involvement in your club, your recent bicycle tour, the latest novel you read, the home decorating job.

Associate with others outside the job arena. Nothing is more confining than people's tendency to limit their social relationships to the people with whom they work.

Don't use your job as an escape. Be proud of your job but don't let it become a crutch or a shield to hide behind. Don't give in to the temptation to use the demands of your job to avoid facing your personal problems.

Develop and maintain outside interests. A good balance of occupational, social, cultural and recreational interests will help you become a well rounded and adjusted person.

Cherish and nurture your individuality.

**What can organisations do to help those facing enfored job loss plan for it?**
Six possible elements of a valid program preparing employees for potential job loss are identified below. They involve in various ways the changing conceptions of work, career and leisure. Many of the elements are not exclusively related to unemployment, and could benefit those still in the workforce. They are portable skills that provide: self-confidence and the ability to make wise decisions that triumph over uncertainty and multiple options; resourcefulness and adaptability in the face of ambiguity and change; personal strengths and interpersonal skills to cope with new demands on self-esteem and identity; communication and relationship skills; and an emphasis on the positive use of leisure to develop new employability skills. An overarching element common to several of the aspects is self confidence or self-esteem. For example, it is important that people not only know about the benefits and rights available to them if unemployed but also have the confidence to claim them. Again, confidence is an important ingredient of job search and job acquisition skills.

*Elements of a supportive training course to help those likely to meet involuntary job loss*

1  **Employability skills**—to equip employees with skills which increase their chances of finding and keeping a job.

   job search skills
   job acquisition skills
   job retention skills
   awareness of factors that may affect prospects of particular kinds
     of employment

2  **Survival skills**—to equip employees with the knowledge and personal skills they need to survive if they are unemployed.

   knowledge of unemployment and welfare benefits
   knowledge of redundancy rights
   knowledge of superannuation/taxation issues
   skills of handling a limited budget
   awareness of 'entrepreneurship' and black economy
   stress management skills for coping with psychological, social
     and emotional effects of being unemployed
   decision-making skills
   positive thinking and self-esteem enhancement skills
   communication skills.

3  **Adaptability awareness**—to extend the knowledge of employment opportunities which employees feel are possible for them.

   awareness of relocation
   awareness of skill training.

4  **Leisure skills**—to equip employees with knowledge and skills which will help them make good use of their increased leisure time if unemployed.

   knowledge of possible leisure activities
   knowledge of local leisure facilities
   knowledge of voluntary community work
   skills of managing own time.

5  **Contextual awareness**—to help employees understand the extent to which the responsibility for likely unemployment lies with society rather than with the individual.

   awareness of the effects of technological change
   awareness of government policies
   awareness of possible alternative patterns of work and leisure.

6  **Opportunity-creation skills**—to equip employees with the knowl-

edge and skills they need to be able to create if necessary their own employment.

    knowledge of job sharing possibilities and procedures
    knowledge of self-employment possibilities
    skills of thinking about work in a proactive rather than reactive
      way
    self-esteem enhancement and positive thinking skills.

There is now a mandatory training requirement placed on employers by the Federal Government and supervised by the Taxation Office. In the 1991–92 tax year all employers must spend 1.5 per cent of their wages bill on approved training programs. A course in some or all of the above would certainly be a valid part of a company's training initiative. However, in designing a training program relating to the issue of how to cope with unemployment, careful attention needs to be paid to the overall aims being promulgated. Such a program could have any of four very different sociopolitical functions.

a.  Social control—adapting individuals to the job opportunities that realistically are open to them.
b.  Social change—making employees aware of the deficiencies in the employment system and of how they can help to change it.
c.  Individual change—accepting the social system as it is and aiming to maximise the chances of individual employees within it.
d.  Non-directive—making employees aware of the full range of opportunities and helping them to be more autonomous in choosing alternatives suited to their own needs and preferences.

These four approaches can be distinguished along two dimensions: whether the approach basically accepts the status quo or is concerned with changing it in prescribed directions; and whether the primary focus of the training is on the individual or on society (Figure 17). The categories and training curricula relationships in Figure 17 are not as mutually exclusive as the diagram suggests. Nonetheless there are tensions between them. It is important that the assumptions and values implied by decisions as to what to include in such a training program be explicitly recognised. For example, a trainer or manager who believes that an unemployed person is usually a layabout may have difficulty dealing with more non-directive elements in a course, such as elements 2 and 4 above. Whatever the ideology of the trainer or manager, the primary focus should be individual needs rather than societal needs. But any training, however focused on the individual, also implies a set of assumptions about the present and future role of work in society and the role of organisational goals.

We have seen from the discussion in the Introduction that the two main causes of the decline in levels of employment are (i) structural

**Figure 17   Relationships between objectives and curricula elements**

|  | Focusing on individuals | Focusing on society |
|---|---|---|
| Change | Individual change approach To maximise students' chances of finding meaningful employment (Elements 1, 2 and 3). | Social change approach To help students to see unemployment as a social phenomenon which can only be resolved by political and social change (Element 5) |
| Status quo | Non-directive approach To make students aware of the possibility of unemployment, and to help them to determine how they might cope with it and use it positively (Elements 2, 3, 4 and 6) | Social control approach To reinforce students' motivation to seek work, and to make them feel that unemployment is a result of personal inadequacy (Elements 1, 2, 3) |

changes resulting from technological innovation and from management practices designed to improve productivity and reduce unit labour costs, and (ii) cyclical changes corresponding to the economic cycle of recession and recovery. In the case of those affected by cyclical unemployment, while attention needs to be paid to providing the skills to cope with temporary unemployment, reinforcing the work ethic is vital too. Positive attitudes to work and to self need to be maintained or even enhanced so that opportunities can be exploited once an upturn occurs in the economy. If unemployment is seen as a long-term structural phenomenon, attention shifts to equipping employees to cope with long-term unemployment. In this context, the promotion of a narrowly based work ethic is highly questionable. It raises expectations that cannot be met and this in turn leads to personal distress and social unrest. For the long-term unemployed, self-esteem, feeling needed and obtaining satisfaction in life will have to come from sources other than work. Employees facing this prospect need help in choosing and developing these alternative sources, so they are encouraged and equipped to create their own work. 'Give a man a fish and you feed him for a day; teach him to fish and you feed him for life.'

*Force-field analysis*

Job loss is usually not a planned, deliberate affair; for the most part we get forced into it. Very few people plan to be redundant, or knowingly take a job with a company that is going bankrupt. Once the immediate shock of impending or actual change has hit, some planning is needed to discover how best to tackle this life transition.

**Figure 18   My personal force-field**

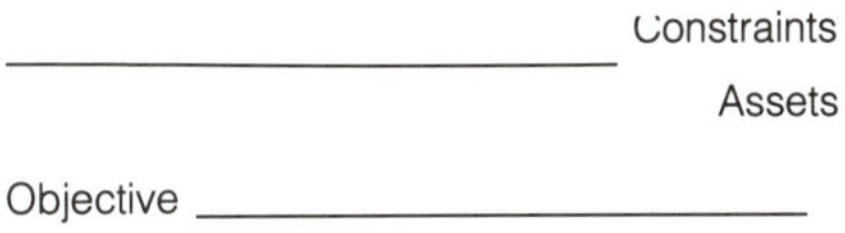

Constraints
Assets

Objective _____

One way of analysing the situation is to use the technique of *force-field analysis*. This technique encourages us to re-evaluate the situation and perceive elements of it in different ways.

To start a force-field analysis draw a horizontal line, with arrows pointing at the line from below and from above. Label the upper arrows 'constraints' and the lower arrows 'assets', as in Figure 18. List against each arrow on the assets side the potentially positive elements in the change situation. Similarly, list against the upper arrows those elements of the situation that you see as constraints. These arrows can be regarded as forces opposing each other. Finally, write down your aim or objective, what you would like to achieve, or be, or do. If the pressure on the top of the line is too great, then the constraints are too great and you are likely to feel overwhelmed and unable to perceive some of the more positive elements trying to push their way through from underneath the mess. If the lists balance you may well feel very frustrated as your advantages are held in check. In this situation, either you have to build up more advantages, adding to the list below until it outweighs the constraining forces above, or re-evaluate or eliminate some of the constraints to permit the push from below. This latter ploy is often easier than you might think, as many constraints are not as fixed or as real as they initially appear.

This is the problem of a production manager in a domestic electrical appliance factory who has unexpectedly been made redundant and cannot see how to cope. His ambition is to be self-employed and run a small business in a field where he has considerable technical knowledge. Previously, he has thought only of the immediate constraints and problems, such as how to pay the mortgage, his lack of formal business training, his loss of faith in himself, how he can continue to help his aged parents. But when he is encouraged to look at his assets, he realises that the proceeds of selling the house, plus the redundancy payment, should come to more than enough to buy outright a small business with a house attached in a small town. The aged parents could come too, and the continuity of strong family bonds would help them all cope better. The secret of the resolution of the problem lay in re-evaluating the various factors and seeing the positive nature of what had initially been some traumatic issues. The assets overcame the constraints.

**Figure 19   Mr Js forcefield**

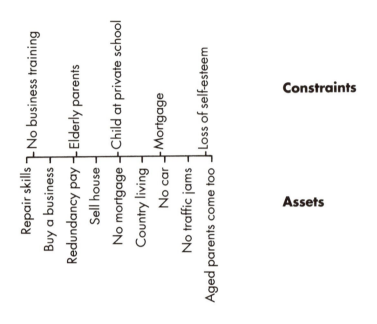

*Objective*:   To own and run a small electrical goods repair shop in a country town

When change hits you, you must evaluate where you want to go with your life. Perceive change, even if forced on you, as an invaluable opportunity to assess the direction you should best take for the sort of life you wish to lead. Of course, in doing this force-field analysis you may have several alternative objectives; draw up a diagram for each of them. One option should start to stand out as you evaluate the constraints–assets balance more closely. All you need to do then is plan your strategy to achieve the goal. Finally, to make the action plan work you must set a timetable, with reasonable deadlines. Establish sub-goals, the achievement of each of which will lead logically into the next step.

## Involuntary relocation and its effects

More managers and employees than ever are having to face the prospect of moving to another part of Australia if they wish to retain a job as companies rationalise, close uneconomic plant, and introduce new technology. Many move out of fear that if they pass up a transfer or a job offer their career, earning ability, lifestyle will all be jeopardised. Therefore few employees feel they can afford to refuse a transfer, despite the psychological effects on all members of the family. Job relocation, whether within the same company or to a different company, is a traumatic event for all members of the family, not just the employee. Relocation often requires the learning of new tasks, 'learning the ropes' in a new work environment, relinquishing old roles, and settling the family in a new community. Adults appear more prone to stress reactions, depression and alcoholism while children suffer from problems of intellectual, social and emotional development.

Job relocation/transfer can be classified as a stressful event because it disrupts the routines of daily life and tears those routines loose from their social context. Uncertainty, anxiety and lack of control surround such moves. We have read earlier that a person's identity is to a large extent a function of the roles he plays and that these roles enable the person to interact with others in a variety of contexts at work, home and leisure. Interruptions to this stream of ongoing daily activity threaten personal identity and relationships with others. This results in feelings of loss of control, loss of valued outcomes of daily behaviour and activities, and uncertainty.

Old routines are prized as they satisfy personal needs for friendships, known ways of working and, for spouses and children, an established secure daily routine involving such activities as shopping at a favourite store, attending a particular school, meeting friends in a coffee shop, club or other setting. All these things are valued and while they may be replaced with new friends, new job, new school and so on, there is no guarantee that the new environment will provide the same satisfaction. There is also a dreadful time lag before setting up new associations, becoming part of a community and generally settling down, during which stress, anxiety, depression, withdrawal, recrimination, soul-searching and health problems often manifest themselves.

Old routines that provided a sense of control may not readily be replaced, so that early in the relocation the family is reacting rather than being proactive. Adjustment to a new environment is usually a lengthy process. It takes less time for employees, as they go out to work, meet colleagues and spend their day maintaining an occupational role and identity. It is harder for spouses left at home in a 'foreign' place, and for children coping with a new school, new curricula, and trying to integrate into existing friendship groups. Some of the initial responses to a move, such as anxiety and depression, unfortunately inhibit positive interaction with the new environment. Figure 20 attempts to summarise the theoretical relationships in the relocation phase.

Research evidence from several countries suggests that the incidence of heart disease is greater among those who are occupationally mobile.

**Figure 20   Theoretical events in relocation**

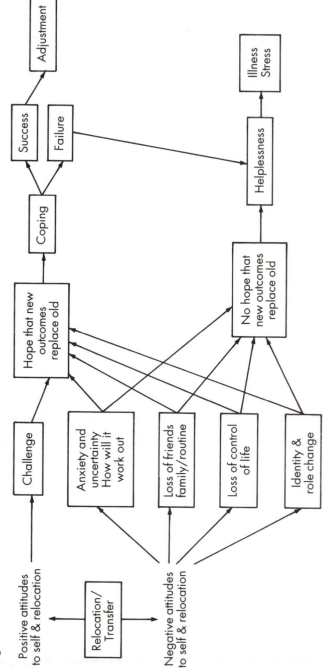

The cause is believed to stem from the tension of uncertainty about discrepancies between ability and performance and performance and outcomes. The performance variable includes such elements as role conflict, role ambiguity and role overload which, as we saw in Chpater 1, are major elements in self-perception. Role overload often occurs when a person takes on a new post because a clear definition of the role may not be available. Difficulty in learning the task also contributes to overload, as speed and efficiency are below optimum. Hence previous training and clear role definition assist adjustment to the work context. These work roles may also be replicated in the family and personal roles as the employee tries to help other members of the family settle down. Thus an employee may experience multi-role overload, conflict between family and work roles, or social role ambiguity.

Research indicates that:

A relocation to a similar work environment is likely to be less disruptive than a transfer to a dissimilar work environment. A different work environment increases uncertainty when, for example, expected dress standards, expected behaviour, leadership style differ between the field office and corporate headquarters. What is acceptable at one is often unacceptable at the other. The relocated employee has to be resocialised. Managers find moves between headquarters and field offices difficult. Research suggests that on average ten weeks is required for the resocialisation.

A relocation to a similar job is likely to be less disruptive than a transfer to a dissimilar job. Uncertainty develops if the employee has to demonstrate new skills and there will be a lack of confidence about ability to perform satisfactorily.

Separation from family at the time of relocation is more disruptive than no separation. Separation does allow the employee to learn the new skills and roles required without immediate home pressures, but it postpones the development of an integrated family–work lifestyle. It also creates tension and conflict between family members as the spouse feels left to cope. There is evidence (particularly from military families) of marital crises among couples who are separated during relocations. The additional roles taken on when the husband is away can result in overload for the wife. Younger children can suffer separation effects from the father and may exhibit regression to babyish behaviour such as thumb-sucking, enuresis, stuttering, temper tantrums. Some preschool children may go into a state of 'mourning'. The loss of a valuable role model for boys is also seen as deleterious by many psychologists. Reintegration as a family can often be a difficult negotiation when the rest of the family eventually joins the relocated employee.

Relocation is more disruptive to the social life of unmarried employees than married employees. Leaving existing social ties behind creates loneliness and isolation for most of us but more so for single people. A relocation is more disruptive if most of the above disruptive factors are present. That is, the individual is most likely to be overwhelmed if several pressures act at once. Coping with a new location is made easier if the job role is similar, and if wife and family are present and supportive.

## The non-working spouse

The non-working spouse is seen as the person who suffers most in a relocation. He, or more usually she, is often the passive victim of an imposed move with no say or choice in it. Most wives are not opposed to relocation when it means bettering the income or a job rather than no job. There is evidence that wives homebound in a new environment tend to report increased drinking, depression, and the use of tranquillisers. While a move can maintain or even enhance the employee's identity and self-concept in the work context, his non-working wife has more difficulty retaining or reconstructing an identity in a new community. It is difficult to engineer role, status and identity in an already functioning community where you are seen as an intruder. Failure to be accepted is often internalised, so that the wife starts to feel she is incompetent, her self-esteem declines, and a negative self-concept emerges, leading to depression and feelings of worthlessness. Unlike the employed spouse, the unemployed spouse can experience total role disruption on job relocation. She is isolated from her past and from her present.

Job relocation is more disruptive to a woman whose identity is bound up with non-family roles such as work and voluntary organisations, than to a woman whose identity stems from mainly family roles. Leaving the old job is a wrench and in a tight labour market there is no guarantee of another one. This can lead to feelings of helplessness and loss of identity. Like her spouse's the working woman's self-concept is to a large extent dependent on the image she has of herself in the work role.

Relocations that break up extended family relationships are more disruptive than those that do not. The emotional, social and even financial support that extended families give their members cannot be underestimated. Distance reduces the possibility of much of this psychological support. This is a loss not only for those who relocate but also for those left behind. Wives often report guilt at moving away from elderly or ill parents, for example.

**Figure 21 Summary of problems facing families**

| Problems | Single | Married with | | | |
| --- | --- | --- | --- | --- | --- |
| | | No children | Young children | Older children | Empty nest |
| The job | X | X | X | X | X |
| Separation from family | ? | ? | X | X | X |
| Housing | ? | X | X | X | X |
| Wife's reluctance to move | | X | X | X | X |
| Wife's adaptation to new environment | | X | X | X | X |
| Children | | | X | X | X |
| Education | | | | X | X |
| Responsibilities to parents | X | X | X | X | ? |
| Social life | X | X | ? | X | ? |

## Children

The effects of relocation on children appear to be related to age. The older the child, the more deleterious the effect, with teenagers having substantial problems. However, research indicates that teenagers who have often faced a forced move are better able to settle at tertiary residential institutions, as they have developed more independence and learnt how to adjust to change. Relocated children report difficulty in making friends and have less-developed peer relationships. Adjustment to new schools with their different rules, ethos, and curricula proves daunting for many, especially if the transfer occurs in the middle of a school term rather than at the start of a new year. Children generally do not like moving. Many children, like wives, report anxiety and depression until they adjust, and may also feel the loss of extended-family members, particularly grandparents.

In summary (Figure 21), it would seem that the main effects of relocation are due to discontinuity. They are:

- job-related stress for employees
- family and social disruption for spouses, and
- social disruption for children.

A useful way to facilitate adjustment to the relocation and reduce its effects on the employee and family is to involve the adult couple in the planning of a move as early as possible, giving them the opportunity to anticipate and organise, and integrating the move into a timetable that fits their needs as much as it does the company's. In the case of a forced transfer within an organisation, employees should be counselled as to how the relocation will fit into their career plans.

There is less trauma, too, if some training is given in the skills and demands of the new post so that employees are not trying to avoid making fools of themselves as they learn a new task or role among new colleagues. With a transfer, the company may enable the employee and family to visit the new area to get a feel for the place, contact estate agents, investigate school facilities and so on, so that by the time the move takes place some matters are well in hand. Anything that can reduce the shock of transfer is beneficial to the organisation, as the employee will be quicker to adjust to job and location and will be under less pressure from other family members as they settle in more quickly. Disruption associated with moving is difficult to avoid, but organisations can mitigate the effects by helping people cope better. Just uprooting a family and suddenly moving it a considerable distance will not enable the employee to give of his best.

Organisations need to plan relocations and enforced retirements. The current management of these in most organisations is best described as ad hoc and knee-jerk. While some workers do relocate and adjust without trauma to self or family, a great majority suffer from personal and family disruption. Relocation and enforced retirement need to be tied in with training policies on succession-planning, corporate goals and strategic goals. We have limited knowledge about the effects of relocation on the employee, on the wife (assumed to be doing home duties), and on the children. The implications for women in professional careers and for dual-income and dual-career couples have hardly been investigated.

Job change linked to relocation is a significant life transition with many potential outcomes, both positive and negative. Given the increasing need for highly trained and multi-skilled staff who can fit into the changing patterns of an organisation's structural development in an era of economic uncertainty, the incidence of relocation can only increase. Thus some way of managing relocation must be developed as part of corporate and personal strategic planning. This should involve, if necessary, the development of a 'mobility culture', i.e. positive attitudes towards job moves and willing acceptance of the inevitability of such moves if one's working life is to continue. In the past, relocations have mainly involved managers or aspiring managers, giving rise to the popular image of the 'nomadic manager' or 'executive gipsy'. But increasingly, relocation also involves blue-collar, technical and office staff meeting short-term demands, or displaced as a result of restructuring rather than any well-thought-out staff development policies.

The important factor in facilitating relocation transitions is the degree of induction and support employees receive. In a recent British study of job mobility and relocation, three out of five employees did not believe their companies were concerned with the welfare, well being and career development of their staff despite the companies priding themselves on being 'people centred'. The study showed that colleagues rather than predecessors appear to be of more help in assisting relocated employees to find their feet. Around 40 per cent of respondents gave negative ratings to the relocation training and induction programs provided, and 25 per cent of relocated employees suffered a decrement in work performance as a result of stress reactions.

As well as financial assistance (if it is an organisation-enforced move), workers facing relocation need visits to the new area, detailed information on the new area, training for the job, the development of wives' groups, help with selling and buying a house with temporary accommodation provided if necessary, information on housing, schools, and transport, and counselling, if required, for any member of the family. The pros and cons of relocation are detailed in Table 16.

Human resource management personnel will need to get more actively involved in the problems, of relocation or else organisations will need to delegate these responsibilities to specialist relocation agencies. The effective management of job relocation within an organisation must be tailored to the particular needs of each organisation in a specific market sector. Such personnel management systems need to be highly flexible and constantly updated in response to changing technological and structural demands.

## Summary

Work fulfils a variety of human needs and to become unemployed is therefore a very complex life transition. Those taking voluntary or planned retirement tend not to suffer the problems of those on whom redundancy is forced. Studies reveal that many of the latter deteriorate physically and psychologically. Health problems, depression and loss of self-esteem destroy the motivation to look for work and can eventually lead to psychiatric illness. New concepts of work, career and leisure may help to reduce the stigma of unemployment. Work is not the same as a job. Leisure pursuits such as hobbies and voluntary work can be used to gain the satisfactions of work, and to learn new skills. The hidden economy can be a source of paid work. Preparation for the future must involve organisations developing portable skills in their workforces.

Relocation, if unprepared for, can also have deleterious effects not only on employees but more so on their spouses and children. Old routines of life are difficult to replace in a new setting, particularly for wives, who often lose close support groups of friends and relatives. Adolescent children are particularly stressed by the disruption

**Table 16   Pros and cons**

| The pros | | |
|---|---|---|
| – Happy in previous job<br>Reservations about<br>new job—e.g.<br>lateral transfer, no<br>salary increase<br>Doubts ability to<br>master new job<br>Wife reluctant to<br>move—e.g. leaving<br>friends or her job<br>Children at important<br>stage of education<br>Family regard present<br>area as home<br>Worried about effects<br>on wife and<br>children | – Extra physical<br>demands of travel<br>and extra work<br>House-hunting is<br>difficult and<br>uncertain<br>Has to travel on<br>business at time of<br>move<br>Separation<br>Wife and children<br>unhappy at his<br>absence<br>Wife jealous of his<br>freedom from<br>responsibility | – New job makes<br>excessive demands<br>Interpersonal problems<br>at work<br>Lacks skills new job<br>requires<br>Needs to prove<br>himself quickly<br>Worried lest unable to<br>afford new mortgage<br>Concerned because<br>wife and children<br>having problems<br>adapting<br>Area doesn't offer<br>desired facilities e.g.<br>sports<br>Finds it difficult to<br>balance competing<br>demands on his<br>time and interest |
| – Happy about new<br>job—it was for<br>promotion etc.<br>Loss of motivation for<br>previous job<br>Wife keen to move<br>The move brings<br>benefits to the<br>family—a new<br>house, better<br>schooling | – Enjoys freedom and<br>'bachelor' social life<br>Involved in new job<br>House transactions<br>accomplished<br>relatively easily and<br>quickly<br>Makes money on the<br>exchange | – Job goes well and is<br>satisfying<br>New work team<br>provide support<br>Family adapt relatively<br>easily |
| Before the move | During the move | After the move |
| – Dislikes upheaval and<br>change<br>Involved in local<br>community<br>Likes current house<br>Works outside the<br>home<br>Children at critical<br>stage of education<br>Children reluctant to<br>move or react badly<br>to change (she<br>worries about their<br>ability to cope) | – Has to cope with a lot<br>of extra work<br>Misses husband<br>Finds she has little<br>social support in<br>the area<br>Feels that husband<br>does not appreciate<br>her problems, is<br>jealous of his<br>freedom<br>Children upset and<br>miss their father | – Feels lonely and<br>isolated—misses old<br>friends and doesn't<br>make new ones<br>Locals are hostile to<br>strangers<br>New house<br>'unsatisfactory' or<br>needs<br>alterations<br>Dislikes characteristics<br>of the area |

**Table 16   (Cont.)**

| | The pros | |
|---|---|---|
| Lives near her parents | House-hunting and timing of move are uncertain and exhausting | Husband too involved in new job to give support<br>No job opportunities for her<br>Lives further away from parents<br>Children have problems at school—slow to make new friends<br>Husband unhappy in new job |
| * Dislikes current situation— geographic area, house etc<br>Enjoys change and seeing new places<br>Likes proposed new location, has friends there<br>Children will benefit— better quality schooling, can start again if problems at school or with social lives | * Friends rally round Separation kept to a minimum by easy transactions etc<br>Finds she can cope and takes pride in her new independence | * Befriended by neighbour or company wife<br>Already has friends in the area<br>Makes friends via established channels—the church, babysitting club etc.<br>Husband and children adapt easily and quickly<br>Moves nearer to parents |
| | The cons | |

of their social ties. Organisations need to help relocated employees by the provision of support groups, help in finding houses, schools and so on.

A useful program complete with videotapes to use with staff undergoing change in the workplace is *A System of Change* produced by Seven Dimensions Pty Ltd, 18 Armstrong St, Middle Park, Vic 3206.

*The Secrets of Finding and Keeping a Job* by R. Burns, published by Business & Professional Publishing, PO Box 5065 West Chatswood NSW 2057 is a practical guide to learning skills for job hunting.

# Finale

Now that you have completed the book, and the activities as well, I hope you are much more confident about your ability to cope with the life transitions that lie ahead both for yourself and for others for whom you may have some responsibility. The book is an attempt, given the current and projected changes in the workplace, to create a subtle shift in emphasis, from using people as a form of capital, to ensuring that staff at all levels are given opportunities to reduce psychological and emotional blocks and enjoy useful and productive lives whatever the future may hold. Both you and they will be strong and resilient, attempting to make things happen, and gaining advantage and opportunity out of apparent adversity.

We cannot avoid change. The problems emerge from the way we perceive particular changes. We must view change positively, look for the advantages in it and see the disadvantages of not accepting it. Only in this way can we make change work for us. Positive thinking creates positive behaviour. The health of each organisation depends on the health of all its constituent parts. One negative, malfunctioning element can start a chain reaction that brings down the whole.

Organisations are changing their shape, size and structure in response to technological, structural and social demands. Life is going to be less secure and less comfortable for those who have limited work skills or whose skills are becoming redundant. For those who have valued skills or are willing to retrain, and for those who enjoy more independence, the world of work is changing to suit them. Contracts, part-time work, small business, self-employment will increase while the old steady career development within one occupation or even one organisation will decline. Retirement, redundancy, unemployment, leisure and career may start to lose their meanings as more people from all levels in the occupational hierarchy become self-employed, work from home, and participate in job-sharing schemes, with work, leisure and life weaving their activities together. Exposure to the realities of the marketplace will increase for managers and workers at all levels. Have you now the optimism to cope with these changes? Can you engender such optimism and confidence in your colleagues? You should now have the skills to do so. By developing your self-esteem, positive thinking, making positive affirmations, managing stress through relaxation, encouraging and involving others through counselling and open decision-making in the workplace, you can reduce much of the tension, resentment and ill-feeling generated in managing change.

Every organisation has three dimensions: economic, social and human. We understand the economic dimension fairly well. The social dimension includes meeting society's demands for the products of change, its environmental impacts, its relationship to the local community. The human dimension has been relatively neglected to date but will achieve far greater importance as recognition is given to the role of people as a major resource of skills. People are an organisation's most important asset in times of change. If they are faced with an uncertain and confused future, productivity will decrease as illness, absenteeism and lethargy take over. The message in this book has been that by developing your own psychological growth you can then build it in others. As a confident, positive and resilient manager, you are not threatened by involving lower-level staff in decision-making or by initiating change with them.

To meet future demands, organisational values may have to change; this requires a prior commitment by management to a set of values and a vision. One major organisational norm covers 'the chain of command'. As flatter organisations develop, with more employees on contract and some even working from home, management will have to plan for a less hierarchical and more facilitative mechanism linking employees together like partners in an enterprise. With authoritative status diminished, management skills will depend on a much more delicate and supportive handling of interpersonal relationships. Another area of values that is changing is the relationship between profit requirements and the quality of working life for employees. This latter aspect will grow in importance for management as managers become more aware of the stressful aspects of working in particular organisations.

One way to bring together all the various strands of psychological growth and management strategies that have been included in this book is to unify them under the concepts of organisational values and organisational vision. These two concepts are inter-related. An organisational value is a prevailing value that guides, directs and constrains the behaviour of an organisation's members. The organisational vision is the aim and forward plan of the organisation. Both values and vision, stem from the behaviour, attitudes and policies of management. Without guiding values and vision, management will have difficulty deciding what direction to take in a changing context or how to enthuse, motivate and support staff through troubled times. Thus, in deciding how to adapt yourself and your organisation to future changes, you can make no better start than review the organisation's apparent value system and vision. By deciding which values need promoting and which are damaging to the health and effectiveness of the members, you can help preserve and develop human beings, promote wellness, eliminate unnecessary stress and improve the quality of working life.

## Activity 70   Organisational vision

Work through this checklist and see whether your organisation and its employees are being prepared for their future by having some vision or plan to aim at.

| | |
|---|---|
| Does your organisation have clear goals for the next two years? | Yes/No |
| Have these goals been communicated to the staff? | Yes/No |
| Have staff at all levels participated in the forming of these goals? | Yes/No |
| Have individuals in the organisation been made aware of their roles within the strategic plan? | Yes/No |
| When new members join the organisation, are they shown clearly their role and their part in the overall vision? | Yes/No |
| Has every member received a simplified summary of the overall goals? | Yes/No |
| Are there measurable/tangible ways in which all members can see that they are achieving their individual goal/group goal? | Yes/No |
| Is communication and feedback between staff at all levels regular and clear? | Yes/No |
| Are staff at all levels encouraged to discuss problems in confidence with their supervisor/ manager? | Yes/No |
| Is creativity and innovation encouraged? | Yes/No |
| Is the organisation sensitive and responsive to new technology, changing markets, etc? | Yes/No |
| Are members of your organisation motivated by feeling that they are part of the organisation and can contribute something worthwhile to it? | Yes/No |

If you record a large number of 'yeses', then whatever changes occur in the world of work you and your organisation's members should manage to steer around the shallows and rapids, maintaining progress, direction and team spirit. Changes should cause little damage to the buoyancy and health of the craft or crew. If there are a large number of 'noes', then your organisation and its members are operating on an ad hoc basis in a context of change, so that individuals have little or no involvement in or knowledge about the direction or lack of direction. Everyone is in the dark with worries and insecurities about their future. Someone like you is needed to lift up your head from the day-to-day crisis and consider what might happen in the future.

## Activity 71   Organisational values

What do you think are the current values and beliefs among your organisation's members? Values and beliefs underlie performance and stress. From the following list, pick four you believe to be strong in your organisation.

You look after yourself here
There's no opportunity for promotion here
I only work here
Management says one thing but does another
Meetings, always wasting time in meetings
Let's keep things as they are
Do the minimum to get by
Rules are more important than initiative
Doing a good job isn't rewarded or recognised
Workers don't seem to matter
Profits govern all decisions
People don't support/help each other here
Customers don't really count.

These are all negative values or beliefs which sap individual motivation and prevent mutual support and preparation for change.
From the list below, select four new values which you feel would ensure that your organisation and its members were more able to cope with change.

We recognise and reward accomplishment
We give the best service possible
Customers count
How can I help you?
We encourage innovation
We can do it
Open communication builds an excellent organisation
We respect the individual

Building a better organisation together
We can achieve a lot working together
A successful organisation builds for the future.

You should now be able to incorporate these positive values in your organisation and its vision for the future.

It is important to remember that a passive reading of this book may give knowledge but not personal development. For the latter, you must not only carry out the activities and reflect on what you are doing, continue with some of the affirmation and relaxation activities for some time to come.

Go out now in confidence and remember that today is the first day of the rest of your life.

# Selected references and
# further reading

Bennis, W., Benne, K., Chin, R. and Carey, K. (eds) (1976), *The Planning of Change*, New York: Holt

Benson, H. *The Relaxation Response* (1976), New York: Avon Books

Berne, E. (1972), *What Do You Do After You Have Said Hello*, London: Corgi

Burns, R. (1979), *The Self Concept*, London: Longman

—— (1992), *10 Skills For Working With Stress*, Sydney: Business and Professional Publishing

—— (1992), *The Secrets of Finding and Keeping a Job*, Sydney: Business and Professional Publishing

Cattell, R. (1965), *The Scientific Analysis of Personality*, Harmondsworth: Penguin

Cooper, C. (1983), *Stress Research*, New York: Wiley

Cooper, C. and Smith, M. (1985), *Job Stress and Blue Collar Work*, Chichester: Wiley

Eysenck, H. and Eysenck, M. (1984), *Personality and Individual Differences*, New York: Plenum

Friedman, M. and Rosenman, R. (1974), *Type A Behaviour and Your Heart*, Greenwich: Fawcett Press

Glasser, W. (1976), *Positive Addiction*, New York: Harper Row

Handy, C. (1985), *Understanding Organisations*, Harmondsworth: Penguin

Kasl, S. and Cooper, C. (eds) (1987), *Stress and Health*, London: Wiley

Nicholson, N. (1984), A theory of work role transitions, *Administrative Science Quarterly*, 29, 172–91

O'Brien, G. and Kabanoff, B. (1978), *Work, Health and Leisure*, Working Paper No. 28, Flinders University National Institute of Labour Studies

Reddy, M. (1987), *The Manager's Guide To Counselling At Work*, London: Methuen

Seligman, M. (1975), *Helplessness*, San Francisco: Freeman

Selye, H. (1956), *The Stress of Life*, New York: McGraw-Hill

Shortland, S. (1988), *Managing Relocation*, London: MacMillan

Sundstrom, E. (1986), *Work Places: The Psychology of the Physical Environment in Offices and Factories*, Sydney: Cambridge University Press

Toffler, A. (1980), *Future Shock*, London: Bodley Head Press

# Subject index

# THE ALLEN & UNWIN BUSINESS AND MANAGEMENT SERIES

*General series editors*:

Dr Bernard Carey
Director
Graduate School of Management
Macquarie University

Professor Elizabeth More
Deputy Director
Graduate School of Management
Macquarie University

*Other title in this series*

*Australian Public Sector Management*
David Corbett

A000015960795